JOURNALISM, ETHICS AND SOCIETY

For my family:
Mam, my late Father, Maureen, Sandra, Christine and Stephen

Journalism, Ethics and Society

DAVID BERRY
Southampton Solent University, UK

LONDON AND NEW YORK

First published 2008 by Ashgate Publishing

2 Park Square, Milton Park, Abingdon, Oxfordshire OX14 4RN
52 Vanderbilt Avenue, New York, NY 10017

Routledge is an imprint of the Taylor & Francis Group, an informa business

First issued in paperback 2020

British Library Cataloguing in Publication Data
Berry, David, 1960-
    Journalism, ethics and society
    1. Journalistic ethics 2. Mass media - Moral and ethical
    aspects
    I. Title
    174.9'0704

Library of Congress Cataloging-in-Publication Data
Berry, David, 1960-
    Journalism, ethics and society / by David Berry.
      p. cm.
    Includes bibliographical references and index.
    ISBN 978-0-7546-4780-5
  1. Journalistic ethics. I. Title.

    PN4756.B49 2008
    070.4--dc22

                                          2008028431

ISBN 13: 978-0-7546-4780-5 (hbk)
ISBN 13: 978-0-367-60324-3 (pbk)

Contents

Introduction

This book grew out of an interest and critical engagement with the academic discipline media ethics. I first taught media ethics as a part-time tutor at the University of Cardiff in 1995 and, like most in a similar situation, my decision to teach this subject was not out of choice but rather out of financial necessity; I was, after all, studying for my PhD. I then secured a full-time post in January 1997 at the Southampton Institute now known as Southampton Solent University where I have taught media ethics on the Journalism degree programme up to the time of writing. Even though I had stumbled upon the discipline by accident, I was fairly well suited to it, at least on the philosophical side: I had studied social and moral philosophy as part of my degree at Cardiff. The realities of journalism appear to be at odds with a discourse in ethics, although there are exceptions, but even where the polarities between ethics and practice appear to be stretched beyond comprehension we cannot escape our inevitable return to morality. It's a gravitational pull too great to resist and potentially dangerous if we choose to ignore it; amorality or indifference isn't an option – at least when power is the centrifugal force of all news discourse.

Media ethics is a broad term encapsulating many varied ethical discussions in relation to practice. However, a recurring theme, implicit as much as explicit, is the relationship between journalism and society, and the impact that news has for shaping our understanding of the environment we inhabit. The majority of its focus is on production rather than consumption; however, a discourse in ethics assumes that practice imposes itself upon public consciousness helping to create perceptions and opinions in the process of engagement. Writers within cultural and media studies will be aware that making assumptions about how consumption proceeds without providing scientific evidence to substantiate claims is problematic; hence the use of ethnographic or audience research in that field of enquiry. Despite the absence of major research projects concerning consumption, writers within the media ethics discipline have commented and continue to comment on standards of journalism and the quality of press performance. Two important features emerge from this: the first relates to purpose of news and the second relates to the meaning of journalism and its role in society. This book therefore begins with a discussion on news in Chapter 1, assessing both historical and contemporary uses. This sits comfortably within the scope of media ethics because moral judgements on standards relate to a definition and purpose of news and its public uses in society. There's also a discussion on newspapers that will help to construct meanings of news that in general terms differs according to which society we choose to study, as well as within different types of newspaper that operate in any given system. For instance, the difference between tabloid and 'quality press' approaches to news in both the UK and, historically, in the US provides examples of how critics approach these products equally as failing or succeeding to achieve the production of content that can be viewed as news.

Chapter 2 takes the meaning of news discussed in the previous chapter and looks at the related context of the meaning of journalism in direct relation to news production. Any moral judgements made with regard to the meaning or definition of news automatically assumes an intrinsic relationship to the actual practice of journalism; journalists after all are partly involved in the dissemination of news, but questions relating to the definition of news and journalism force us to further deliberate on their respective purpose and function in society, for surely news must have a purpose. Defining journalism is a direct consequence of an engagement with ethics because, at its root, ethical deliberation concerns itself with 'right' and 'wrong', 'good' and 'bad', which are natural products of normative approaches to news and journalism.

Chapter 3 assesses liberalism, which is the political philosophy that has dominated meanings and functions of both news and journalism. Liberalism is the framework of how news and journalistic practice proceed and is also the framework within which news and journalism are perceived by the public. The liberal *idea* of the fourth estate is central to meaning because it structures practice as a social activity. Liberalism is also the reason for the many criticisms of journalistic practice that have emerged within the field of media ethics, as well as the reason for a defence of individual rights to practice when confronted with the realities of monopoly ownership. The liberal notion of 'individualism' is therefore perceived either negatively for destroying the collective fabric of society, or positively in that it can salvage freedom of speech from the ravages of monopoly capitalism. Thus depending on the philosophical view, it's either demon or saviour. In this latter context what I term the *spirit of liberalism* lives on, despite a turn to neo-liberalism.

Chapter 4 assesses media ethics as a formal discipline in more depth and argues that, above all else, it can be viewed as creating an academic space that perceives journalism as a process of enlightenment. There is a discussion in this chapter on the US-based public journalism[1] 'movement', which was born out of a critical reaction to liberalism. Where the latter places strong emphasis on the individual, public journalism emphasizes the collective or community. There is also a discussion on the European Union's (EU's) view towards news and society that serves as an interesting comparison to public journalism. Briefly, although the EU's media policies seek to serve the interests of society, both nationally and throughout Europe, it doesn't offer a criticism of the liberal notion of individualism

---

1   Public journalism is also referred to as 'civic journalism' although some writers claim that there are differences, subtle or otherwise. For the purposes of this book I shall refer to 'public' rather than 'civic' journalism, although in Chapter 4, 'civic' is used, but only in direct relation to the works of various writers or groups.

that is so pervasive in public journalism. Rather, it seeks to enforce the *spirit of liberalism* as a dynamic against the forces of neo-liberal conditions.

Chapter 5 provides a discussion on truth and objectivity, which are seen as central to a discourse in the ethics of journalism. Truth and objectivity also help to provide some understanding of the issues in relation to the definition of both news and journalism. Objectivity is seen as *means* (method) and *end* that constitutes the fundamental elements of news production, which structures the meaning of journalism; objectivity is equally seen as a means to achieving truth. Critics argue that objectivity is unattainable with some, such as the former BBC journalist and war correspondent Martin Bell, preferring 'attachment' rather than the apparent 'detachment' that objectivity infers. Subjectivists argue a similar case. Whatever the differences and disagreements, objectivity forces us to critically confront the meaning of news and the purpose of journalism in society.

Chapter 1
History and Context:
News and Newspapers

Such is our hunger for news of all kinds, it would seem, that it is frequently described in terms of a physical or pathological 'need'. (Basner 2000, p. 271)

News

Newspapers developed initially as extensions of other forms of communication, such as verbal exchanges and were indeed necessities to fulfil appetites for news; perhaps the only real difference that emerged with the development of newspapers and journalism as a social practice was *specialization* and *power*. From an early period humans have exhibited an extraordinary interest in news and although it is difficult to scientifically trace the history of news to its actual beginnings, we can nevertheless safely assume that one aspect of our being, what determines human kind and separates us from the animal world, is our appetite for news of events. One could argue that this appetite for news is an intrinsic part of our human nature, and irrespective of the form it has taken historically or in modern times, most receptions of news require trust in authenticity.

Understanding what constitutes news appears to be more complex today with an emphasis on global communication networks dominating lived experience. On one important level, news is intrinsically connected to journalist productivity; on another broader plain, news is everywhere. News in relation to mainstream press and media organizations dominates social landscapes, which requires an analysis of power, influence and the ability to shape our understanding of the world we inhabit. In this context news in relation to journalistic activity is a central concern to a discourse in media ethics because the focus is on how news is produced and for what purpose, and this is premised on the privileged position that journalists and news organizations occupy and their ability to distribute news across time and space.

Burns (2002, pp. 49–51) under the sub-heading 'Defining News' explains that: 'The word "news" to describe the things journalists write about has been in use for at least 500 years, well before newspapers were around.'[1] Although human interest

---

1   It is worth reading Lynette Sheridan Burns's book *Understanding Journalism* (2002) on what constitutes news. At the time of publication Burns had been a journalist for 25 years and there is, despite some contradictions and contentious points in the book, a genuine

in news underpins current journalistic activity, it has underpinned the activity of other non-journalistic mediators in the past, such as chroniclers of events and more commonly peoples travelling between places:

> Human beings have always been curious about the world around them, and anxious to know about events that will have an impact on their lives. For most of human existence, this curiosity and anxiety were fulfilled by travellers' tales and gossip ... . Early forms of transmitting news began with word of mouth; news was limited to what someone told and retold ... . (Hastings 2000)

Moreover, people have and continue to produce news relating to personal, working and family lives. This shared social system is referred to as 'oral culture' where a community of speakers, coordinate information by means of the spoken word. Stephens (2007, p. 17) calls this early form, 'Oral news systems' that had particular dynamics, and says that: 'The roots of our own journalism lie in such methods', but, residues of oral cultural continue to exist throughout the world. Historically, oral cultures used memory to solidify tradition, customs and spoken narrative, and without print, oral culture was pure; with the introduction of print, oral culture was diluted but not annihilated. Print may condition oral culture in the modern context; that is a probability.

In Ancient Greece oral culture produced an intense intellectualism demonstrated by the *Socratic dialogue*, which was based on memory and then memorizing learnt theory for future dialogue. The *dialogue* was based on one's perception of lived experience of the concrete world; this was no metaphysical exercise. Insight, a central element of the *dialogue*, could be achieved but only through the explicit dialectical process of statement made and actual experience – this was a process of self-realization. The *Socratic Dialogue* was based on interpersonal (collective) understanding between participants by testing statements against one's personal experience.

Even though the spoken word dominates oral culture, this doesn't negate power in discourse and the ability to persuade. Rhetoric, the art of persuasion, was taught by Greek sophists to fee-paying students. Sophists argued that humans could be taught to better themselves by learning the art of persuasion. Aristotle expanded on the use of rhetoric, maintaining that rhetoric had practical uses in civic affairs using *ethos, pathos and logos* to demonstrate its persuasive power. The fact is the study of rhetoric (rhetorical analysis) continues today through communication theoreticians in the study of persuasion in mass communications and advertising

---

attempt to grapple with the complex character of news. Although there is an emphasis on ethical conduct and self-responsibility, the book lacks a clear discussion on ideology and power in relation to news selection made by powerful mainstream media bodies that condition a public agenda. Despite these shortfalls, I would certainly recommend the reader to engage with pages 49–124, particularly the sections titled 'Finding News', 'Choosing News', 'Gathering News', 'Evaluating News Sources' and 'Constructing News'.

(see Hornig-Priest 1996; Berger 2000). Sophists travelled from city to city taking news with them and distributing it amongst their pupils. Socrates, who was accused of being a sophist, would have used news from other parts as a key element of the *dialogue*, which would have conditioned the lived experience of participants. News was the staple diet of the Greek Agora (market place), which played an essential part of Greek democracy from around 600 BC; news in this sense was a major part of Greek politic and much later in the Roman Forum where handwritten sheets were posted daily adding to the spoken news during the Caesarian period (Stephens 2007).

Today, oral culture continues to survive in various degrees according to cultural contexts through memory, narrative and dialogue and much of what is past off as news amongst cultures in the oral tradition is based on traditional modes of mediation. Memory is an aspect of the human condition that writers such as Jésus Martín-Barbero firmly believe constitute an essential part of human nature, particularly the memory of popular culture that continues today in the form of residues from the past that dialectically interweave in modern times to form and shape new cultural forms. And in Latin America, at least, what partly constitutes the popular culture of the people is the interpersonal form of transmitting news of communities and local happenings within a context of fast trans-national communications.

Until the technological advances of the mid-nineteenth century onwards, news moved slowly, but today, with modern technology, as Barker (2000, p. 2) states, news is largely perceived as 'information on recent events'. Barker also alludes to a narrower definition today with regard to content than was previously disposed in eighteenth-century England 'when for some, all types of gossip, anecdote and fashionable, moral or religious discussion were deemed worthy of being termed "news"'. This historical perspective on what constituted news, and Barker's rejection thereof, raises important concerns for contemporary forms of journalistic practice, particularly when we consider what it means to be a journalist and what journalism as a social practice is meant to be achieving. It is, after all, no coincidence that many academics accuse the tabloid press of 'dumbing down' culture because of the content, where political news is seen as having less value than gossip and entertainment. Tabloid editors for their part will argue that news is defined by public taste, which interestingly has historical roots, as have ethical concerns of what is preferred as news over and above the interests and tastes of the public as Black (1991, p. 42) demonstrates with regards to the English press and weeklies in particular during the eighteenth century:

> There were clearly some serious disputes within newspaper managements over the issue of content. A recent study of Arthur Young and the *Universal Magazine* in 1762 has detected a tension between what the readers apparently wanted and the solemn, heavy pieces that Young thought they should be given, which ended with the purchase of the magazine by booksellers, and the lowering of its tone.

As Black further explains (ibid., p. 44), there were heated debates over content:

> Clifton's *Medley* attacked the style and content of Mist's *Weekly Journal*. He accused it of being lewd ... Referring to Mist's 'vast success among the lower class of readers', the *Medley* claimed that it had promised never to appeal to Mist's readers by printing puns, conundrums, and *double entendres*, and that it dealt with people of sense.

This informs us more about the ethics of 'good' news, according to Clifton, than it does about a clear definition of news; suffice to say that news at its vaguest is information about people and events. However, the emphasis on what apparently constituted proper or acceptable forms of news in history also informs us of how writers in media ethics currently perceive the social responsibilities of journalists today.

There have been claims that the word 'news' is an acronym formed from the letters **N**orth, **E**ast, **W**est and **S**outh, although this isn't convincing. The word 'news' is seen to represent the 'new', therefore the emphasis is upon 'current events' (*Oxford English Dictionary* 1989) with the additional 'important, or recent interesting happenings' tagged alongside. Who decides what is both important and interesting is very much a key part of the discussion on ethics because, as stated earlier, it invokes a discussion on responsible action. To complicate matters further, the word 'new' is an adjective and, in English at least, rarely do adjectives have plural forms as the word 'news' obviously implies.

Some writers believe news to be of the moment and thus time becomes an indication of whether something constitutes news and, in this context, whether it therefore reflects an act of journalism. Using an historical analogy Stephens (2007, p. 48) states: 'Writing was for tortoises such as Thucydides; news is spread by hares', adding that 'Socrates, a contemporary of Thucydides, was capable of playing the hare' because Socrates according to Stephens 'wanted to be brought up to date on the *current* state of philosophy (a form of specialized news)' (ibid.; my emphasis). Barker (2000, p. 2) has also argued that news is essentially characterized by 'current events' in relation 'of interest to the public', which apparently 'forms the subject matter of public debate', ideally perhaps and certainly not in all cases. However, although 'current' isn't entirely inappropriate for defining news; perhaps the *act of revealing* for the first time is more appropriate. If the *act of revealing* constitutes news then time, in terms of the 'new' and or 'current' isn't privileged. If, as an example, a three-year long investigation into historical Nazi war crimes reveals new evidence then surely this constitutes news, for what else is it? This may come as a surprise to some, but even historians are engaging in the production of news; the style of writing and approach to reference systems may differ, but revealing something hitherto unknown is an act of news.

The *Oxford English Dictionary* reminds us that news derives from the fifteenth century 'newes, plural of newe ... on the model of Old French *noveles* or Medieval Latin *nova*' meaning 'new things'. News that reflects the new is information being disclosed and revealed for the first time – hitherto unknown – a revelation; otherwise it's old news, if I am permitted to use what is a contradictory term. Old news is news that has been previously disclosed and once had the value of news at a point in history – that value depletes over time making news (new) more valuable both in terms of merits of disclosure and status. News can have an historical and reflective dimension, and whether or not it is news from the deep past as opposed to the recent is irrelevant, for it is *disclosure* that is a defining moment of what constitutes news. Those that claim news can only be so if it is deemed to be interesting and important, as the *Oxford English Dictionary* states, can be said to adhere to a paternalistic model of defining news, for this assumes a social value bestowed upon society of which benefits are derived.

Similar to Barker above, Conboy (2004, pp. 6–7) also argues that news is distinct from 'gossip' and 'rumour', although Conboy's account is hardly convincing because news is never thoroughly defined here and it is merely taken for granted that it has superior value to gossip and rumour:

> Before the formalisation of communication in various forms of newsbooks and newsletters, at which point we can begin to identify certain characteristics of early journalism, all levels of society had been lubricated by the more informal exchange of information known as rumour and gossip.

This point is also documented in Mott (1962, pp. 8–9) stating in relation to the Massachusetts-based title *The Present State of the New-English Affairs*, 1689 that: 'Its sub-head, "This is Published to Prevent False Reports", is an acknowledgement that one of the great functions of the printing of news is to correct the inevitable abuses of rumour.' This position contrasts with Emery's (1972, pp. 2–3) account stating that news is a combination of gossip and information: 'news was exchanged long before there was even the most primitive form of newspaper. One of the great attractions at the country fairs of the Middle Ages was the opportunity to exchange gossip and information.' Emery continues: 'News had a structural effect as part of that flow of information which reshaped Early Modern European societies' (ibid., p. 8) and with reference to Habermas, the author alludes to the idea that reliability defines news, but in what way exactly? And how reliable is gossip? There are, however, some contradictions or points of tension because Emery also pays reference to 'high quality news' (ibid., p. 7), as distinct from what exactly?

Although it is true that people throughout history have been engaged in exchanging news either within localities or from far-flung places, the relationship between journalist and news is seen to be not only different, but one that is far more complex, and this is despite the fact that some newspapers provide highly contentious versions of news. Perhaps the most fundamental element that conditions something we may safely and trustworthily perceive as news is 'truth' that reflect facts of any case in hand. A truthful recording of events, however, makes no ethical judgements on what is interesting or important and is therefore neutrally defined. Any salacious, pernicious and harmful content can therefore be justified as news as long as it is based on truth and factual observation, so the normative axis becomes much greater when we deliberate over what constitutes news as well as deliberating on its truthfulness. This can deteriorate into subjective evaluations of what constitutes news based on personal taste and acceptance – one may say tabloids are 'dumbing down' culture, or on the other hand that they are wonderfully inventive!

For example, with respect to the introduction of the 'yellow press' in the US during the late nineteenth century, particularly Randolph Hearst's 'new journalism' (Keeler et al. 2002, p. 48), a new ethical debate emerged on what constituted news. As the authors argue this was a debate on ethics concerning 'right' and 'wrong' or what is acceptable or not according to the values of different press people of that time. The yellow press published sensationalist stories, focusing on crime and sex amongst other matters, and was seen to belong to the culture of the people or what has been described as the 'great unwashed'. This approach to news can be seen in all its glory in the UK today; the *News of the World* and *The People* are two amongst many examples. However, the content that was published in the yellow press forced members of the elite to pass comment and judgement on standards, definitions of news and the meaning of journalism:

> Higher classes were critical of newspapers for pandering to and perpetuating working class values, presenting trivial and tasteless news, lowering moral standards … . In addition, journalists should be well educated and of high moral integrity. (ibid., p. 49)

Whether they truly represented working-class values is open to debate and seems a gross generalization and stereotype, but the point has been made; there were differences over what constituted news in relation to personal judgements and moral positions. This debate continues today and with respect to the US, Keeler et al. (2002) state that what constitutes news in the contemporary US is governed within a much broader and often dubious framework: 'A great deal of "news" is being derived from "reality" programs, call-in talk shows, and news greatly tailored to narrow audiences in an increasingly fragmented media environment' (ibid., p. 53); in other words, anything goes. In the UK the *Daily Star*, *Sun* and *Daily Mirror* often publish accounts of soap operas that is passed off as news. This condition reflects the ideas set forth in Umberto Eco's (1998) work *Faith in Fakes: Travels in Hyperreality* where the reproduction of fictional accounts brings forth events that produce far more gratification than the real. In this context the realities of everyday life are exhumed from their actual social conditions and the fake is passed off as the real. In ethical terms the point of critique rests upon the departure or the negation of news practice that bases itself on factual accounting. The films of UK director Ken Loach (social realism) have far more basis in reality, irrespective of whether the films are produced from a value-judgement on society. Eco had argued that fabricated reality was sold to the public as being better than the real. Whether it is reality game shows in the US or tabloids in the UK, what isn't being sold is news, but rather it is a simulation or an invented world. This isn't perhaps so shocking when we consider Eco's work on Disney, for the latter attempted to reproduce the real through ideologically generated strategies, but in the context of newspapers, with the apparent emphasis on news, it not only becomes more shocking, but certainly raises the debate over ethics on what constitutes news and on what constitutes a newspaper, which are after all organs of news – or at least that is the theory.

The assumption that real news is to be discovered outside the cosy, manufactured confines of reality television or even reality newspapers is an argument for distinguishing between what can be satisfactorily referred to as news and non-news. For instance, Mott (1962, p. 788) under the sub-heading 'What's the news?' argues that it is something created by a trustworthy and serious newspaper, and provides a list of newsworthy events that have shaped historical events. Mott also argues that it is the approach to events that helps define 'The News and its Status' which is the chapter heading (ibid.), and the approach is principally defined as a method, which is at the heart of understanding journalism that structures news; for Mott the required method that creates news is objectivity:

> DESPITE INCREASED EMPHASIS UPON INTERPRETATION, THE NEWS itself – the objective news facts as nearly as an honest and skilful reporter can ascertain and record them – continued to be the fundamental business of American journalism. It is as difficult to generalize about newspapers as it is to make sweeping statements about human nature; there are unscrupulous papers which distort the news, as well as highminded journalists who suffer in the cause of truth, and prejudiced observers can make a case for either distrust of the press or faith in it by choosing suitable examples. But in 260 years of American journalism, newspapers have, in general, been read chiefly for the news; and in general, they have furnished the news to their readers faithfully. (ibid.)

This emphasis on objective news differs significantly from the idea that news can be used to agitate and subvert as a revolutionary tool to propagate change: 'A contemporary historian of the Revolution, William Gordon, assumed that "In establishing American independence, the pen and press had merit equal to that of the sword ... To rouse and unite the inhabitants"' (Rutland 1973, p. xii); not so dissimilar from Lenin's theory of the press, at least in the short-term, and identical perhaps to John Pilger's *campaigning journalism* or even US director Michael Moore's film-making techniques. Moore's 2007 film *Sicko* about the US health service was primarily used to agitate and provoke a reaction from the audience to invoke change.

For many, defining what exactly constitutes news has always been problematic, but this, I would argue, is because of a misunderstanding of the social processes involved that distorts the original meaning of news. Sarah Niblock epitomizes this view that news is an extremely complex word to understand: 'Ask any journalist how they would define "news" and most would find it a very hard question to answer' (1996, p. 3). However, I would argue the complete opposite; news is very easy to understand. The word 'news' is a noun and there are two seemingly opposed explanations of news in the *Oxford English Dictionary* that help towards one part of the misunderstanding. First, it states that news is 'Current events, important happenings or interesting recent events'; then, it states: 'Interesting or important information not previously known or realized, *it's news to me.*' As stated above, my preferred meaning of news is partly based on the latter definition because this reflects the idea that news is something revealed for the first time irrespective of when, and also that news can be value free perceived in pure abstract terms. The words 'interesting' and 'important', however, are adjectives that invariably involve *subjective interpretation* on the meaning of what may or may not constitute news and it is these words that lead to the misunderstanding and over-complication of the meaning of news. What Niblock does is to solely associate the word 'news' with 'newspaper' and thus anything that is omitted from the authoritative press does not have the value of being news. What makes an item or event news for a newspaper can be legitimately viewed as news, but it is news based on selectivity and *subjective interpretation* when in reality news is everywhere. This *monopolization* for defining news is one pertinent criticism of journalism because it is able to shape society and what Theobald (2004) called *The Media and the Making of History* is one of the primary reasons for establishing critiques of the media.

Niblock uses a familiar term that defines news, 'newsworthiness', which describes 'any event or issue meriting coverage' (1996, pp. 3–4), but who decides and what are the criteria that determine coverage? This notion of newsworthiness is ultimately based on news values, which are often conditioned by press organizations that reflect a paper's 'house-style' or moral and even political viewpoints. Moreover, once values are asserted, news can be a reflection of ideology, which corrupts objectivity. Using an historical analogy, Rutland (1973, p. 22) more or less argues a similar view to Niblock whereby news can only be so, and will be authentic only if it is mediated from the printed word, the original source being of less importance: 'News isn't news until it's printed. Print turned rumour into fact, created a visible record of that fact, and became a saleable item in a society on the periphery of mercantilist England.' In contemporary times the assumption may be that journalists produce 'official news', which has an air of 'authenticity' and 'reliability' about it and is sanctioned by the relationship with the medium and news organization that provides legitimacy over other non-journalistic types. This, then, doesn't negate other forms of news, but they are viewed by the industry as less reliable and perhaps have the potential to veer off into rumour, gossip and hearsay. However, once we posit this privileging of news production towards journalism and acknowledge its limitations and power, we must then begin to think in terms of applying normative procedures that alert us to such noble ideas as responsible journalism, truth, objectivity, standards and quality of performance, for there is always a propensity for abuse and to mislead unwittingly or otherwise.

Frost (2007, p. 22) dedicates a chapter titled 'News: Towards A Definition' stating that understanding how news works is important for understanding ethical debates in journalism. The author states: 'There is a difference between a newsworthy event and news. A newsworthy event will not necessarily become news'. In a similar vein to Niblock and Rutland the author further claims: 'We can define news as an event that is recorded in a newspaper or a broadcast news bulletin' (ibid.).

Michael Skapinker said: 'I occasionally speak to school students and they usually ask the same questions … What do you do if there is no news? (There is always news.)' (Skapinker 2007). Indeed, as Skapinker alludes, news is everywhere; it's endless; a pit of infinite events that we make and inhabit; it's just that Skapinker doesn't care to mention two correlative words that are central to our understanding of production in the journalistic context: 'omission' and 'inclusion'. News, however, isn't divinely delivered nor is it a result of miraculous reification; rather, it is the product of human invention and more often than not, human interpretation of a series of events mostly conveniently bundled into a coherent linguistic package that is humanly recognized as news. We can all make news if we so choose; it's just that some make the headlines rather than others, and some are more able to condition the social space on which opinion and sometimes knowledge is built. News can be value free; news can be fermented with ideology and intent; both contain different intentions. Values and beliefs that underscore the very selection of information that constitute the primary strands of news lead us to questions of power and influence: the very stuff of a discourse in the ethics of journalism. Burns (2002, p. 49) states:

> For most inexperienced journalists, the idea of 'finding' news is the most daunting part of the job. Their uncertainty about where to begin is not helped by the language used by journalists to describe 'news'. They talk about having a 'nose' for news, and 'seeing' the story they later write … . Few journalists, when pressed, can find a standardised definition of news but all would say they know a good story when they see it.

It's also interesting, if not totally reassuring and convincing, to note that Burns on the one hand admits to having no confirmed notion of what actually constitutes news whilst simultaneously, and perhaps contradictorily, stating that almost by nature or dint of character in relation to *the job*, journalists somehow know exactly what news is. How can this be so? How can one recognize something if something isn't recognizable? This for certain is a complexity of mammoth proportions. Perhaps we should all just shut up about the meaning of news and get on with it … if only; for the debate on what constitutes news goes right to the heart not only of the meaning and constitution of journalism, but perhaps more importantly for this book, it is pivotal to the discourse on media ethics. Burns's final statement, however, atomizes the *idea* of news, splitting and fragmenting it into a multitude of subjective positions and viewpoints, and places the emphasis on production rather than needs of consumption. In other words, the producers of news, journalist and newspaper, become the authority that overrides public requirements, and they act, as they so often do, on the public's behalf; they call this the public interest, an amorphous concept if there ever there was one, but widely used and mostly determined by news agencies.

Deliberating on the relationship between journalism and news requires an understanding of what constitutes news and why it's important for society and its democratic needs. Journalism is a social process of transferring news from one point to another and Allan (2004, p. 8) alerts us to the fact of the problem 'in defining precisely what should count as a news account'. Thus, understanding the meaning and dynamics of news allows us to understand what constitutes journalism and being a journalist, which further allows us to understand or at least appreciate why academics and journalists become concerned for ethics in practice. The issue concerning how information becomes news (headline or otherwise) or how news is finally selected is well documented. Amongst others Hall (1981) has pointed out that journalists often define news 'as if events define themselves'.[2] Under the sub-heading 'News Selection', McQuail (1993, p. 217) details varying criteria for making judgements on news and uses Hetherington's (1985) study on news values to highlight how choice is made:

> He [Hetherington] concludes that journalists, consciously or not, base their choice and treatment of news on two criteria (i) what is the political, social, economic and human importance of the event? And (ii) will it interest, excite and entertain our audience?

Point (i) is extremely general and rules nothing out, and point (ii) is mostly based on *perceptions* of the audience, sometimes stereotypically applied. Either way, news is what journalists believe it to be and more often than not based on spurious notions of what is euphemistically referred to as 'newsworthy' based on equally but ideologically determined notions of news values conditioned by the news organization. Accordingly, news values condition news based on the further and equally spurious notion of the public interest; each principle connected umbilical-like to each point.

Historically, the emergence of printed news has been associated with the emergence of a specific type of practitioner. Although this has greatly varied throughout history, the association is not based on public participation but rather was and is associated with minority figures. Printed news meant official news in that it wasn't the product of ordinary people, at least not in any significant numbers. One fact is that news of this type was distributed over large geographical areas and the ability to reach wider audiences raised concerns in history as they still do today. These concerns range from the possible impacts that news may have had on both religious

---

2   See also John W. Robertson's (2006) 'Illuminating or Dimming Down? A Survey of UK Television News Coverage' for an up-to-date discussion on news values.

and royal governing bodies in late sixteenth to early seventeenth century England where home news was banned; hence the *corantos* of this period were restricted to foreign news, were printed abroad (Netherlands) and subsequently imported to England; this was safe news – to the ethical concerns over falling standards and a lowering in the quality of performance today; hence media ethics. Whatever the differences of emphasis, the ability to reach and impact a wide audience has been a distinguishing factor of practice and the determination of news.

However, the internet has disrupted that convenient truth; ordinary people now have the power to reach a wider audience and the only difference is the way in which news is mediated. We, the public, can take liberties; they the journalist are, in theory at least, expected to mediate *their* news by objective means for us the public to consume, whilst we the public can also mediate news in the most extreme and distorted fashion, thus the many scathing attacks upon the net and in particular *blogs* for their apparent unreliable production of news. This not only informs us of the changing character of news, but equally informs us of the changing character of journalism and what it means to be a journalist.

Two writers amongst many others who have launched attacks on the internet and blogging in particular for failing to produce news based on factual accounts is the journalist for the UK's *Independent*, Robert Fisk, and Andrew Keen, who wrote the *Cult of the Amateur* in 2007. In an interview with Justin Podur, Fisk commented on how newspapers were far more trustworthy as sources of reliable news and using the Middle East as a context of news stated:

> the *New York Times, Los Angeles Times, Washington Post* version of events doesn't satisfy millions of people. So more and more people are trying to find a different and more accurate narrative of events … . It is a tribute to their intelligence that instead of searching for blog-o-bots or whatever, they are looking to the European 'mainstream' newspapers like *The Independent*, the *Guardian*, the *Financial Times*. (Podur 2005)

With regards to *The Independent*, Fisk added 'I'm not just running some internet site' and with regards to readers world-wide Fisk claimed 'that a British journalist can write things they can't read elsewhere but which must have a considerable basis in truth because otherwise it wouldn't appear in a Major British paper'. Finally, Fisk claimed that the internet was 'unreliable'; ironically this interview appeared on the internet at http://www.rabble.ca – as the Disposable Heroes of Hypocrisy once sang: 'Hypocrisy is the greatest luxury, raise the double standards.' It is therefore not problematic to see that Fisk, and others who share his views, believe that certain sources of information, not just the internet either, are not producers of news, because despite all of the complexities surrounding its actual meaning, there is the belief that authenticity is a central feature in the production of news and more often than not authentic and reliable sources of news are often characterized by the relationship of journalist–news organ.

Keen disparagingly refers to internet space as the 'blogosphere' where it is fast replacing the mainstream media and threatening the ethos that underpins news. For Keen the criticism is summed up by his reference to bloggers as 'amateurs' and contrasts this with the 'professionalism' of traditional newsmakers. Keen views web-world as a dangerous place creating pernicious criteria for what constitutes news; it's a post-modernist's dream come true. In web-world the amateurs reign supreme criticizing mainstream journalists for creating unreliable news whilst remaining blissfully truthful; Keen attempts to convert this state of being.

Both Fisk's and Keen's views are contentious and controversial; however, to understand what it means to be a journalist as opposed to an ordinary citizen conveying a news story, we need to investigate further the structures and the guidelines that characterize practice, for without them journalists would simply be ordinary citizens conveying the same news as us but by a different means. The editor of UK newspaper *The Guardian*, Alan Rusbridger (Pritchard 2007), argued at the annual meeting of the Organization of News Ombudsman at Harvard University that new technology is fast blurring the boundaries between hitherto distinct 'journalist' and 'citizen', with the former now contributing to news rather than being the definitive author and definer of news. Rusbridger also claimed that changes were perhaps occurring too 'rapidly' in our contemporary world, a point also made by Joseph Hatton back in 1882!

> The history of the newspaper press changes almost as rapidly as the effects which a landscape artist vainly tries to fix upon his canvass in a permanent form and colour. (Preface to Hatton 1882)

At the same meeting, Jeff Jarvis stated that 'collaboration with the public' was the way forward, and this would certainly be perceived as progressive, democratic and ethical for supporters of the main media ethics school of thought in the US, namely Public Journalism, who have called for some time now for more involvement from citizens in constructing news for their communities. Perhaps the important issue to bear in mind is not so much defining news, because news is everywhere, but rather to focus on those who are able to dominate public news agendas by addressing a large number of people.

The Newspaper

> Newspapers did not create news; news created newspapers. (Emery 1972, p. 3)

Understanding the tri-partite relationship between news, newspaper and journalist is fundamental towards understanding the social function of journalism. Although Emery's quote nicely demonstrates the relationship between news and newspapers, there is, however, a problem with emphasis in that news appears to have been reified into a living–acting organism capable of producing a form of communication independent of other things and beings; the fact is humans created newspapers and, moreover, humans create news. Whatever the social and cultural context of news, in historic and/or contemporary times, its uses and modes of production and consumption, what we know is that gathering and distributing news as a part of oral culture doesn't necessarily transform the speaker into a journalist. Moreover, what we can say with a degree of certainty is that journalism is intrinsically tied to newspaper, although not confined to it. Even though new technology is changing the meaning of news and journalism, the fact is that the development of newspapers helped to define news more specifically and, what's more, newspapers defined the context of journalism as a social practice.

When we assess the historical texts on journalism we can see that three distinct but interrelated forms emerge; news, journalism and newspaper. If we are to understand journalism as a social function and the concerns of academics with ethics and standards, we need to understand this tri-partite relationship because it forms the basis of responsibilities. The three forms are distinct in so much that, (1) news can be a product of non-journalists; and (2) journalists and/or early writers of news have and continue to use other modes of expression other than a newspaper to express news. The newspaper, however, by definition, incorporates both news and journalism and within this printed space a series of ethical issues arise concerning how production of news proceeds, particularly in relation to the purpose of journalism in relation to society. Defining what constitutes a newspaper therefore has served to provide us with some indication of journalistic practice, particularly the idea that newspapers are authentic, reliable and trustworthy organs of communication. In contemporary times there are many within as well as outside journalism that despair at the idea that new media, the internet and blogs provide authentic, reliable and trustworthy news. It's claimed that the new media is threatening true journalism and the place where it rightly belongs, the newspaper. This fear is captured in UNESCOs 'Student Journalism Competition' to commemorate the UN World Press Freedom Day, 3 May 2008, entitled 'Is New Media Killing Journalism?' in association with *The Guardian*.[3]

To understand contemporary concerns it's worth reviewing some of the important texts that have provided meaning on what constitutes a newspaper in relation to the historical constitution of practice. Perhaps the earliest account for defining a newspaper can be found in Frederick Knight Hunt's *The Fourth Estate: Contributions Towards a History of Newspapers, and of the Liberty of the Press* originally published in 1850; republished in 1998. Hunt (1998) explains how *The English Mercurie*, first published in 1588, was widely thought to have been the first newspaper, but disputes this. Equally for Hunt, news-books and pamphlets published in 1603 and 1607 are dismissed as constituting a newspaper proper. Rather, whilst sharing certain characteristics with news-books and pamphlets such

---

3   See http://www.unesco.org.uk/pressfreedomcompetition.htm.

as relative freedom to speak and propagating news, newspapers were nevertheless to be defined in very different terms.

Certainly, the oral news that Hastings (2000) had spoken of changed dramatically during this period with the development of both single-sheet *corantos* and the multiple-sheet news-books; the latter according to Herds (1952) were the forerunner to the development of the newspaper. Similar to Hunt, Herds also states that 1622 was the defining moment for the emergence of the newspaper in British society.

Whilst the tradition of relaying news informally, without hard evidence, barely changed, the form certainly did. News-books were mainly distributed within localities but curiously covered international news rather than local news, and were often translated from foreign languages. News would come from as far afield as Italy, Germany, Holland and Hungary. Bringing news in this fashion had always existed with the migration of peoples or of travellers moving from place to place; the difference was form and the written rather than the spoken word began to emerge as king with the aid of transit.

News-books and pamphlets certainly contained news, and both were thin books of a few pages. News-books contained between four to eight pages and differed from pamphlets in the manner in which discourse was conducted. Pamphleteers tended to be more critical and radically minded than the authors of News-books, but both shared a common arrangement: irregular publication. This irregularity in publication became a central point for Hunt's analysis and he doesn't hesitate in providing an exact moment in British history when the very first newspaper emerged in society:

> The is no reason to doubt that the puny ancestor of the myriads of broad sheets of our time was published in the metropolis in 1622, and that the most prominent of the ingenious speculators who offered the novelty to the world was one Nathaniel Butter. (Hunt 1998, p. 9)

The title of what Hunt claims to be the first newspaper was *The Weekly News*, and it is distinct from its predecessors that had emerged in the mid to late sixteenth century. This perspective was also shared by Fox Bourne (1887) who had claimed that 1820 had marked 200 years of newspaper history using Nathaniel Butter's '*Courant* or *Weekly News*' (p. 373) as the chief indicator 'in what appears to have been the first attempt to give in said form and at regular intervals' (ibid.). The defining characteristic of the newspaper for Hunt was regular publication coupled with 'connection' (Hunt 1998, p. 10) between each weekly copy. The word used to describe the orderly fashion in which publication proceeded is 'systematic' and Hunt takes note of how weekly editions were systematically numbered. Frank's (1961) work on the English press between 1620 and 1660 came to similar conclusions placing emphasis on print runs at regular intervals. Frank also stressed the reporting of current events in providing a clear definition of both news and newspaper.

Here too emerges a new moment for Hunt, who argued that Nathaniel Butter was for reasons of regularity a 'news-writer' (1998, p. 11) and during the mid-1600s news-writers of various persuasions emerged to do battle with each other, or what we term in modern times manoeuvre for hegemony. Hunt referred to this historical event as a 'paper war', which the 'first newspaper writers waged with each other' (ibid., p. 111). The business of journalism then, according to Hunt, had begun in earnest. Bleyer (1927, p. 8) also notes a change in production but doesn't refer to Butter's publication as a newspaper:

> At the close of the year 1624, Butter and Bourne headed their news-book *The Continuation of our Weekly Newes* ... . As this designation was continued for at least twenty-three successive weekly issues, it may be regarded as the first instance of the use of a title for a coranto news-book.

Hunt's account of the emergence of newspapers and news-writers, or to use the modern term journalist, is disputed by Alexander Andrews in his book *The History of British Journalism*, published nine years later in 1859, republished in 1998. Andrews argues that the history of newspapers can be traced much further back to Ancient Rome and by implication the practice – or shall I say *spirit* – of journalism can also be located to this period. Here, too, regular copy can be found: 'The Romans had their daily reports of public occurrences called *Acta Diurna*, spoken of by Senaca' (Andrews 1998, p. 9). The fact that the *Acta Diurna* 'were issued "by authority" of the government' (ibid., pp. 9–10) was for Andrews irrelevant for disputing the claim of being a newspaper. In fact, Hunt probably wouldn't have disputed this either recognizing that in the seventeenth century newspapers were the tool of government, Church and others. For Hunt, the people responsible for content and copy were not of importance, but rather the regular issuing of publication was deemed to be the defining characteristic. Andrews, however, uses Hunt's model for defining a newspaper and states that the *Acta Diurna* 'make good a claim to be regarded as a newspaper, if periodical publication and the promulgation of news are ... the essential points of difference between newspapers and proclamations, or pamphlets' (ibid., p. 10).

The regular distribution and orderly numbering that Hunt believed distinguished newspapers from previous copy was made possible because of technological development and control over the means of production. Nathaniel Butter, after all, was publisher, printer and writer. However, Andrews was critical of this claiming 'types and presses do not constitute a newspaper' (ibid.). Not only does Andrews claim that Ancient Rome is the birthplace of the newspaper, but astonishingly that it is equally the place in which we can legitimately trace the origins of journalism: 'Italy – whatever may have been the real character of the *Acta Diurna* – can still claim to have been the birthplace of journalism' (ibid., p. 12) and the reason for this is because Rome was the first place to have a 'public newspaper' (ibid.). Accordingly, making news *public* in print defines the role of the journalist regardless of who owned the means of production.

Hastings (2000) makes a similar if not identical claim arguing that the process of newsgathering can be traced to classical times, but makes no statement about whether the form of mediation was a newspaper or not, or whether the mediator could be perceived as a journalist: 'even as far back as classical times, attempts to record news in written forms occurred. Under Julius Caesar and his successors, a daily record of political news and acts was recorded at Rome and distributed to the Roman colonies.' This account of recording and making news public in print is perfectly reasonable in relation to Rome. The issue of whether the writers of news could be perceived as forerunners of journalism, however, is more contentious. We only need look at contemporary debates regarding journalism to understand that autonomy is a defining feature of a journalist's work. Herman and Chomsky's (1988) 'propaganda model' is an apt reminder that journalists who simply transmit government spin can hardly be regarded as autonomous or even have *relative autonomy* from governmental constraints. A journalist that simply peddles government spin, knowingly or unknowingly, wittingly or unwittingly, is a propagandist, by default or other means. Using Joel Feinberg's (1973) model, autonomy translates into freedom *from* constraints and this enables a journalist to be free *to* work independently; perhaps realistically this can only translate into *relative autonomy*, but even that is preferable to absolute dependence on powerful elites.

Using Allen (1930) as a starting point, Emery (1972, p. 3) lists seven points as criteria for a newspaper of which the first point states that 'it must be published at least once a week'. Point 6 states 'it must be timely, or relatively so' and point 7 states 'it must have stability, as contrasted by the fly-by-night publications of more primitive times'. Similar to the English writers Hunt and Fox-Bourne, the American historian of journalism Edwin Emery has argued that the *corantos* of early sixteenth-century England also constituted a newspaper:

> It was not until 1624 that the corantos began to be identified by name, thus supplying something of the continuity required of a true newspaper. The earliest known coranto published by title was *The Continuation of Our Weekly Newes*, from the office of Bourne and Butter. Because this title appeared on at least 23 consecutive issues, the offering marks another step in the development of the newspaper. (ibid., pp. 9–10)

He then claims that the '*Oxford Gazette* in 1665 ... was, strictly speaking, the first periodical to meet all of the qualifications of a true newspaper' because of the regularity of publication, which was twice-weekly, a point equally made by Mott (1962, p. 8), stressing that the *Gazette* was 'regularly issued' as opposed to Almanacs, which 'were issued only once a year' (Rutland 1973, p. 20). However, despite the time spent between producing almanacs, Rutland argues that they did contain acts of journalism: 'Broadsides were an important form of eighteenth-century journalism', but are not defined as newspapers because of the 'irregular' (ibid.) publication.

Bleyer (1927, p. 13) also states: 'The period of the news-book may be said to end, and that of the newspaper begin, with the publication in 1665 of the single-sheet, semi-weekly *Oxford Gazette*, the first English newspaper', whilst the 'first daily paper, the *Daily Courant*, appeared on March 11, 1702' (ibid., p. 16). Undoubtedly, most historians of the press see regularity of publication as an important criteria for determining whether an organ of information is perceived as a newspaper or not. What distinguished the *Gazette* from the *Courant* is time, one semi-weekly, the other daily and like their contemporary counterparts there are the weekly *Sunday* press and the daily press. Whatever the differences in time, both groups of newspapers provide news, which could be historical as well as up-to-date, if the former is *revealing* something to the public for the very first time. But surely what also binds these groups are the actions or practices that people are affectively engaged in; namely, journalism. Thus, time or regularity are in my opinion not as important, if at all, as the *practice* and *method* in determining what constitutes a newspaper. For surely what really conditions and constitutes a newspaper is journalism, and the debate in media ethics and media criticism of whether a publication reflects good practice and serves society well is indeed a matter of ethical debate over what constitutes an act of news that has societal value beyond the act of journalism.

It's believed that the earliest *corantos* to be published in England was in 1621 but according to Bleyer (1927, p. 6) there 'were doubtless reprints of corantos published in Amsterdam'. Bleyer continues: 'The earliest extant prototype of the newspaper printed in England is a coranto, issued by Nicholas Bourne … 1621' (ibid.). Many of the known *corantos* were printed on both sides of a single sheet but: 'In 1622 the single-sheet was superseded by the news-book coranto, a pamphlet consisting of eight to forty pages' (ibid.).

Stephens (2007, p. 131) has claimed that: 'To qualify as a newspaper, most journalism historians would agree, a publication must be available to a significant portion of the public, as were the news-books or news ballads with which Europe was already familiar', adding as criteria 'regularity', 'frequency', 'variety of different stories' and 'consistent and recognizable format', further arguing that the 'Venetian gazettes' of the sixteenth century contain many of the above criteria and are therefore 'perhaps the oldest direct ancestors of the modern newspaper' (ibid., p. 134). For Stephens, 'news-books or news ballads' (ibid., p. 142) cannot be described as newspapers where the *corantos* could because they managed, amongst other things, 'to squeeze in late-breaking developments' (ibid.). Shifting the emphasis, Emery (1972, p. 1) has claimed that:

> It is now generally conceded that the modern press is the gift of no one nation, and that it was already in the process of development in other parts of the world long before the corantos began to be read in London … The oldest known and preserved copies of a primitive newspaper were published in Germany in 1609 …

Black's (1991) work on the eighteenth century English press stresses the importance of adopting a 'pragmatic approach' (ibid., p. xv) towards the assessment of newspapers. Two of the defining characteristics thus far discussed are 'regularity' and 'up-to-date news', but the issue of content was also important and Black notes that the broad content and issues that were included in newspapers were also apparent in magazines:

> Items characteristic of the eighteenth-century magazines can be found in abundance in the newspapers of the period. The distinction between the two is more one of size and frequency than of content. Essay-sheets, journals devoted to a single essay and bereft usually of news and advertisements, are not regarded by some as newspapers. (ibid.)

Black goes on to state that: 'Any rigid definition ignores the fluid nature of the eighteenth-century press, titles changing their format, content and frequency of publication' (ibid.). Regularity and size for Black are less important than the reporting of news, thus: 'Essay papers appearing at least weekly' that report news are included within the broad view of newspapers whilst magazines that are published at similar intervals, but negate up-to-date news, aren't. Editorials were in the eighteenth century, and continue to be, a key characteristic of newspapers and, as Black explains: 'Many newspapers increasingly offered a distinct editorial', however, content 'could be found in papers prior to 1789' (ibid., p. 281). Although editorials are a means to convey opinion that in theory attempts to be distinctive from that of competitors, for our purposes they are only useful to distinguish them from the debate over the practice of journalism.

In the US, some writers have claimed that the first newspaper was produced by Benjamin Harris in 1690 titled *Publick Occurences, Both Foreign and Domestick*. For instance, Mott (1962) in the chapter titled: 'First Newspapers in "The New England"' states that it was the 'first American newspaper', a point similarly made by Stephens (2007, p. 163) who has no problem with comparing *Public Occurences* to the *Boston News-Letter* as 'a newspaper' (ibid.) even though the former had only one issue, whilst the latter 'survived for 72 years'. Equally, for Mott the single issue of *Public Occurences* seemed not to matter for he refers to it as 'the first American newspaper' despite the fact that he acknowledges that it 'ended summarily after the publication of only one number' (1962, p. 9). So too for Bleyer (1927, p. 45) referring to it as a 'newspaper' and comparing it in this way to 'colonial newspapers of a later date' despite the fact that is was 'one issue' where later colonial papers were published more regularly.

Emery (1972, p. 27) positions himself very differently, arguing that 'one of the qualifications of a newspaper is periodicity, or continuity' and this being the case would appear to disqualify *Publick Occurences*, whilst Mott's (1962, p. 11) sub-heading in relation to the *Boston News-Letter*, 'The First *Continuous* American Newspaper' (my emphasis) suggests that longevity isn't an issue for defining a newspaper and stating in relation to the *Mercury* in Philadelphia that it was 'the third continuous paper in the colonies' (ibid., pp. 24–25). For his part, Emery (1972, p. 21) argues that 'there was printed on the morning of April 24, 1704, the first genuine American newspaper. It was called the *Boston News-Letter.*'

Tabloid

The historical debates concerning regularity, consistency of title, and volume or number of pages are in the main technical issues. These provide us some understanding of what constitutes a newspaper but they are far from complete. What is clear however are the differences in emphasis on what constitutes a newspaper regarding these points. Differences are not however related solely to these technical issues but also concern practice and content. Thus, whilst it's important to review the historical debates on what constitutes a newspaper, the concerns within the field of media ethics over newspaper production broadens this debate to consider ethical issues over content, standards, quality of performance and responsible journalism. Whether or not specific concerns are acceptable is not of interest at this stage, but they do, however, highlight the issue of what constitutes news and what's more what journalism *should* be about. The newspaper therefore becomes a battleground of ideas as we observe the legitimacy of content.

Size and shape hasn't and continues not to be a consideration in the determination of a newspaper. However the 'tabloid' format has brought and continues to bring with it a controversy that strikes right at the heart of the meaning of news, the definition of newspaper and the meaning and social function of journalism. In the UK today, most, but certainly not all of the ethical concerns over standards and quality of performance are directed towards tabloids and they reflect the historical ethical concerns over the yellow press in the US with its similar tabloid approach to news.

The term 'tabloid' today has connotations beyond its original meaning and academics have added the awkward sounding term *tabloidization of culture* as a result of the tabloid type of newsgathering with its particular form of content and specific mode of address. Many argue that content is salacious and that tabloids lower journalistic standards; so much so that it is arguable whether or not certain newspapers in a tabloid format actually are newspapers or even represent an act of journalism. The *tabloidization of culture*, however, is a consequence of specific actions or the effects of media. It isn't a term that allows us to understand the specific processes of news in relation to elements of tabloid newspapers.

Mott (1962, p. 671) with reference to the development of the tabloid press in the US during the early decades of the twentieth century provides us with such a term where the author states: 'This was the beginning of the end of the worst phase of "gutter journalism". The eight-column papers had been protesting for a year or two against the excesses of *tabloidism*' (my emphasis). *Tabloidism* as a mode of address and conveyor of a specific form of information, sold as news, raises interesting issues about whether certain tabloids can be verified as newspapers. If we are to judge a newspaper on the basis of regularity of production and continuation of title then certainly all tabloids fit the criteria of being a newspaper. However, when we shift the emphasis to content and practice it becomes highly suspect that certain tabloids can be effectively defined as newspapers. We've already seen above how many UK tabloids use television soap operas as news items and this is unacceptable because it negates facts of actual life; hyperreality rules over reality. Indeed in 'Sensationalism and Tabloidism', Pribanic-Smith (2002, p. 267) argues that tabloid is not only a matter concerned with size but with a specific mode of address relating to journalism:

> Sensationalism by its very nature exploits the unusual … . Historians have long argued the definition of sensationalism in journalism. A consensus of the arguments includes an appeal to baser emotions – excitement, titillation, shock, astonishment, horror, and so forth.

Although Pribanic-Smith doesn't explore further the issue concerning base emotions, the fact is that they have been and continue to be associated with the lower classes in society. In the UK there are class readership categories that signify the differences in readership levels: 'A' is the highest and normally readers of, for example, the *Daily Telegraph* and 'C' and 'D' are amongst the lowest and normally reading, for example, the *Sun* and *Daily Star*. The former is broadsheet with more words; the latter two are tabloids with minimal words and thus less intellectually taxing. In this context sensationalism and tabloidism are seen as modes of address mainly for the less educated classes. The issue of tabloid news therefore impacts on the meaning of journalism because it has shifted the focus on news practice.

One of the interesting criticisms against *tabloidism* is that it is contrasted with the so-called 'quality press' and the argument that it is the audience that conditions content. Many writers have claimed that the lower educational standards of tabloid readers account for the lowering of taste and content in the press and that readers of the quality press have a superior cultural capital at their disposal. This apparent distinction is summed up by Rutland (1973, p. xxi) with reference to Wilbur Schramm:

> news audiences have generally fitted into one of two categories. The 'immediate reward' audience seeks immediate gratification of the senses, delights in scandal and small talk, and has no worries about what is news and what is entertainment – all are of a piece … . On the other hand, the 'delayed reward' audience is composed of merchants, professional men, scholars … . (ibid.)

This notion of distinct audiences based on distinct modes of address has a long history. In many ways, both the content and mode of address that is found in contemporary British tabloids or the penny and yellow press in the US is reminiscent of the broadsheet ballads and chapbooks produced in sixteenth-century England and even though a variety of content is indicative of both, the broadsheet ballads and chapbooks nevertheless contained the stuff of tabloids today with their focus on the sensational. As Bleyer (1927, p. 3) states, the content covered news on 'crime, catastrophe, scandal, battle or death' and continues: 'Contemporary criticism shows that some of these ballads were regarded as quite sensational, and quite as often concerned with trivial events, as were some newspapers of a later date' (ibid.).

In relation to the US press, Mott (1962, p. 666), under the chapter heading 'The Tabloid Newspaper', rightly states that the tabloid has a long history and that: 'The term "tabloid" as applied to newspapers at first referred solely to small page-size.' Early American newspapers were small in size mainly for lack of news, but other important reasons for remaining small was linked to economics. Smallness was also indicative of the early English newspapers and today in the UK former broadsheet newspapers, which were associated with 'quality', are now formatted in tabloid size such as *The Times* (founded as *The Times of London* in 1788) and *The Independent*. The *Guardian* changed its format to *Berliner* style, which in terms of size is somewhere between tabloid and broadsheet. Whether the new tabloid-sized newspapers such as *The Times* and *Independent* are changing the way they approach journalism is beyond this discussion, but their transition to a tabloid size highlights the complexities associated with tabloid formats and the supposedly 'dumbing down' (tabloidization) of culture through the lowering of standards.

This complexity can also be highlighted with historical reference to *New York World* in the US and the *Daily Mirror* in the UK, although for very different reasons. As Mott (1962, pp. 666–667) has stated, Alfred Harmsworth, later to become Lord Northcliffe, established the *Mirror* in 1903 and persuaded Joseph Pulitzer to publish a copy of the *New York World* in January 1901: 'Its editor called it a "tabloid newspaper"', but the paper was published in tabloid format style only for one day. If regularity can be used as a determining factor for a newspaper then so it should apply to a tabloid newspaper and this being so in terms of time-scale, the *World* had more in common with Benjamin Harris's *Publick Occurences* in 1690 than the *Mirror*, which was in tabloid format and produced on a regular basis. Therefore, the *World*, according to the criteria of regularity, was not a tabloid – at least not in terms of format – but prior to that one day change and thereafter it continued to produce yellow journalism that, as a journalistic style, has all the hallmarks of *tabloidism* producing news in a sensationalist way. It is also worth remembering that the accusations that a newspaper is sensationalist has characteristics pertaining to *tabloidization*, and the accusation that such newspapers are 'dumbing down' culture are in the main, but not always, confined to, elitist critiques. For instance, in relation to Harmsworth's *Daily Mail* and *Daily Mirror*: 'Lord Salisbury remarked that "having invented a daily newspaper for those who cannot think, Mr. Harmsworth has now invented one for those who cannot read"' (Mott 1962, p. 667). What the *New York World* had proved was that a style of abrasive journalism not associated with the so-called 'quality press' had little to do with size or tabloid and it opens up an interesting debate on the constitution of journalism as a social practice.

But the complexities over the *Daily Mirror* deepen particularly when we consider the transformation that the paper underwent throughout its existence. It began as a paper for women in 1903 then became a pictorial paper in 1904. Alfred Harmsworth sold the paper to his brother Harold (Lord Rothermere) in 1913 using the paper for his own ends by supporting the British Fascist Oswald Mosley in the 1930s. But in the late 1930s Cecil King radically transformed the paper from a 'respectable' middle-class paper into a left-wing paper campaigning on behalf of the working-class, and the form of journalism that emerged in this tabloid was popular journalism as opposed to the *tabloidism* that it is associated with today.

Carter and Allan (2000, p. 132) in '"If it bleeds, it leads": Ethical questions about popular journalism' refer to the American journalist Carl Bernstein who rightly claimed that: 'Good journalism is popular culture, but popular culture that stretches and informs its consumers rather than that which appeals to the ever descending lowest common denominator.' They also referred to the British journalist Matthew Engel claiming that good popular journalism 'has become debased' (ibid.). Therefore, the distinction between popular journalism and commercial journalism, irrespective of format, is a distinction and argument over both the meaning of journalism and news.

Unfortunately, Stephens (2007, p. 112) under the sub-title '"Popular" Journalism' conflates *tabloidism* with *popular journalism*: 'Most of us would probably agree, however reluctantly, that there is an inverse relationship between level of education – and therefore to some extent social class – and susceptibility to the more *emotive* and *fanciful* forms of journalism' (my emphasis) before highlighting a difference between 'popular' and 'serious' journalism' (ibid., p. 114); the former wrongly associated with *tabloidism*.

The term *tabloidization of culture* through a mode of address associates *tabloidism* primarily with commercialism. When we compare the mode of address and content of *tabloidism* with popular journalism, size indeed does not matter. But it informs us of the struggle over both the meaning of journalism and certainly the value of news. Moreover, regardless of views, the fact remains that tabloids have had a profound impact on the constitution of journalism and certainly upon the social function and purpose of journalism, and this has provided rich material for academics concerned with media ethics as well as journalists who disassociate themselves from the activities of people who are deemed to be responsible for inauthentic, debased journalism.

Chapter 2

Journalism

In its origin, journalism was not the child of the printing press. The germ of it is to be found in the circular letters sent round after Agincourt and other medieval battles; and the profession of a writer of 'letters of news' or 'intelligence' dates from the establishment of regular postal services. Long before this, however, statesmen had found it necessary to have a constant supply of news. In the days of Queen Elizabeth, Robert Devereux, Earl of Essex, founded a staff of clerks in order to provide himself with news. His establishment for this purpose vied with that of government itself. His clerks, Anthony Bacon, Sir Henry Wotton, Cuffe, Reynolds and Temple, so plentifully supplied him with intelligence that they were one of the sources of his power. But these were not journalists writing for the public … .
(Williams 1901–21)

For Williams, the distinguishing factor between a journalist and other writers is that the former write for the public, which in modern times translates into the idea of the public interest, more often than not defined by news organizations. It's a problematic concept, but the point Williams makes is one of principle. Williams is right to attach journalism to the provision of news, and equally correct to point out that other (non-journalist) sources can also supply news, which complicates matters concerning the identification of core factors that constitute the practice of journalism from other sources of news both historically and in modern times. For instance, the latest academic material concerning the 'citizen journalist' – the ordinary person armed to the teeth with new technologies able to submit texts and images (news) without formal training, either through industry or university – is yet another, if rather unconvincing piece of the complex journalistic jigsaw puzzle, for it requires us to re-evaluate what journalism is and what distinguishes journalism from other forms of information provision.

Although the term 'journalist'[1] wasn't used in the UK at least until the early nineteenth century (Conboy 2004), as Williams alludes to above, the practice of gathering and distributing news has been a human condition for some considerable time. What we know so far is that journalism *as a practice* is intrinsically connected to the gathering and distribution of news via varying degrees of technologies throughout the ages, but it isn't exclusive to journalists, and therefore this rudimentary fact doesn't inform us much about what distinguishes a journalist from an ordinary member of the public who also gathers and distributes news. Non-journalists, if I can use that term, also select, omit and deceive, and are rarely

---

1   'Journalism' derives from the French word *journal*.

objective in their everyday accounts, and in doing so all reduce news of events to a bare minimum; we all self-edit, sometimes conveniently so. Journalists have been criticized for doing something similar, that is, reducing news to convenient sound bites, of not being objective; of not providing a full and truthful account of news. Yet we may be forgiven for taking convenient shortcuts, whereas journalist practice is at times held up to the closest of scrutiny, and not just in relation to the end result (distribution), but equally the means by which news is gathered.

Defining journalism is a central concern of media ethics and Conboy's (2004) study of journalism, although interesting, is mostly analytical, never normative. The following quote from Rutland is also analytically evaluated:

> The term *journalism* has been variously interpreted. Journalism in pre-radio days might consist only of a printed page issued on a regular schedule. In this volume the assumption is that journalism is a spoken, printed, or visual report of timely interest to a mass audience. Thus, while the town crier's messages were not recorded, they were a rudimentary form of journalism. Indeed, journalism, particularly before 1800, included not only newspapers and magazines but broadsides, almanacs, and pamphlets as well. (Rutland 1973, p. xii)

So is this:

> These corantos, first as single sheets, then as news-books, containing only foreign news gleaned largely if not entirely from Continental news periodicals, constitute the *first stage* in the evolution of English journalism (Bleyer 1927, pp. 8–9)

I am not attempting to undermine analytical approaches, for they inform us of the historical roots of practice. Furthermore, they form the basis of normative evaluations of practice. But the question to consider is why are academics and journalists so concerned with quality of performance and standards in journalism? Sociological-analytical observations are important but they are limiting in this context; moral philosophy can go beyond the purely analytical to intellectually engage with the *meaning and social function of journalism*. However, this isn't an argument for separation, but rather is one supporting an *interdisciplinary* approach to the practice of journalism; for where moral philosophy in relation to media can go beyond a sociological approach, it is also limited, particularly where it tends to negate questions of power and ideology.

The question above isn't difficult to answer because the concern with ethics in journalism is one based on both production, that is, methods of newsgathering (objectivity or not, for instance) and the way in which news is framed for consumption (truth or not). Interestingly, within the discipline of media ethics, the focus of analysis heavily leans towards the production side; rarely if ever does it engage with consumption. For instance, I'm not aware of any substantial ethnographic account within media ethics that has produced empirical data detailing how news is consumed and what value it has *vis-à-vis* a democratic process. However, it is assumed that in theory at least there are substantial benefits that emanate from journalism to the advantage of society; hence an ethical concern with practice. However, these benefits are negated if practice lacks the required standards set out by some critics within the field of media ethics, thus a concern with normative principles to set matters on the right course; so the concern with practice is one evidently based on the relationship between journalism and society.

When we view the development of journalism throughout various places and within different periods of history we note that differences in what occurred and in what *should* occur vary from place to place. What is so interesting about a discourse in media ethics is the view that good ethical practice should become universal regardless of place. The contemporary ethical analysis of journalism in the UK for instance is one that invokes historical developments in journalism, so to attempt to thoroughly come to terms with the meaning of journalism and offer new insights we need to understand its history. In relation to the development of journalism in the UK, Herds (1952, p. 11) states:

> BRITISH journalism as we know it today is the product of a slow-moving evolution in the seventeenth and eighteenth centuries – a development that was watched with unfriendly eyes by kings and Parliament alike. There has never been a period in our history when authority has genuinely liked the idea of full publicity for its activities and unchecked criticism of its conduct, though in modern freedom of expression; but in the seventeenth century the dislike of journalism was violent and unconcealed and took the form of repressive measures varying from censorship to suppression and from fines to imprisonment for those engaged in writing, printing and distributing news of, and comment on, public affairs.

Herd's comments tally with those of Hunt discussed earlier in Chapter 1, not just in terms of Hunt's belief that the first newspaper in Britain can be located in the early seventeenth century, but rather the belief that the origins of British journalism can be located in this period in relation to newspapers. Hunt's argument is that newspapers are distinguished from pamphlets because the former were produced regularly, whilst the latter were published sporadically. Hunt made no point on content, purpose or practice, so theoretically a pamphlet published regularly, regardless of size, could be considered as a newspaper and as an expression of journalism.

Pamphleteers are associated with the dissemination of political discourse and one of the best known was the English radical Thomas Paine (1737–1809) who vigorously campaigned for American Independence. Depending how we define journalism and its purpose, it could be argued that Paine wasn't a journalist, if we are to take objectivity as *the* defining characteristic, for Paine was an agitator and propagandist. The subjective context of *gonzo journalism* and its supporters would dispute objective accounts, claim that Paine was a journalist because his writing was honest and that's as truthful as one could get.

Other writers such as Jonathan Swift, Daniel Defoe and John Milton were also, amongst other things, pamphleteers. Swift wrote for *The Examiner*, a periodical founded in 1710 and published on a weekly basis. Swift's style was similar to the modern-day columnist and, typical of that period, Swift would reference ancient works such as Virgil's *Aeneid* or the poetry of the Roman poet Horace.[2] Swift was a part of the Tory political establishment and could be viewed as a conservative writer and even a political 'spin doctor'. However, this is too simplistic, for Swift was also a writer in the spirit of Irish causes and wrote *The Drapier's Letters*, a collection of pamphlets written under the pseudonym of M.B. Drapier, so sensitive was the subject matter.

Defoe was also a pamphleteer and agitated with a radical spirit. One of his pamphlets, *The Shortest Way with Dissenters*, was a stinging critique of the 'High Church' tradition within Anglicanism. The word dissenter derives from the Latin word *dissentire* meaning 'to disagree'. Dissenting and radicalism are but two sides of the same coin; the word radical derives from the Latin word *radix* meaning 'root' and radicals are known for 'leaving no stone unturned' (Button 1995, p. xiii) in their quest to question and critique establishment by means of dissent. The purpose of radical journalism, and we see it in Defoe, was to question authority in order to affect social, political, cultural and economic change.

John Milton also produced pamphlets but to a lesser extent and these were, to all extent and purposes, polemics aimed against the institution of English marriage law in which Milton sought to broaden support for divorce. However, Milton believed that pamphlets should be used for subversive purposes and he vigorously contributed to their production by typesetting the print. As a supporter for Puritan causes, Milton supported the heady mixture of political agitation and news, not that dissimilar from Lenin's theory of the press in which Lenin saw the press and journalists simply as a means to propagate revolutionary ideas.

The seventeenth century was certainly a unique period in British history and not only because of the English Civil War in the 1640s, but for our purposes the explosion of the press and pamphleteering that grew out of that experience. The war had spurred the development of diverse political and religious ideas, which entailed the plurality of pamphlets (Harris 1995). The seventeenth century witnessed a huge growth in printing presses and collectively the plurality of diverse ideas equally witnessed a new moment in journalistic development, namely a wider public interest and an intensification of public opinion. This period of pamphlet growth also witnessed a development of distribution networks widening the readership away from the towns, which were by and large the domains in which pamphlets were both produced and consumed. As Griscom states:

---

2   See *The Examiner*, No. XIII, Thursday 2 November 1710 for references to both Virgil and Horace.

The most prolific, not to mention, democratic form of expression on an individual level was undoubtedly the pamphlet. Once it was printed in London, a pamphlet would be sold on street corners or in print shops or carried to more rural locations and sold for next-to-nothing. Some copies were either bought by retailers for resale in the country, carried by their owners on travels away from the capital, or sent by 'post' to friends in the countryside. Once a copy reached a village or town it would be posted for greater consumption. (Griscom n.d.)

Defoe is not only currently viewed as a pamphleteer, a novelist and a satirist, but equally associated with journalism, and it has long been held that Defoe was the first to develop 'economic journalism'. However, to associate pamphleteering with journalism in every case appears to be problematic. Surely one defining feature of journalism is independence from powerful establishment elites. This is not to argue that journalists do not have sympathies with political ideologies, although forcefully expressing them in news text is arguably controversial, but rather to recognize that autonomous activity is necessary to avoid political spin and propaganda. Journalism, after all, is not only based on a relationship *of* power, but more importantly is a relationship *with* and *against* power. So, when the establishment uses printed copy to propagate its views, as previously discussed in Chapter 1 with reference to the daily edicts of Roman politicians, then it can no longer be described as journalism, because quite evidently this is an abuse of political power and privilege. A similar problem emerged with the pamphlet:

Many of the pamphlet responses exhibited a fear of the new media by attacking the very rise of scandalous pamphlets. Charles I, himself, was known for authoring pamphlets in response to various charges, and lamenting the noxious anarchy of expression. The king responded defiantly in a broadside to charges that he was complicit in the Irish Rebellion. (ibid.)

In an interesting work by William Bowles, the author claims that Paine was in fact not only a journalist but also an early day 'blogger'. The latter term is interesting because Bowles argues that any individual, in the modern sense, can become a blogger, if they have access to the Internet, and therefore, by definition, anyone can become a journalist:

the 'Blog' has at long last enabled us to challenge the long-held assumption that to be a journalist you need to have some special dispensation from some higher power that enables one to stand aside from the human race and cast an 'objective' eye over events. (Bowles 2005)

Bowles's approach to the practice and meaning of journalism is located in the historical development of a form of practice. Bloggers are the new pamphleteers, but equally the 'citizen journalist' can also be included in this schema even though the approach to news may differ in force or form. This raises very important issues for journalism because, as we can see, Bowles castigates objectivity as an essential constituent for journalistic practice; perhaps more interestingly, however, he also dismisses training, either industrial or university, as unimportant and quite possibly irrelevant criteria.

Bowles's article is another intriguing twist in the discussion on what constitutes a journalist and to make his point *vis-à-vis* blogging Bowles states that: 'Blogs have been with us for some 400 years although obviously their form and means of distribution has changed' and 'early "bloggers" like Thomas Paine' (ibid.) confirm the long tradition of 'blog journalism'. To push this point further he states:

> Ultimately, what the Web represents is in some way a return to the days of Swift and Paine, before the time when corporations and the state had a monopoly on the flow of information but in order to retake this space it has first been necessary to challenge the orthodoxy of the unholy alliance between the corporations and academia. (ibid.)

For Bowles, the self-publication of the pamphlet is akin to and has the same status as the self-ownership of the computer, and its value partly lay in the fact that it transferred the ownership of the means of communication away from media corporations to citizens. This perspective takes its lead from Marx's notion of the ownership of the means of production.

The chief criticism against blogs is that they aren't reliable because discourse is based on an absence of facts. However, many media critics accuse the mainstream media for doing something similar. For instance, John Pilger published how the BBC used government spin and passed it off as fact in the run-up to the war in Iraq in 2003 (Pilger 2006). The belief that facts are central to journalism has a long history: 'The first newspaper journalist to work in English appears to have been Pieter van den Keere, a Dutch map and print engraver in Amsterdam' (Stephens 2007, p. 141). What according to Stephens qualifies Keere as a journalist? With reference to the Dutch *corantos* of the early seventeenth century, Stephens states that opposed to the 'melodramatics of the news-book or news ballad', the *coranto* 'was dense with facts' (ibid., p. 142); the latter defining journalism.

Emery (1972, p. 2) has claimed that ' … England had no special claim as the home of the modern press, even though it advanced beyond all other countries journalistically'. Although, Emery is referring to the early development of the newspaper, it is the second part of the quote that is interesting for my purposes here: for what exactly is meant by being advanced journalistically? And what is it that Emery is comparing to that is not advanced, in other words primitive and non-journalistic?

Theory and Practice

Is journalism a generic term that encompasses many different journalistic forms or is there an underlying ethos that defines its essential characteristic? Towards the end of chapter one under 'tabloids' I briefly discussed how some writers see tabloids and the popular press as sensational forms that report the trivial. This perception of content is an argument that tabloids do not engage in news or at the very least it is not serious news and therefore not worthy of serious contemplation; it is then to all extent and purposes either non-news or news of little value. This perception has implications on what journalism is *meant* to be hence the division between 'tabloid journalism' and 'journalism'. Tabloid journalism is thus seen today as a sub-category with its unique mode of address and style of presentation that has led to the accusation of 'dumbing down' culture and society. This distinction between modes of address is nothing new as Bleyer (1927, p. 4) states with reference to broadside ballads in sixteenth century England:

> As the ballad maker was the journalist for the masses, so the educated intelligencer in Elizabethan and Jacobean England served as news-gatherer and news-letter writer for the statesman, or man of affairs, who desired to be informed regarding the news of London.

Here we see the notion that there were and are by definition two distinct groups or audiences with different interests but perhaps more importantly two distinct ways of addressing the groups. As we shall see this approach to news and journalism is central to the ethical debate on the function of journalism in society with emphasis on bringing tangible benefits to any given community, particularly in relation to expanding a democratic order.

Although we perceive newspapers today as being intrinsically bound-up with journalists this wasn't always the case. During the 1790s papers lacked a 'corps of journalists …' (ibid., p. 283) and relied upon the public to 'send items in …' (ibid.). Invariably, items sent would have been opinionated pieces, perhaps ironically not that dissimilar in structure and form from that of the editorial. In other words, they would have lacked an objective-scientific approach to events. Interestingly, Jeremy Paxman, the lead presenter on the BBC's flagship news programme *Newsnight* was scathing in early 2007 of the proposal by his editor Peter Barron that the public send in items for their consideration. Paxman was clearly signalling that only properly trained journalists with the correct skills could achieve the best results for what constituted news. Barron's suggestions followed BBC Radio 5's lead on asking the public for contributions, not that dissimilar from many local newspapers who, for purposes of boosting sales, often reach out to the community, all of which has an impact on understanding what it is that distinguishes journalism as a social practice from the everyday uttering(s) of the public. Paxman's point wasn't necessarily to do with methods and approaches, but perhaps rather ability. However, readership involvement in one form or another has been intrinsic to journalistic practice for some period of time, as Bleyer (1927, p. 15) explains:

> A popular innovation in journalism was introduced in March, 1689/90, by John Dunton, a London bookseller, when he began the *Athenian Mercury*, a weekly publication devoted to questions asked by readers and answered by the editors.

Even though newspapers in one form or another had existed since the 1620s, the term 'journalism' as Conboy reminds us, was only 'introduced into the English language rather late in the day ... in the 1830s' (2004, p. 1). The idea that to be a journalist one needs to be objective arrives much later and primarily began in the US. Paxman's point doesn't reflect objective accounts as a trustworthy source, but rather reflects the long-standing notion that to be a good journalist one should be able to write with panache irrespective of content, which is reflected by Conboy's following statement that despite the word journalism only entering the vernacular by the 1830s, 'many of the practices and traditions of this form of public communication had been well established by then' and that such practices came to be 'formally defined as journalism' (ibid.), which for Conboy reflects a broad rather than narrow range of practice. Commenting on the difficulty of finding a singular definition Conboy states that:

> there is not and never has there been a single unifying activity to be thought of as journalism. On the contrary, journalism has always been associated with dispute – dispute about its value, its role, its direction, even its definition – and journalism has always been constructed as a diverse and multiple set of textual strategies, differing practices attempting to champion or challenge whatever has been the dominant version ... . In any history of journalism it is important to banish any thought of a predetermined agenda to its evolution. There have been significant shifts in its practice and content ... . For instance, it has moved from a private exchange of intelligence to the public consumption of information, as well as from the clandestine operation to an officially sanctioned activity ... journalism has always evolved pragmatically; according to social and technological determinants. (ibid., p. 3)

This statement isn't entirely unreasonable, but neither is it entirely satisfactory. Journalism is certainly a disputed practice and contested site over its social and political function; see Lenin's theory of the press or the debate in the US over public journalism as examples. It's not that difficult to understand what journalism *has* and *is* doing and *how* it does it, but more difficult is what it *ought* to be doing as a social and political practice. If anything, a discourse on the ethics of journalism takes us to the heart of what is socially and politically acceptable. Just because the children are running amok in a self-regulated manner doesn't make their behaviour morally acceptable and in the case of the press this is one reason that either laws or codes of conduct, however satisfactory or otherwise, exist as an agent to control the excesses of practice.

It's worth commenting on Conboy's concluding remarks in this context. He dismisses Franklin (1997) as 'negative criticism' and refers to Langer (1998) as 'idealised', preferring to use Dahlgren's (1988) term 'cultural discourse', which reflects the amorphous condition that Conboy prefers: 'The "cultural discourse" of contemporary journalism is to be observed in the media-saturated everyday life of its audience both as citizens and consumers' (Conboy 2004, p. 224). Although Conboy describes journalism in terms of being a very broad church having 'a range of competing and overlapping functions' (ibid.), he also states: 'If it is able to survive, journalism must be able to assert a specific location within this media sphere, demonstrate that it can deliver a particular form of service to the public' (ibid.), then speaks of journalism as having 'core practices' (ibid., p. 225).

Although there is a lack of ethical debate and engagement in Conboy's work, the focus being mainly descriptive, the last two references at least hint, if insufficiently, at a discourse on ethics for they are a call to good practice. Sadly, Conboy doesn't expand on what is meant by 'core practices' nor does he explain what a 'particular form of service' *should* be; nor does he explain why journalism *should* be in the service of a public. All these issues are central to ethics in journalism; for instance, as we shall see later, one crucial core practice for many writers that doesn't feature at all in Conboy's index, is the concept of objectivity. We don't have to be satisfied with certain definitions of objectivity or as to whether it exists or can be practised, but we do, however, need to engage with it if we are to believe that underlying the practice of journalism is, as Conboy alludes to, *a service to society*.

What is really missing from Conboy's account, considering his tentative concern with core practices, is a serious engagement with method as a basis for newsgathering; after all, 'a particular form of service' would heavily rely on a *particular form of newsgathering* when we further consider Conboy's belief that journalism if 'it is ... to survive' must act on behalf of the public. This reflects the point made above by Williams and can either be seen as translating into the poorly defined notion of the public interest or more interestingly into the notion that the press must act as a critical fourth estate.

This concern with how journalism *should* act in contemporary times is addressed more efficiently and thoroughly in the US with some contributions from the UK. In order to understand the contemporary concerns, it's worth revisiting some of the main historical arguments concerning journalism because this allows us to critically engage with the debates concerning method as an underlying principle of practice and its subsequent function in society. One of the earliest statements on method and function/purpose came from Fox Bourne (1887, p. vi) providing the following description:

> Though journalism is a branch of literature, moreover, it has *rules* and *methods*
> of its own; and much that may be good as journalism is faulty as literature. But

journalism has progressed as a phase of authorship, no less than as a powerful engine for the *political advancement of the community*, during the past two centuries and more. (my italics)

This notion of journalism working for the 'political advancement of the community' relates to its democratic function in society, whilst rules and methods relate not only to an ethical-acceptable approach but also identify journalism as a distinct practice, in this instance at least, from literature. However, what rules exactly and by what method and means exactly? Even though Fox Bourne had congratulated both Hunt (1850, republished 1998) and Andrews (1859, republished 1998) for their fine historical accounts, he also added 'but diligent as their writers were, they left many things unsaid and said many things inaccurately' (Fox Bourne 1887, p. vii), and surely we can apply that in this instance in relation to rules and method to Fox Bourne himself. Debates on rules and methods eventually developed more thoroughly in the US, both within journalism and academia, and within an ethical context. However, Fox Bourne's statement in my mind is an extremely useful starting point from which to build a discussion on journalistic practice and its social function.

Pondering on the meaning of journalism is invariably bound up with the question: *what is the social function of journalism?* Function relates to the idea of purpose, so is function in this context teleological? For us to properly engage with journalism's social and political function we need to begin with its origins, for we can only assume that the birth of journalistic practice was a defining moment of the role it was to play in life – why else introduce it to society? The historical beginnings of journalism were conceived then out of a design of somehow helping humans achieve a purpose. Function is related to purpose in the teleological meaning of the word, because it can be viewed as a means to achieving human goals or ends.

The methods and rules Fox Bourne alludes too aren't dealt with in any great detail; however, method is a primary indicator of good practice in relation to objectivity as a means to revealing the truth, and these principles underpin the discussion on the meaning of journalism as a social practice *vis-à-vis* society and the benefits it may bring as a consequence of method. This being the case, we can begin to trace the origins of journalistic practice back to the writings of Thucydides in his book titled *The History of the Peloponnesian War* (republished in 1978). In an intriguing article by Keith Windschuttle (1999), the author argues that in order to understand the practice of journalism we need to investigate the contribution made by Thucydides who is normally associated with being an historian rather than a writer of news. A crucial part of Windschuttle's argument is based on his critique towards the position advocated by John Hartley who has claimed that journalism is essentially a modern invention:

However, the idea that journalism is essentially modern is contested by the fact that there are examples of journalism that long pre-date the modern era, and that it is possible to identify a tradition of journalistic writing that extends back almost to the origins of Western civilization. While journalism certainly expanded enormously because of the demand for freedom of speech that arose in the seventeenth and eighteenth centuries, and because of the mechanization of printing during the industrial revolution, it is a genre of writing that is much older than either of these developments. In fact, both journalism and the production of daily news reports are more than two thousand years old. (ibid.)

As we'll discover shortly, there is ample evidence to support Windschuttle's claim, but for the purposes of this book my interest lies not solely in dating or deep history, but more importantly in the objective approach to newsgathering in order to strive towards the truth. Both objectivity and truth are fundamental issues and concerns within the field of media ethics; the fact that they have deep historical roots is indeed interesting; the fact they serve as a social purpose is profound!

Windschuttle further maintains that: 'The origins of journalism lie in exactly the same place as the origins of history' and the eternal fountain for the journalistic source is Thucydides' account of the Peloponnesian war. Accordingly, '*The History of the Peloponnesian War*, is not a history of past events but is, rather, a running commentary on the course of the war as it unfolded' and moreover Thucydides was a 'war correspondent' as well as a historian. This raises some interesting ideas relating to observing, accounting and documenting evidence, and perhaps it's not that fanciful to suggest that Thucydides was expressing sociological tendencies. Fishman (1980) after all had claimed that journalists and sociologists share many characteristics in common, such as the pursuit of factual data and accounting for it in a rigorous fashion.

Whilst Windschuttle may well be the first to connect Thucydides to the practice of journalism, he wasn't the first to connect Thucydides to the art of writing that bore resemblances to journalism, as detailed by George Colman in the eighteenth century:

> We writers of essays, or (as they are termed) periodical papers, justly claim to ourselves a place among modern improvers of literature. Neither *Bentley* nor *Burman*, nor any other equally sagacious commentator, has been able to discover the least traces of any similar production among the ancients; except we can suppose that the history of *Thucydides* was a retailed weekly in six-penny numbers ... (George Colman, *The Connoisseur*, in Black 1991, p. 1).[3]

---

3   George Colman 'the elder' (1732–94), as distinguished from his son George Colman 'the younger', was a founding member of *The Connoisseur* a weekly paper, along with Bonnell Thornton. *The Connoisseur* was launched as a 'plebeian' alternative to Edward Moore's periodical *The World*, published around the same time, which was produced for aristocratic tastes. George Colman 'the elder' was both a dramatist and essayist.

This is probably one of the earliest accounts that the ancient writer Thucydides was not only an historian, but also an early, pioneering journalist. We can argue over the differences between essayist, or as Colman states 'writers of essays', and journalist, but perhaps the telling phrase is 'of any similar production', indicating that Ancient Rome wasn't the original source of printed news, but rather that goes much further back in time to Ancient Athens and to Thucydides' compelling account of *The Peloponnesian War* between Athens and Sparta.

Thucydides (460–400 BC) is more commonly associated with being an historian, and a quote taken from the text appears to bear this out: 'My work is not a piece of writing designed to meet the taste of an immediate public, but was done to last forever' (Thucydides 1978, p. 48, I, 22); in other words as an historical document and not news for the moment that would appear ephemeral in form. However, the book or more to the point, the *method*, which Thucydides adopted in order to document the war appears to complicate the issue of the title that he or we should attribute to Thucydides as a documenter of facts. And herein lies the interest and perhaps, for the moment at least, a tenuous connection to the world of journalism. Thucydides' aim and conviction was to use facts as a basis for truth, and in doing so, he was critical of mythology that pervaded ancient Athenian and Spartan societies. This was a man not entirely interested in the oracles that dominated both these systems, but rather he was interested in documenting events, sometimes from first-hand experience and on other occasions from human sources, and then relaying that information to the reading public of the time.

In relation to first-hand experience or direct observation of events, Carey's (1987, pp. 1–2) book on reportage provides an extensive list of writers who have contributed to this field of writing. The list begins with the 'Plague in Athens 430BC' attributed to Thucydides. In the introduction Carey begins by providing a definition of reportage:

> Before editing a book on reportage you need to decide what reportage is, and how you tell the good from the bad. I decided early on that for my purposes reportage must be written by an eye witness, and I have stuck to this most of the time, though occasionally I have let in a piece that is not eye witness itself but based on eye-witness accounts. (ibid., p. xxix)

Thucydides certainly used both of these methods (direct and indirect accounts) for collating and documenting information, and with respect to the plague, it appears as a first-hand account. In *The Peloponnesian War*, Thucydides used both methods not only in order to provide a truthful account based on evidence, but also to justify a critique of other forms or writing that based itself on myth and self-indulgence:

> I do not think that one will be far wrong in accepting the conclusions I have reached from the evidence which I have put forward. It is better evidence than that of the poets, who exaggerate the importance of their themes, or of the prose

chroniclers, who are less interested in telling the truth than catching the attention of their public. (Thucydides 1978, p. 47, I, 21)

Here we see the first reference to 'evidence', which provides for Thucydides a more authentic and honest account of events. Moreover, this is clear evidence of an attempt to produce factual accounts of events by objective means, which is for many writers the route to establishing the truth. But finally, and perhaps more importantly, we witness the very first implicit reference to a public interest. All in all, we see an attempt at detachment, not to fulfil the self-indulgent fantasies of vanity, but rather to create unselfishly for others outside of the self. Evidence for Thucydides is scientific and less vulnerable to be disputed or to use Popper's term less vulnerable towards falsification. With reference to first-hand accounts and the use of sources of information, here is what Thucydides says: 'In this history I have made use of set speeches some of which were delivered just before and others during the war' (ibid., I, 22) and then he states:

> And with regard to my factual reporting of the events of the war I have made it a principle not to write down the first story that came my way, and not even to be guided by my own general impressions; either I was present myself at the events which I have described or else I heard of them from eye-witnesses whose reports I have checked with as much thoroughness as possible.

As Carey (1987, p. xxix) states: 'One advantage of insisting on eye-witness evidence is that it makes for authenticity. All knowledge of the past which is not just supposition derives ultimately from people who can say "I was there".' Of course, being 'there' is no absolute guarantee for producing a truthful account, unless truth is merely an account based on value-judgement and interpretation. Besides, there is always the type of language used to describe selected events that may indicate bias, but to be fair to Thucydides he was fully aware of descriptive terms used to convey a message. His manner was dry and exact, and purposely so in order to convey accuracy as he put it, which is the hallmark of objectivity. There was no place for the flowery language used by the hapless romantics who were for Thucydides submerged in mythology, to which we can perhaps add ideology.

Thucydides certainly displayed the working practices and conventions we associate with modern journalism: he sought out independent sources of information and then both recorded and documented information for publication. More importantly, the rationale behind Thucydides' method was to distance himself from the event, in other words to attain an objective and more authentic account. But Thucydides also displayed everything that is unethical about modern journalism; he filled in absent gaps for his own purpose. The 'Melian Dialogue' (pp. 400–408) is evidence of Thucydides' subjective analysis. There are no names attributed to this debate and it appears as a figment of his imagination. Equally, in the discussion in the 'Oligarchic Coup' Thucydides states 'in my opinion' and also passes judgement on the change of government: 'During this first period of this new regime the Athenians appear to have had a better government than ever before, at least in my time' (pp. 598–99). Perhaps we could forgive Thucydides certain indiscretions in light of the fact that collecting information during this period would have been slow and laborious, but it's fair to credit him with a *spirit* of journalism, to produce information that would serve a civic debate.

However, the important issue is the emphasis on 'method', 'rigour', 'discipline', 'source', 'calculation', 'documentation' and 'purpose' of information that Thucydides was attempting to achieve in his own indomitable way and to a large degree succeeded. News, as opposed to journalism, has always existed. News between people existed prior to Thucydides and during his lifetime. The important issue was that Thucydides was attempting to create a new form of mediation through method and application, and Windschuttle rightly calls this journalism, and journalism was a new way of distributing news. Stephens (2007) would emphatically disagree with this, however, arguing that Thucydides was a historian and not a journalist. Perhaps this is less important than the common approach that both historians and journalists (sociologists also) use towards revealing the fact and truth behind events, and as we shall see later in this study, for most, not all, academics within the media ethics tradition the *method* of approach to events *should* always be *objective* – time, as an indicator of news, is in this context less important than *method*.

The differences between the integrity of Thucydides' methodological approach towards news discourse and the promulgation of political ideologies of the pamphleteers in seventeenth century England are indeed vast and are moreover, indicative of the differences of opinion between supporters of objective and subjective journalism. Carey's work on reportage is a stout defence of subjective accounts of events as long as the language used to portray matters isn't based on generalizations. Individuality for Carey and the idiosyncratic use of language that individuals may bring to documenting is key to 'good reportage'. Reportage can literally be 'on-the-spot pieces' or 'instant-response stories', referred to as 'Rushed reportage' (Carey 1987, p. xxx), but they can also be reflective pieces, written long after the event. Which is more truthful?

It's worth mentioning that whilst Stephens (2007, p. 47) acknowledges the contribution of Thucydides as a 'Greek writer of non-fiction prose', Thucydides wasn't according to Stephens a news writer because he wasn't gathering or distributing news: 'News lives for the moment and its applause' (ibid., p. 48), and further: 'There is no evidence that it was circulated to or even intended for contemporaries' (ibid.). Although earlier Stephens admits that Thucydides 'did in fact write about the events of his lifetime' (ibid., p. 47).

Carey's view of subjective journalism reflects the style of journalism developed by Hunter S. Thompson referred to as 'Gonzo Journalism' and a part of the 'New Journalism' movement in 1960s US. Thompson, it could be said, took liberties with news accounts by exaggerating narrative that reflected a novelistic style in order to convey the power of a message. Gonzo Journalism was often written in the first person and often included the experience of the narrator within the narrative, and Thompson claimed that this style of journalism was more sincere, honest, but above all, a more truthful account of events. Above all else, Gonzo Journalism blended fact with fiction into a storytelling narrative and opposed the idea forwarded by *objectivists* that truth existed independently of perception; for Thompson, truth lay within and manifested itself externally by using events as opportunities to express an intense form of individualism.

More recently, the former BBC war correspondent Martin Bell developed his 'journalism of attachment', which is itself a form of subjective journalism, although different in style and outcomes from Thompson's Gonzo Journalism. Bell's 'journalism of attachment' is about involvement, immersion and even intervention into a story that may empathize with the subject matter, denouncing neutrality in the process. It's important to understand that the roots of this belief emerged from Bell's experience covering the Bosnian War in the 1980s, although Bell draws upon other previous experiences arguing against detachment from the subject matter.

Bell's argument is that journalists are human beings with feelings and values and similar to Thompson, argues that to pretend otherwise is insincere; so the idea of detaching oneself from a story is ludicrous and to a large extent deceptive. Bell argues therefore in favour of making moral judgements; journalism, he states, 'must be informed by an idea of right and wrong' (Bell 1998, p. 18), previously claiming that journalism is a 'moral enterprise' (ibid.), therefore the journalist is a part of the story with opinions and beliefs attached. I'll return to Thompson in Chapter 5 on objectivity, because Thompson was scathing of the *false idea* concerning objective accounts believing them to be insincere, and also to Bell whose 'journalism of attachment' stands in contradistinction to objective accounts.

The debate over whether journalism is based on either objective or subjective accounts has reached new heights. For instance, in a reference to the ubiquitous technological devices at our disposal in contemporary times, similar to Bowles, Bew (2006, p. 200) proclaimed 'We are all journalists now', and similarly with reference to the new fashionable and hip term 'citizen journalists' Allan (2006, p. 168) has claimed that the persons in the street armed with their 'mobile telephone cameras' are able to capture and document happenings and events thus becoming a type of journalist in the process. Allan based his observations on the images captured of the scenes of the London underground bombings of July 2005 whereby 'citizen journalists' were able to snap and post these scenes on the worldwide web, thus acting as journalists and documenters of events. This is not too dissimilar from *reportage*, which stresses 'being there' and 'first-hand accounts' as an essential prerequisite for defining journalistic activity and subsequently transferring the data to a medium that the public are able to access.

This has echoes of the Marxist notion of having access to the *means of communication* written all over it. Having access to technology, whether primitive or advanced, and the *means of communication* is essential to journalism, however, 'being there' with the means of communication doesn't guarantee effective or ethical journalism. With reference to the impact that new technology is having

on our understanding and perception of contemporary journalistic practices Allan
goes onto state: to a close friend. This hardly constitutes what we believe we
know about journalism, that is, reaching an audience above the figure of one. With
reference to the impact that new technology is having on our understanding and
perception of contemporary journalistic practices Allan goes onto state:

> This ... was made possible by the Internet. A number of extraordinary 'phonecam
> snapshots' of passengers trapped underground were posted on Moblog.co.uk, a
> photo-sharing website for mobile telephone images. (ibid.)

But was this really journalism or just the end product of someone who just
happened to be there? I posted my holiday snaps of Poland on the web but I
wouldn't be so bold as to say they were the result of journalistic practice. Doesn't
journalistic practice entail method, training (university of otherwise)? Doesn't
journalism have a social function beyond the ordinary expressions of individuals
who may disclose, for reasons of vanity, self-interest and self-indulgence? It is true
that images and narrative provided by the public have been used in a journalistic
context for some considerable time and in reality the only real difference today is
technology and the web, which allows for expressions to be displayed over *time*
and *space* more efficiently reaching larger audiences in the process. But if it's true
that anybody can do this and thus become an instant journalist, is this to deprive
journalism as a social practice of a number of defining elements that constitutes
its practice? Elements such as objectivity, truth and ethical responsibilities for
instance? Just 'being there' with a mobile camera is not the same as having a
rationality that is fundamentally based on critical self-reflection, or at least that's
the theory. The issue concerning new technologies that apparently allow us all to
become 'citizen journalists' raises some interesting questions about journalism as
a social practice. After all, training, whether on-the-job or university, entails to a
large degree a relatively deep understanding of what it means to be a journalist and
what function and responsibilities journalists have in society, whereas the average
Joe can just happily snap away without any prior considerations, not that dissimilar
from tabloid journalists who believe ethics is a colony for the seriously deluded.

  And what of blogging? In an article titled 'Disruptions in the Fourth Estate',
internet blogger Daniel Harrison argued the web has become a 'disruptive
technology' not only unsettling the practices of journalism but positively changing
them for the good: 'Nowhere have such examples been more prescient ... than ...
in the field of journalism, ... [with] two high-quality, equally highly acclaimed
weblogs published well-written, erudite and ... professional pieces of investigative
journalism' (Harrison 2006). Harrison claims that 'the landscape of journalism' is
changing and quotes Glenn Reynolds from another news-based website, Pyjamas
Media, to ferment this view: '"I think that blogging is the wave of the future, and
consequently, I think we're going to see journalism moving from a profession,
back to being an activity"' (ibid.) à la William Bowles. Reynolds continues:

We used to say that a journalist was somebody who wrote a journal, and a correspondent was somebody in a distant city who wrote you letters, and corresponded. Now it means somebody with good hair and a microphone. But I think that the traditional meaning of journalism is what it's going to be like again ... It's more a case of who's on the scene and who can report – or journal – what happened, as opposed to somebody who makes a profession out of reporting and opining. So it's driven by the activity; it's driven by the nature of events, rather than by your paycheck, if that makes sense. (ibid.)

Click onto OhmyNews International and you'll find a section titled 'Citizen Journalism' proposing: '10 Citizen Reporter Commandments' plus the eight points of the, 'OhmyNews Reporter's Code of Ethics' (OhmyNews International 2007). This website (and others) plus the comments by Reynolds, Bowles, and so on, certainly confirm the corrupt nature of mainstream news organizations, but they do not answer what the social meaning and function of journalism is in relation to society and democracy; after all they are as guilty for producing non-factual accounts or repeating news from other 'official' sources as the mainstream press and media.

If anything, their impact may only be positive in that they have forced the mainstream to re-evaluate their role in society. This point is addressed by the Assistant Editor for News of *The Guardian*, David Leigh who in an article titled 'Are Reporters Doomed' (Leigh 2007), claimed: 'Citizen Journalism is here to stay. But in the rush to embrace new media we risk destroying the soul of traditional reporting.' The references to citizen journalism are often obscure, for it is never really clear if citizen journalism is a form of journalism distinct from journalism proper. Does citizen journalism for instance have its own separate rationale from 'traditional reporting' as Leigh states? If it does, what is it? Or perhaps it's so anarchical that it doesn't have one. Leigh goes onto state: 'The internet is an incredibly rich information resource, and a great tool for worldwide sharing. But it degrades principles.' So for Leigh the 'soul of traditional reporting' is governed by 'principles' that journalists are aware of. This may in most cases be wishful thinking, but Leigh's point is to separate citizen journalism as a practice from traditional journalism as practised by real journalists, or what he confidently calls 'proper reporters', which has its roots in 'investigative journalism'. 'Slow journalism' Leigh states, as opposed to the rush of the net, presents the 'reporter as a patient assembler of facts'.

On the face of it, the issues raised by Leigh are not entirely unreasonable; suffice to say that unfortunately the 'proper reporters' he refers to often produce biased information (see medialens for numerous examples).[4] That being so, one interesting aspect regarding ethics is that it always insists on discussing the *ought* factor in journalism; it stresses the normative perspective against the brutal realities of the multi-media revolution or the commercial-industrial journalism

---

4   http://www.medialens.org.

with its emphasis on getting the story necessary for the continuation of commodity production or other purposes. Keen (2007) has contrasted the amateur of the web with the professional journalist distinguished by the latter's ability to be objective and factual. In an article in *The Guardian* (Dowling 2007) titled 'I don't think bloggers read', Keen explained that there are however bad examples of journalism exemplified by the *Sun* newspaper in the UK and Fox news in the US, both owned by Rupert Murdoch.

David Leigh's reference to investigation is intrinsically bound up with method and truth. For some writers investigative journalism is a form of journalism that delivers particular results through a rigorous and in-depth approach to news. What isn't clear in many texts is whether investigative journalism is an abstract method of approach that is applicable to regimes of journalism such as politics as opposed to fashion journalism, or whether it is a method that is applicable to journalism irrespective of regime difference.

Stephens (2007, p. 233), for instance, addresses the thoroughness for which investigative journalism is renowned – to 'go beyond the official sources' – but also states that it is: 'Reporters with an *inclination* to investigate' (ibid., p. 238), suggesting that it is limited to 'fact-hungry reporters' (ibid.), with which hard news is connected. Equally, Aucoin (2002, p. 209) in a paper titled 'Investigative Journalism' claims that 'The methods of investigative reporting are traditional reporting techniques amplified' stating that in the US it was at one time labelled 'detective journalism' during the 'late 19th century' (ibid., p. 210). One term used to describe this activity was 'muckrakers' (ibid.), and although Aucoin claims that the 'investigative spirit' had existed since 'colonial times' (ibid.), it wasn't officially formalized at least in the US as 'investigative journalism' until the 1970s. Aucoin goes onto state that the organization known as the Investigative Reporters and Editors (IRE) declared that:

> Investigative journalism ... is journalism that exposes information about an important public issue that someone or some organization does not want the general public to know ... IRE later expanded its definition to include journalism that does not expose secrets, but instead reveals information not widely known before. (ibid.)

However, similar to Stephens, Aucoin also states that: 'Investigative reporters found a niche for themselves within the general practice of journalism' (ibid., p. 215). At the very least we have, according to Stephens and Aucoin, two, not one, notion of journalism; on the one hand, there is investigative journalism with its in-depth approach to news and on the other there is journalism with it various regimes, which similar to Conboy's perception of journalism is a broad church applying various forms of practice according to the subject of enquiry.

Pilger's approach is different, but mainly because there is a normative principal involved. On purely descriptive accounts, both Stephens and Aucoin are correct to point out that investigative journalism has not involved all journalists in every newspaper, whereas Pilger has argued that all journalism *should* be investigative, therefore only true journalism has its roots in investigation and in-depth enquiry and therefore all other forms are but merely representations of the real thing; in other words, if it isn't investigative, it is fake journalism. Pilger's idea of investigative journalism is identical, however, to the point that Aucoin made in relation to Carl Bernstein, the investigator on the US Watergate scandal, who had a 'suspicion of the established power structure' (Aucoin 2002, p. 216).

Character and Discipline

What is the difference between journalism and a journalist? On the face of it, there shouldn't be any relative distinction; for surely it is true that a person referred to as a journalist is a person that practices journalism? Once we say that a person isn't a journalist we are admitting that they do not practice journalism. Is it possible that some who work for newspapers could be misconstrued as journalists? In Chapter 1 it was claimed somewhat obviously that newspapers have played and continue to play an important role in the production of news, but can anyone do this or do they require special skills to operate effectively in order to be referred to as a journalist as opposed to a layperson or 'citizen journalist'. Some people occasionally write for a newspaper but wouldn't refer to themselves as a journalist. Some people are hired by newspapers as journalists only to be accused of not being one because of their modes of operations and apparent lowering of journalistic standards. Some writers have even claimed that it is the person that makes the position, rather than the position turning the person into a journalist. Those writers who subscribe to the former view tend to emphasize the 'character' of an individual with *innate-biological* abilities and skills, naturally able to cope with the rigours of practice, effectively and competently. These writers, normally individuals that refer to themselves as journalists, have worked in the newspaper industry and some of them have transferred into the world of academia. This belief in innateness is subsequently a belief in talent; one either has it or not and talent and determination are perhaps not more important than journalism as a socially defined practice, but are more able to make it work more effectively. Perhaps, at the very least, we are speaking in terms of a 'good' journalist as opposed to those less competent. On the other hand, a belief in innate talent is ultimately an argument that not everyone can practice journalism, and that some people are therefore ill qualified to be called a journalist because they are unable to meet the criteria believed to be essential for effective practice.

'Character is also key to good journalism' states Sanders (2005, p. 162), reflecting David Randall's (1996) view that above all else what separates the good journalist from the average and mundane is the notion of 'character'. Whether character is innate in the biological sense or can be taught isn't discussed here in Sanders's work, although later she states that some people are disposed 'with "flawed" characters', but the 'Key is to find ways of showing them that being good is also a kind of enlightened self-interest' (2005, p. 163) indicating that discipline through training and education is possible for changing character. However, I must stress Sanders does not convincingly explore this or how it might be possible. Perhaps the main indicator here is the reference to 'enlightened self interest'; after all, many attached to the discipline of media ethics perceive it as a space for producing *enlightenment journalism*. Presumably, Sanders's character is not flawed and my question is why not? And what is more on what basis does she judge others to have flawed characters?

Frost (2007, p. 57) has also claimed that 'it is possible to produce a list of characteristics that a good journalist should possess' but it is up to the individual to decide which are appropriate even though somewhat contradictory Frost states that they have a 'moral duty' (ibid.) to do so, although duties as opposed to responsibilities are externally imposed, so it's unclear whether Frost is expressing an existentialist approach or a communitarian approach to practice. Suffice to say, character is seen to be important, naturally or otherwise.

One writer who has stressed innate character is Nick Tomalin, who wrote 'Stop the press I want to get on' (1997), arguing that character and innate talent are the main ingredients for becoming a journalist. There isn't any discussion of what journalism (as opposed to journalist) is meant to be, but it is abundantly clear that Tomalin believes that, similar to other areas such as music, philosophy, and so on, a good journalist is one that has natural skills. Tomalin's piece is a scathing attack on schools of journalism in universities and the training provided therein. Tomalin argues that the essential requirement for a good journalist to survive and ultimately be successful is a 'ratlike cunning' (Tomalin 1997, p. 16). This view of character has its supporters: 'As Sir David English, editor of the *Daily Mail*, says "Journalism is a skill that can only be acquired on the job and at the end of the day it depends on whether someone has a burning individual talent"' (Keeble 1995, p. 342). Tomalin also lists other qualities that are 'helpful for the pursuit of good journalistic practice' (Tomalin 1997, p. 16). As Tomalin states: 'These include a knack for telephones, trains and petty officials; a good digestion and a steady head; total recall; enough idealism to inspire indignant prose ... well placed relatives; good luck' (ibid.).

In terms of the US, Upshaw (2002) in an article titled 'Characteristics of Journalists' also notes that there are certain qualities required to make a journalist but is not as opprobrious as Tomalin is towards university training and nor should he be, for Upshaw was at the time of writing a Professor of Broadcast Journalism at San Diego State University. In fact it's not entirely clear what Upshaw's position is *vis-à-vis* character and training; one would assume that he is indeed sympathetic towards training, but when we scrutinize his text more closely there appears to be a leaning towards character and innate talent – unless one can develop that through training also.

For instance, Upshaw begins his work by stating: 'News professionals write a great deal but only rarely seem to reveal their *true inner nature*' (ibid., p. 66; my italics). There could not be a more emphatic statement supporting the idea that human nature with all its diverse complexities primarily and fundamentally conditions personality and character; this is nature over nurture, for to have a true inner nature is something we apparently cannot resist or affect because it governs our actions. If one were to support this philosophical view, it could be argued that we all have a true inner nature, but what the relationship is between a person's true inner nature and their apparent capability to write and act as a journalist remains unclear.

Although Tomalin and Upshaw certainly do not place their arguments in the context of philosophy, they are, however, whether they are aware of it or not, discussing matters that are deeply entrenched within a philosophical tradition. The innate talent that they refer to is akin to having the natural ability to have practical knowledge within oneself. This perception of inherent practical knowledge is what is referred to as *a priori*, which is a belief that knowledge cannot be learnt from experience and that any known knowledge of values, which are in this context linked to practice, are either the products of pure reason or intuitive. A direct consequence of their writing is therefore to consider how *a priori* practical knowledge manifests itself in practice and what uses it has for society.

In relation to printers in the colonial period in the US, Upshaw argues that overall although most at the time they were successful and had similar objectives towards the purpose of public writing, they nevertheless lacked the 'Other characteristics – political passion, resistance to authority, and a "sense of history"' that Upshaw believes to be essential ingredients for a journalist. Later, after assessing various historical periods and figures, Upshaw states that: 'Indeed, if a single characteristic can be traced through the history of journalism, it probably is a complex, ineffable, obdurate love of the craft' (Upshaw 2002, p. 73), which is hardly conducive to innate talent, leading me to suggest that Upshaw's position is at least ambiguous and at most ill-thought-out and poorly defined. Upshaw then states: 'Researchers rarely target this emotion' (ibid.), but we are all capable of that emotion; it tells us nothing whatsoever. Finally, Upshaw produces yet another characteristic, which he claims is conducive to journalism, that in fact a large percentage of the human race have had during a lifetime: 'Journalists, avoiding maudlin self-disclosure [another trait], even more rarely state it plainly' (ibid.).

American writer Joseph A. Mirando (2002, p. 82) provides an account of journalism education and training in the US and whilst he appears sympathetic to technical vocational training within university, he does nevertheless detail criticism of training within academia:

> ABC News *Nightline* anchor Ted Koppel's modern criticism was just as biting as Greeley's and Godkin's when he told a student audience, 'Journalism schools are an absolute waste of time. You cannot replicate true journalism – genuine pressure – in an academic setting.'

Niblock (1996) would have us think differently judging by the training manual she has written for university students that outlines a 'how to get successfully by guide to a career in journalism'. There's even a chapter titled 'What is Journalism' to inform and guide students of the nuances of journalism. Niblock's book is titled *Inside Journalism*, a part of the 'Career Building Guides'. It makes for uncomfortable reading! In a critique of the position advocated by Tomalin, Cole claims that:

> The idea that journalism is instinctive, based on innate ability and flair which cannot be improved upon by training is manifestly as absurd as suggesting that world-class athletes simply compete and have no training which fills 99 per cent of their lives. (Cole 1998, pp. 67–68)

Cole has also argued that technological skills are required by budding journalists, but are not necessarily central to practice:

> Journalists require computer skills, electronic communication skills. The page planner and modern equivalent of sub-editor requires more advanced computer skills … . But these computer skills are not central, necessary, but little to do with journalism itself. For all the technological changes, for all the changing attitudes towards content, journalism remains the identifying, collecting, selecting, ordering, and presentation of information. Much of this can be taught, and is taught. (ibid., p. 68)

More recently Cole (2006, p. 75) has returned to the issue of training in 'Education and training local journalists', and once again is supportive of university degree courses in journalism. However, as Cole notes, there is scepticism from some parts of the industry towards university training: 'There is still a residue of local editors who believe apprenticeships was and is the only way', and 'There remains some employers who are suspicious of degrees' (ibid., p. 79).

Former Australian journalist turned academic Lynette Sheridan Burns (2002) also places strong emphasis on the process of student training, particularly the recognition and understanding the importance of critical thinking seen as *the* positive trait in good journalistic training. Together, both training and critical reflection is a form of enlightenment for students of journalism and as Burns enthusiastically claims: 'Critical self-reflection is a hallmark of good professional journalism' (ibid., p. 12). Burns is clearly advancing a moral dimension to the process of training, but more importantly is arguing that irrespective of the imposition or the inculcation of a house-style, journalists have the power to negotiate the journalistic terrain.

Even though Mirando (2002, p. 83) has acknowledged criticisms levelled against university training, the author nevertheless is broadly sympathetic towards it stating that the 'technical/vocational approach was intended to give journalism education a sense of acceptance and legitimacy among the media industry'. Mirando also notes that within the vocational approach, journalism schools offered 'speciality areas' within the curriculum, one of which is 'ethics' (ibid.).

Belsey (1998) has expressed an alternative suggestion to either character or training in the sense discussed thus far, although interestingly it would involve character and training albeit with a different emphasis. In 'Ethics and journalism: Can they coexist?' Belsey clearly recognizes the constraints that 'industrial journalism' places upon ethical practice and the production of good journalism. The resolution to this conflict is neither an appeal to innate talent or university training, but rather 'virtue in journalism', which is a 'disposition to act in an ethically correct way' (ibid., p. 13). Belsey doesn't address the issue of academic training but rather appeals to journalists to educate themselves in virtue ethics. For academics and practitioners who are concerned with lowering of journalistic standards and in quality of performance, many see the teaching of media ethics within academic schools of journalism as the only option for developing good practice, but there are no guarantees. However, the teaching of ethics goes right to the heart of training in general and whether one can be trained, or whether one has a so-called natural disposition towards practice, because one's moral compass so to speak is equally about character and discipline.

Much of this debate on training concerning character and discipline has deep historical-philosophical roots in psychological behaviour in relation to human nature. Quite evidently there isn't the space to do this debate any justice here, but it's worth reviewing some work at this juncture because the debate on media ethics is not simply about duties, responsibilities, and so on, but is also about whether ethics can be learnt with any degree of effectiveness *vis-à-vis* the debate on innate talent ('character') and 'discipline' that is imposed externally. For if it is true that competent journalists are naturally endowed then what happens if they are unreservedly and unapologetically amoral or immoral? In other words, can naturally talented writers learn to be good moral persons with social responsibilities to others external to themselves, or does that also depend on innateness?

John B. Watson (1924) in his work *Behaviourism* attempted to turn psychology into a serious scientific field and therefore rejected speculative theory based on unobservable evidence. Much of what had preceded Watson's work, particularly Freud's speculation on 'id', 'ego' and 'super-ego' were redundant in Watson's work, for only observable facts could inform us of human behaviour. Moreover, Watson rejected outright the speculative notion of 'instinct', claiming that these were merely fantastical expressions of academics imposing their will onto others. Watson also claimed that basic bodily functions that enable humans to act and think served as the only innate feature; all else was learnt. Humans were accordingly the product of their relations, not that dissimilar from the ideas of Karl Marx. This, then, was nurture over nature, where social-environmental activity conditioned behaviour: 'Everything we have been in the habit of calling an "instinct" today is a result largely of training.' Watson claimed further: 'there is no such thing as an inheritance of *capacity*, *talent*, *temperament*, *mental constitution* and *characteristics*. These things again depend on training' (ibid., p. 94).

B.F. Skinner (1965) also rejected inner mental causation precisely for the same reasons as Watson because they were unobservable; but does this make them any less probable? Skinner also rejected 'inherited' factors and took the idea of 'training' to such a degree that, like Watson, any human could be trained to perform any act. The fact is we do not know for certain the relationship between nature and nurture in each individual and to what extent one conditions the other. As opposed to *a priori*, the opposite, *a posteriori*, posits the notion that we learn things through experience, which is difficult to deny.

In an article titled 'The Training of Journalists', Peter Hinchliffe (2007) recounts the futility of his own training experience thus:

> 'There's a notebook in the bottom drawer' said the chief reporter, pointing to a metal filing cabinet. 'Help yourself'. So began and ended my initiation as a newspaper reporter.

Chapter 3
The Liberal Theory of the Press: *Spirit* of Liberalism and Residual Meanings in the Present

Liberalism and Individualism

In a critique of individualism and extreme forms of *hedonistic egoism*, Brown (1986, p. 155) has claimed that we must have:

> rational concerns for the welfare of others in *our community* for their own sake and not merely as a means to the pursuit of our own narrow concerns or private projects. Without something like this we could not convince everyone of the merits of a particular social practice, for there will always be someone with a (narrow) interest in some alternative wherein he would be better off. The man who ruled a world (and liked it) could not easily be convinced of the benefits of democracy unless he was convinced of the merits of a democratic life for himself.

The critical debates within media ethics are either based on a sympathetic view of liberalism or more often than not a critique of liberalism and the position that the individual journalist occupies within the system. In Chapter 4 we shall see that the latter is chiefly represented by the US public journalism school of thought and the former by existentialist thinker John Merrill. There is also the relatively new position advocated by the EU with its various media policies to consider. This serves as an interesting contrast to the US public journalism view on press and media responsibilities, where it is argued that technology can effectively democratize European societies and manage the *unfortunate* excesses of press and media development according to the logic of liberal theory. The point I am emphasizing here is that despite differences, and there are others not included just yet, liberal philosophical theory has dominated, and continues to dominate, the press and media landscape, which can also be applied to the internet if we are to believe in the rights of individuals to express themselves via technological applications and in the name of free speech – a highly held value according to liberal philosophy. The fact that free speech is negated on Google China or by the monopolization of press and media outlets, whilst of concern, is immaterial, because the point to grasp is that the *spirit of liberalism* continues to occupy contemporary life. This *spirit* is not necessarily benevolent but can be pernicious, destructive and inherently contradictory; it can also be used to justify monstrous abuses in the context of media ownership and power under the dubious claims that it represents a fourth estate, seemingly independent from state authority and apparently working on behalf of a public interest. So let us begin by addressing the salient points of liberalism:

> The study of liberalism is both simple and complex. It is simple because liberalism is a pre-eminent ideology in Western political thought, extensively articulated and amplified, and a familiar component within the ideological spectrums of the past century and a half. It is complex because its permeation into rival families, both socialist and conservative, makes its unravelling difficult, and because its diffusion has led to an extraordinary range of variants that, unlike the many nuances of socialism, tend to present themselves under the same name, without qualifiers such as 'evolutionary', 'Marxist', or 'democratic'. Indeed, many theorists as well as laymen assume some vast homogeneity that adherence to liberalism bestows on its supporters, often described as an attitude of mind rather than a distinct set of political beliefs, without being alert to the conceptual permutations which those beliefs display within a recognisably liberal morphology. (Freeden 1998, p. 141)

The use of morphology in context of political theory is interesting and perhaps safer than its original application towards biology because, in relation to the latter, there is always a risk involved, mainly because classifying organisms according to morphological applications can, in theory at least, negate unrelated biological structures. In the former, on the other hand, there are normally core concepts that define a political theory and the rest is inflection and interpretation. That said, I use Freeden here to alert us to the fact that liberalism isn't a theoretically cogent and coherent political philosophy, but rather, as the author states, is complex, to which I would add varied. Bearing this in mind will help us therefore to be aware that references to individualism and free speech, for example, are contingent on the possible various liberal viewpoints. Nevertheless, even when we take into consideration the possible variations, we do so by simultaneously acknowledging that both concepts are core concepts that constitute the morphology of liberal thought, and for the purposes of this chapter they form the basis of the liberal theory of the press.

The difficulties of assessing liberalism are not simply restricted to the variations within the tradition, but are also rooted in notions and accusations that today we inhabit a 'neo-liberal' political and economic environment dominated by monopoly capitalism and large state infrastructures. Whilst the latter two points are quite evidently true, depending on which society we study, it is also true that core liberal beliefs and concepts continue to permeate contemporary societies that are indeed governed by monopoly business practices and large state infrastructures. Monopoly includes newspaper ownership, which impacts upon the autonomous individual journalist with political and moral rights to exercise so central to liberal thought. But even here it is not the case that interference into news practice is universally applied. Murdoch, after all, is on record for saying that where he does interfere into the working practices of the *Sun* (Britain's biggest selling daily paper) and the *News of the World* (Britain's biggest selling Sunday paper) he doesn't to the same degree with *The Times* or *The Sunday Times*. With regards to the *Sun* and *News of the World*, Murdoch informed the Lords Communication Committee in September 2007 in New York that he acted as a traditional proprietor determining key political policy in the process:

> Minutes of the House of Lords communications committee ... acknowledged he had 'editorial control' over the *Sun* and *News of the World* ... . They read 'Mr Murdoch did not disguise the fact that he is hands-on both economically and editorially. He exercises editorial control on major issues – like which party to back in a general election or policy on Europe. (BBC News 2007)

The Times and *Sunday Times* according to Murdoch weren't subject to the same attention but 'He explained he "nominates" the editors of these two papers ...' (ibid.). This contrasts with *The Guardian* newspaper where the paper is beholden to the Scott Trust. On 18 July 2007 the presiding editor Alan Rusbridger made the following statement to the Lords Communications Committee on the process by which he was appointed:

> It is an unusual if not unique process ... I had to stand for selection and the first stage was a vote of the journalists themselves. There were four of us, all internal, who stood. We did hustings, we set out a manifesto and there was an indicative vote conducted by the Electoral Reform Society, which went to the Scott Trust. (United Kingdom Parliament 2007)

Two related questions followed: 'You are responsible as editor for the editorial policy of the newspaper?', answering 'Yes', then: 'That independence is guarded by the trust?' answering 'Yes' (ibid.). The contrast between these three examples reveals the clear tensions and contradictions of liberalized and neo-liberal perspectives towards the production of news. The differences in terms of levels and degrees of interference, however, is, in the round, partial, and the continuance of liberal thought in practice is what I refer to as the *spirit of liberalism and residual meanings in the present* and that is how I would like to proceed with the following discussion. The contemporary development and meaning of journalism therefore continues to be connected to the liberalized *idea* of the fourth estate and to the various levels and degrees of interpretation of rights and responsibilities therein. The *idea* of the fourth estate therefore is de facto a site of political struggle over hegemonic meanings premised on the foundations of the liberal theory of the press.

Edmund Burke first introduced the *idea* of the fourth estate during the eighteenth century, but it was later in the nineteenth century that the basic principles of the fourth estate began to emerge in the works of Thomas Carlyle. It's here that we can see the *idea* of the fourth estate becoming intrinsically linked and a product of liberalism, and to understand the former in relation to media ethics we need to clearly understand the mechanics of the latter.

A good reason for understanding liberalism, and perhaps the more important in this present context, is because the discussion on media ethics and responsibilities in some academic and journalistic circles is born out of a critique of the liberal theory that dominates journalistic practice. This critique, however, is not directed at the liberal *idea* of the fourth estate as an autonomous body, which more often than not is seen as a necessary element of society irrespective of philosophical differences within media ethics. Rather, it is a critique of the status that individualism has within liberal theory and what is exposed here is an essential contradiction and tension between the rights of press owners pitted against the rights of individuals working within the industry. The *idea* of the fourth estate has helped to shape and define the parameters within which journalism operates; thus, understanding the meaning of journalism requires an understanding of the political theory that defines the fourth estate and, perhaps more importantly, to recognize the limits that the liberalized *idea* of the fourth estate set on such definitions and meanings of journalism in this context.

Understanding liberalism in relation to the *idea* of the fourth estate is vital for two reasons. First, we can trace the origins of liberal thought back to the English philosopher John Locke, whose contribution to the *idea* of the fourth estate was twofold: (1) Locke discussed 'economic liberty' concerned with property rights, detailed in his *Two Treatises of Government* (reprinted in 1990); and (2) Locke discussed 'intellectual liberty' in his essay written in 1689 titled 'A Letter Concerning Toleration' (reprinted in 1955). With respect to the former, it is in my opinion the ability to widely interpret Locke's contribution on property rights that becomes highly significant in the changes in economic ownership of the press from liberal to neo-liberal conditions. For instance, Habermas (1989) had argued that the essential characteristics of liberalism were being eroded around 1870 with the collapse of small multiple business centres towards the emergence of monopoly capitalism, mass media systems and concentration of ownership. Habermas also argued that this reflected a shift from literary journalism, whose formal emphasis was cultural, to commercial journalism, whose formal emphasis was profit dictated by the rise of proprietors who sought position in the market place over what Locke had previously termed 'intellectual liberty'.

However, despite these structural changes this period was less a definitive break with liberalism, but rather a new defining moment in the liberal dialectic; one which re-characterized liberalism but not totally annihilating it. The alteration in the mechanics of liberalism simultaneously introduced new moments whilst maintaining older traditions, and ensured the *spirit of liberalism* was maintained in some circles whilst becoming obliterated in others; in essence the core subject of dialectical movement!

In terms of the press, the shift from liberal to neo-liberal framework can be conceptualized with reference to Locke's work concerning 'economic liberty' and 'intellectual liberty' and the contradictions therein; contradictions that strike right at the heart of liberalism and to the *idea* of the fourth estate with pole interests of individual property rights on the one hand and freedom of speech on the other, if we are to assume that exercising the latter is free from formal constraints, that is, press owner's commercial interests. Therefore the 'economic liberty' of Locke's thought detailed in this transition from liberal to neo-liberalism automatically clashes with his second point concerning 'intellectual liberty' or *freedom of conscience*, which underpinned the introduction of the *idea* of the fourth estate later in the eighteenth and nineteenth centuries.

Embedded in Western Enlightenment philosophy was the right to free speech and the free exchange of ideas; to be free to exercise thought meant autonomy from state power and economic restraints. What we have here is a contradiction and tension between the individual economic rights of ownership that have led to monopolization of the press and rights of expression (conscience even) by individuals within this system; something that liberalism allows and cannot resolve. Thus the liberalized *idea* of the fourth estate is constituted from this tension, and both historically and contemporarily it is the *idea* of the fourth estate that has defined, and continues to define, journalism. So when we ponder upon the meaning of journalism, more often than not this process is conditioned by an empirical reality rather than abstraction.

Thus, despite the economic structural changes, the *spirit of liberalism* continued and we can understand this process in terms of what Raymond Williams referred to as *archaic*, *residual*, and *emergent*: 'The *archaic* is of the past; the *residual* is "formed in the past [and] is still active in the cultural process … as an effective element of the present". The *emergent* is the process by which "new meanings … values [and] practices" are created' (from Berry 2006, p. 201). So whilst the economic conditions of the press changed at the end of the nineteenth century and continue to change today, they impact upon the historical *idea* of the fourth estate as an apparent autonomous body in a critical relationship with power and the establishment. In other words, the *archaic*, *residual* and *emergent* continue to collide in defining the relationship between the press, journalism and power, which strikes at the heart of media ethics when the emphasis on normative activities are considered.

For writers such as Francis Fukuyama (1992) in his oft-discredited work *The End Of History And The Last Man* the liberal *idea* was seen to be triumphant when the former Stalinist states collapsed in 1989. This position is highly significant because what Fukuyama was arguing was that liberalism is *the* true reflection of human nature, thus, challenging the premise or basic structures is to invalidate the true essence of humanity.

For journalists, this transfers into the reality that one has the right to question and be of a critical mind, but one cannot legitimately use the means, that is, a newspaper within a liberal economic system, to call for the overthrow of that system from within, and primarily the reason for the suppression of free speech, that's assuming that one would want to articulate it in the first instance, is the defence of *property rights*. A Fukuyama view of the fourth estate therefore is functional; watchdog rather than revolutionary or even radical reformist, and ultimately its purpose along with other existing structures of capitalism is to ensure the recognition of humans; 'Man', claimed Fukuyama enthusiastically 'wants to be recognized. In particular, he wants to be recognized as a *human being*' (ibid., p. xvi). All this is based on the rejection of Marx's economic interpretation of history, 'historical materialism', and supportive of Hegel's 'non-materialist account of History, based on the "struggle for recognition"'(ibid.).

This view is also greatly influenced by the modernization theory of the 1960s, which can be traced back to Max Weber's thoughts on developing a new value system for society. Modernization Theory's view of media was one that coordinated national development according to liberal philosophy; the media is not only placed in context or *vis-à-vis* property and individuals' rights to gain property, but more importantly it is there to protect this most central tenet of liberalism, and there is no more contentious issue than the notion that an individual, let's say Murdoch for example, who is searching for *recognition* in private ownership, can govern journalistic practice in a dictatorial manner, the result of which is ideology over ethics.

It is to Locke that we look to find the origins and defence of property as a natural human condition where Locke states in relation to the main objective of the political state, 'the chief end whereof is the preservation of property' (Locke 1990, p. 158). Under the section titled 'Property', the following quote provides an explanation of the rights to ownership:

> God gave the world to men in common, but since He gave it them for *their benefit* and the greatest conveniences of life they were capable to draw from it, it cannot be supposed He meant it should always remain common and uncultivated. He gave it to the use of the *industrious* and *rational* (and labour was to be his title to it) (ibid., p. 132; my italics).

So here we have the promotion of the rights to property, which in reality the few and not the many acquired, but in order for owners to profit and for rights to gain greater legitimacy, Locke confirmed the exploitative relationship between owner and labour that would seal the imbalance in power between people, but moreover would be the source of the contradictions and tensions that are inherent in liberal theory because what eventually develops over time is a struggle by the oppressed for gaining greater rights in an unequal class-driven society: 'Master and servant are names as old as history, but given to those of far different condition; for a free man *makes* himself a servant to another by selling him for a certain time the service he undertakes to do in exchange for wages he is to receive' (ibid., p. 158). What Locke was trying to achieve was the justification of a move from the *state of nature* to a *political society*, governed by law and, despite the seemingly egalitarian overtones of the *Two Treatises of Government*, the reality was that *universal consent* by all to a system based on ownership of property and selling of labour power was absent. Locke attempted to resolve this by introducing the notion of *tacit consent*, which simply meant that by living within the authority of government, people automatically consented to rules, even though in reality the system was an imposition by an elite onto the many. The basis of people's obligation to the state or the justification of the system was pencilled under what Locke called the 'original compact', which according to Locke was determined by the majority, but in reality the majority was in fact a minority of elite individuals who could dictate policy.

It is this system that provides the framework for modern-day media and journalistic practice and it is in this context that the liberal thinker John Stuart Mill wrote his works on the role and 'liberty of the press' that served 'as one of the securities against corrupt or tyrannical government' (Collini 1989, p. 19) in society during the nineteenth century. In Mill's work *On Liberty* there is only a fleeting reference to the press; however, the importance of this work is to place the press in the context of achieving liberty. Thus, liberalism, according to Mill, is a political theory that establishes, benefits and maintains society. As Freeden (1998, pp. 144–145) states in relation to Mill's work:

> Mill formulates the object of his essay so as to place the preservation of liberty at its centre. Liberty, however, is positioned in immediate proximity to a dual decontesting of individualism. First, because 'over himself, over his own body and mind, the individual is sovereign', the individual is the unit of analysis. As Mill categorically states, deliberately dismissing the role of groups in social inquiry, 'The worth of a state, in the long run, is the worth of the individuals composing it'. Parallel to this emphasis on the individual is an appreciation of the personal attributes that individuals possess, what Mill terms 'character', and the expression of which is 'one of the principal ingredients of human happiness'.

The press is a means to express both character and more importantly opinions, thus allowing for maximum expression, and this vast distribution of ideas not only brings rewards to society but perhaps more importantly emanates from society; after all, Mill wrote for various newspapers and periodicals. For Mill, the expression of free opinion enriched the notion of individualism that always stood in contradistinction to the state and its monolithic apparatus. Interestingly, Mill's work titled *Chapters on Socialism* reveal the campaigning nature of the press as vital for the working classes to pursue their 'political aims' (ibid., p. 224). Mill was no Margaret Thatcher, who once famously claimed that there is no such thing as society; society for Mill certainly existed but Mill's concern was that 'society has now fairly got the better of individuality' (from *On Liberty* in Collini 1989, p. 61) going on to state that 'Even despotism does produce its worst effects. So long as "individuality" exists under it' (ibid., p. 64). As Collini (1989, p. vii) has stated, above anything else, *On Liberty* is concerned with the 'value of human individuality.' Society, according to Mill's interpretation of liberalism, is a system of individuals with rights who may speak and act freely without causing undue harm to others.

But it's important to emphasize the political differences and philosophical distinctions between the terms individual and individualism. The recognition of the individual as a distinct social entity precedes liberalism, but it is used to demonstrate the validity of individualism as a philosophical notion. I would suggest that individuality is the bridge that connects the individual as a living social entity and individualism as a philosophical construct. The political and moral philosophy that prioritizes individuality is based on a view of human nature and is therefore teleological because it quite evidently expresses purpose.

As Heywood (2004, p. 26) expresses: 'In the most obvious sense, an individual is a single human being', further stating that the individual is an 'independent and meaningful entity, possessing an identity' and one who is 'autonomous'. This view is largely unacceptable because in reality an individual both inhabits and shares a social-collective space with a greater number of other individuals. The individual in this sense isn't an isolated being (Robinson Crusoe theory) but rather one in a *community of speakers*. In other words, the identity that is created within the individual is a social-collective-group process where experience and influence is shared. Heywood continues by claiming that 'individuals are not merely independent but they are also distinct, even unique' (ibid., pp. 26–27) going on to state: 'to understand human beings as individuals is usually to believe in universalism' (ibid., p. 27). This last point stresses a universal acceptance of the individual as distinct, unique and possessing a 'personal identity' (ibid.). With respect to individualism here is what Heywood says: 'Individualism does not simply imply a belief in the existence of individuals. Rather, it refers to a *belief* in the *primacy* of the individual over any social group or collective body'(ibid.; my italics).

This notion or belief in individualism that has primacy over the social-collective isn't formed out of any natural process or human nature, but rather is a constructed piece of ideology and is therefore questionable. Nevertheless, individualism is central to liberal theory and its view of the practices of the press that materialized in another ideological invention of liberalism known as the fourth estate. For the moment, all we need to observe and bear in mind is that the liberal view towards individuality is simply that, and is prime material for critique and perhaps the basis for alternatives. In Chapter 4 we will see how the US-driven view of communitarianism uses the liberalized view of the individual as a basis of critique and the rationale for expressing an alternative view of how the press *should* operate according to justifiable ethical standards.

The question posed by Hampton (1997, p. 170), 'What is Liberalism?', leads into a discussion on the various perspectives that have dominated liberal theory. The answers and positions are indeed multiple and complex encompassing Locke, Rousseau, Kant, Rawls and Feinberg to name but a few, but what they have in common are inflections on the individual and its value within society. As

Heywood (2004, p. 29) correctly states in sum: 'Liberal thought is characterized by a commitment to individualism, a belief in the supreme importance of the human individual, implying strong support for freedom.'

Liberalism forcefully expresses the rights of individuals, but where do these rights come from and is it the case that all are equal? Mill was certainly one of most forceful advocates of individualism, expressing the 'different from the herd', and was vociferous in arguing against the morality of Victorian Britain. Mill argued passionately against conformity and perceived the desires within individuals and their realization as true reflections of individual freedom, and although individuals should hold responsibilities not to harm others as the following clearly demonstrates: 'The liberty of the individual must be thus far limited; he must not make a nuisance of himself' (ibid., p. 56), this doesn't detract from what Mill perceived as *the* fundamental right of humanity. This is proved by the following reference to Baron Wilhelm von Humboldt where the objective of individual freedom is based on 'freedom, and variety of situations ... individual vigour ... originality' (from ibid., p. 58).

We shouldn't underestimate the power of conviction in Mill's words and the deeply held belief that individuality was a force against all oppression. Similar to some of the later writings of George Simmel concerning culture and human development, Mill vociferously argued that individuality, or what Simmel referred to as 'subjective cultural development' (from Berry 2000) was the building block of humanity and to interfere with these rights of the individual is to halt the natural progression of humankind: 'Human nature is not a machine to be built after a model, and set to do exactly the work prescribed for it, but a tree, which requires to grow and develop itself on all sides, according to the tendency of the inward forces which make it a living thing' (from Heywood 2004, p. 60). The important point here is that Mill was convinced that individualism had a better chance of survival under capitalism than socialism; the latter he much admired but believed that it tended to lean towards the collective, thus having a tendency to thwart individualism. Capitalism wasn't perfect, so Mill in effect was *hedging his bets*; in other words there were no guarantees.

It is this liberal view of the individual set amongst capitalist structures that has translated into the ethics of practice in journalism. Perhaps the greatest exponent of this is John C. Merrill (1997, p. 56) who, in a critique of communitarian ethics and politics of which more is discussed in Chapter 4, states:

> I am a firm believer in individualism. The individual is prior to the community, not the other way around; individual perfection is the goal; as individuals get better, society will improve. I believe in journalistic autonomy, in journalists having the maximum freedom in their decision making.

This indeed is a powerful statement on the rights of the journalist as a moral individual, and on first reading this appears to be perfectly reasonable as a form or protection from external forces, reflecting both Locke's view of individual liberty and Mill's thoughts concerning liberty. Indeed, a part of Merrill's commitment to individuality is based on a condemnation of codes of ethics and the communitarian belief that the individual be subjugated to the will or indeed whims of the collective. Both for Merrill unnecessarily meddle in the ultimate rights of humanity, in this case an individual journalist's right to decide for themselves. But it's a very misleading statement, for what does Merrill mean by securing or protecting a journalist's maximum freedom? Merrill points out that:

> Kierkegaard argued that a person who forsakes personal freedom, follows the crowd, and does not choose his or her own identity as an individual cannot even be said to exist. I heartily concur in this sentiment and highly recommend it (ibid., p. 64).

Merrill's contrast of the individual with the crowd is revealing and it forms the basis of what he terms *existential journalism*. The notion of the crowd was originally used by thinkers such as Gustave le Bon, Gabriel Tarde, Sigmond Freud, Wilhelm Reich, Ortega y Gasset and Oswald Spengler to signify a *mass* of people who thought in collective, often gullible terms as a 'herd', as Wilfred Trotter so eloquently put it, as opposed to the rational-reasoned intellect of the individual. What became known as social psychology during the later period of the nineteenth century was the study of how public opinion was formed and psychoanalyst Edward Bernay experimented in the 1920s to prove how perceptible the crowd were to media messages by persuading women to smoke cigarettes through mass advertising regimes. The quote above by Merrill with reference to Kierkegaard places individualism within this context and is one of the prime reasons for Merrill's stout defence of *existential journalism* against the policies of one of the most influential group of thinkers in the field of media ethics, namely those of public journalism, who collectively launch a stinging attack upon the liberal notion of individuality.

It's not entirely clear whether Merrill supports all the views of the writers above in their oft-uncomplimentary statements concerning what they termed or referred to as the 'crowd'. For instance, le Bon in the chapter titled: 'General Characteristics of Crowds – Psychological Law of Their Mental Unity' from *The Crowd* begins by stating:

> In its ordinary sense the word 'crowd' means a gathering of individuals of whatever nationality, profession, or sex, and whatever be the chances that have brought them together. From the psychological point of view the expression 'crowd' assumes quite a different signification.

Further addding:

> What constitutes a crowd from the psychological point of view – A numerically strong agglomeration of individuals does not suffice to form a crowd – Special

characteristics of psychological crowds – The turning in a fixed direction of the ideas and sentiments of individuals composing such a crowd, and the disappearance of their personality – The crowd is always dominated by considerations of which it is unconscious – The disappearance of brain activity and the predominance of medullar activity – The lowering of the intelligence and the complete transformation of the sentiments – The transformed sentiments may be better or worse than those of the individuals of which the crowd is composed – A crowd is as easily heroic as criminal. (Le Bon 1920)[1]

With reference to the supposed gullibility of the crowd, Wilhelm Reich (1946, p. 10) asked 'How is it understandable that a single Hitler or a single Djugashvili (Stalin) can control eight hundred million people? How is this possible?' Ortega y Gasset viewed the crowd as vulgar, steeped in mediocrity, shallow and, similar to Reich, conformist in character. For Ortega y Gasset (1933) the masses represented the 'vertical invasion of the barbarians' and they had become 'visible' where once they were on the margins of society. For Oswald Spengler, what was termed as mass society contributed towards *The Decline of the West*, the title of his huge book originally published in 1928 (reprinted 1980). Freud had spoken in terms of group behaviour and Gustave le Bon said a crowd can be defined as 'a psychological phenomenon in which individuals with different lifestyles, occupations and characters are given a *collective soul*' (ibid.).

However, what is perfectly clear is Merrill's firm belief that it is only the individual, strong and resolute against the crowd, and its infectious-contaminated ways that can only *ethically* resolve the inherent problems that besmirch journalism today; in other words, left to their own devices a virtuous journalist is more able to produce news that best brings rewards and benefits for liberal democracy. There is an assumption in this view that there is something rotten in contemporary society and whilst Merrill may be less vitriolic in his condemnation of a decline in 'culture', he nevertheless shares the views of many of the above that culture requires urgent attention. *Existential journalism* therefore is deeply embedded in knowledge and epistemology, as it can only reveal the truth on which the world apparently turns; the crowd is the negation of truth and truth is the seat on which journalism rests its lofty behind in this philosophically determined view of practice. Culture via *existential journalism* can therefore rediscover itself faced with the attack of the *barbarians*.

Merrill's view on journalism reflects Kierkegaard's philosophy on individualism in that the individual should be responsible for philosophizing the empirical world relatively free from abstraction; this is philosophy on a personal level. There are comparisons here with Ortega y Gasset and Nietzsche, particularly concerning

---

1   The English translation of Gustave le Bon's book *The Crowd: A Study of the Popular Mind* (1920) can be located at http://etext.virginia.edu/toc/modeng/public/BonCrow.html where this extract was taken from. I would personally like to say a big thank you to the Electronic Text Center at the University of Virginia Library for making this available.

their respective views on *perspectivism*, more of which is discussed in Chapter 5 on truth and objectivity. Kierkegaard's philosophical existentialism therefore transfers into the *existentialist journalism* forwarded by Merrill. In Kierkegaard's work *Either/Or* (1992), the author proposed that we inhabit two 'existence spheres'; the first is what Kierkegaard called 'aesthetic' and the other was 'ethical'. For Kierkegaard both spheres were hardly satisfactory for perfect self-development because they entailed compromise with others, but at the time of writing he was reasonably satisfied with the way in which liberal-bourgeois society was progressing. There are echoes here of Schopenhauer, particularly Kierkegaard's firm belief that individualism is about taking risks in defying socially accepted practices. Schopenhauer was fiercely 'individualistic' (Janaway 2002, p. 9) condemning Hegel's view of his beloved state as an end-goal of human existence and perfection. Schopenhauer was anti-establishment and anti-authority; fiercely protective of the rights of the individual and, as Janaway states: 'Independence of spirit is the trait most characteristic of Schopenhauer' (ibid., p. 1). Nozick's (1974) work *Anarchy, State and Utopia* can be interpreted as a reflection of Kierkegaard's philosophy where, whilst not ideal, nevertheless one must accept that the state exists and whilst the state in theory is a threat to individuality, as also in Mill and his critique of despotism, one must therefore greatly reduce its influence and power, hence Nozick's notion of the 'minimal state'. Nozick argued that individuals have a moral space where, unless consensual, no other can invade: As Nozick (1974, p. 149) states:

> The minimal state [limited to the narrow functions of protection against force, theft, fraud, enforcement of contracts and so on] is the most extensive state that can be justified. Any state more extensive violates peoples' rights.

For Merrill, although he doesn't specifically refer in this context to Nozick, the minimal state transfers into the *minimal press organization* with limited interference from owner and editor into the daily working practices of a journalist; thus for Merrill the perfect liberal press is expressed in terms of maximizing individual rights to speech and expression and minimizing external interference. Staying with Merrill for the moment, it is disingenuous of him (1989, p. 21) to state that Mill 'saw capitalism as the system best suited to bring the most happiness to the public' as if this were currently applicable because of the changes that have occurred in the structures of capitalism since Mill's time; once diverse, presently monopolized. Similar to the way Marx wrote on capitalism before the development of imperialism, I am sure that Mill, like Marx, would have revised his philosophy according to the changes that occurred. What appalled Mill more than anything else were powerful dictatorial institutions not too dissimilar from the multinational corporations that dominate the news and media industry today. Perhaps there are two possibilities to consider here in light of the corporatism that dominates the media and journalistic landscape that suppresses the individual freedom that Mill aspired too; first, and assuming Mill continued in his belief of protecting individuality, he may have devised a new strategy for journalists to push back the frontiers of tyrannical power; a call to arms for *enlightenment journalism*, a moral crusade for the rightful place of individual freedom but *only* within present structures, that is, a reformist line, or, second, perhaps Mill could have admitted that he had got it wrong, that capitalism couldn't be reformed. Consider the following quote from Collini (1989, p. xxii) in reference to the *Chapters on Socialism*, which I feel is a much better reading of Mill than Merrill has offered:

> it would not be too misleading to say that while Mill found the *ideal* of socialism infinitely more attractive than the often unjust and selfish *reality* of capitalism, he believed that the *actual* practical and moral difficulties of socialism in the present stage of social and moral development meant that a greatly *improved* capitalism held out the more realistic hopes for human betterment in the short term.[2]

Herein lay the essential problem facing Mill: how to improve capitalism and any leanings towards governmental/state despotism. It's perfectly reasonable and fair to interpret Mill and argue that he would have been equally outraged by large media corporations that sought to impose their will onto individuals who work within them. What is referred as 'organizational imperatives' are company directives that determine news policy, and these invariably negate the expression of individual free-will; Merrill's view, perhaps naïve, is to argue for a greater expression of individuality within journalism, but how realistic is this view in the current corporate climate? It's difficult to know what Mill would recommend, but perhaps he may acknowledge that the problem primarily lay with a fundamental contradiction within liberalism itself that has its roots in John Locke and his preferred emphasis on bestowing legalized individual rights to own property; media owners are, after all, expressing these rights. So how do liberal thinkers resolve the tensions and dilemmas between individual free speech and economic rights of ownership? And what do liberals say about a company-determined organizational imperative as news policy that is expressed in the public interest? Finally, what do liberals say about the natural swing towards monopoly control in the market place that has systematically undermined a plurality of voices in society? It seems perfectly reasonable to argue that there is very little in way of resolving the inherent

---

2   It's clear in *Chapters on Socialism* that Mill perceived the possibility of a particular form of socialism in very favourable terms as the following demonstrates: 'The *practicability* then of Socialism, on the scale of Mr Owen's or M. Fourier's villages, admits of not dispute' (Mill 1989, p. 62). Mill therefore was supportive of small scale cooperatives where the means of production could be held in common, but was against the idea that production should be managed by, 'one central organisation' (ibid.), a critique of what actually developed in the USSR under a one-party Stalinist dictatorship, which in essence led Mill to argue that the jury was very much still out on the verdict between 'public' or 'private' ownership (ibid., p. 273).

contradictions between individualism and monopoly without state interference into the rights of property ownership, but as liberals call for minimal state interference into the rights of individuals to own property and express their will therein, *the song remains the same* and no ethical code of conduct can be enforced, especially into the pure notion of individualism, because this too is an external force similar to the state. Thus, in the UK at least self-regulation of the press remains firmly intact with the largely ineffective Press Complaints Commission's voluntary Code of Practice detailing guidelines for editors and journalists to follow; the National Union of Journalists has a Code of Conduct that is broadly similar.

There is no dispute over the thoughts of Mill, which are clearly outlined in his works on socialism, but for our purposes, and that's assuming that the reader accepts this view, it leaves the discussion on the value and the role of the individual journalist *vis-à-vis* corporate media power and the increasing gap in wealth and political power between elites and the rest in society in a state of confusion, for what are journalist responsibilities in such undemocratic circumstances, and what's more, if a journalist's right and freedom to speak, what Pilger in reference to Primo Levi calls the subversive truth, is curtailed by the organizational structures in which they practice, what action then?

What the liberal view of individualism provides is a debate on the very essence of humanity or human nature, for what is it to be human? What are the characteristics that define our humanity that significantly differ from the animal world? These are indeed big philosophical questions, which have yet to be resolved as a result of converging views of human nature and indeed whether human nature actually exists! The issue of individuality, human nature, rights and freedom go right to the heart of journalistic practice because they infer a system of responsibilities, for the trade-off for awarding such rights is that an individual doesn't misuse or abuse them. But this says nothing about the *social responsibilities* to the community or towards democracy whatsoever, and it only speaks of the individual. This sense of individuality was discussed in another of John Locke's (1996) books, *An Essay Concerning Human Understanding*, where Locke discusses the cognitive processes that constitute the 'self', which is 'consciousness' and 'thinking'.

Although Locke doesn't directly speak in terms of individuality, the philosophical notion described here as the 'self' assumes a human right to be able to think differently from others; in other words, what defines the self is what I call the *distinction of difference*. Locke called this condition 'personal identity', and what gave it its true power and value was its interrelationship with rationality; to be an individual or to have personal identity meant one had the biographical structures on which rational beings could thrive. Strip away our sense of individuality and you sacrifice the personal identity that opposes tyranny and collectivism; it's the stuff of Patrick McGoohan in the *Prisoner*: 'I'm not a number, I'm a human being'. It's the critique of Stalinist rule, which trampled violently upon the individual.

In a discussion on philosophy and its application to journalism, Hodges (1997, p. 48) says 'we are indeed freestanding individuals possessed of a serious measure of independence' whilst recognizing our social commitment to others. Of course, the central issue here is whether the commitment to the community outweighs the journalist's apparent right to protect and administer a personal will against the rights of the community and the public interest. In other words, can forces exogenous to the individual compel them to a duty beyond self-interest? Such external forces are codes of ethics, which are institutionally formed; the very bodies that opposes liberal individualism because they are not the product of the moral-agent and of self-experience. In this sense, institutional bodies that seek to impose ethics upon the individual in the name of duty and obligation are seen as tyrannical by liberal thinkers, there to be opposed if one wishes and justified on the basis of personal choice.

The Fourth Estate

Hastings's (2000) account of the history of journalism doesn't distinguish satisfactorily between news and journalism, only that technological advances in human development such as the printing press by Gutenberg in 1456 allowed for a 'wider distribution of news'. This account places emphasis on technology, not method and certainly not on ethics; news is what it has always been, but now it's transmitted in greater quantities and over greater swathes of space, hastened of course by the development of railway networks in the nineteenth century. But whilst this is a perfectly reasonable account of news, that is, humans accounting for events regardless of the means used, it is nevertheless an inadequate account of journalism as a social practice; in other words news and journalism are conflated and connected like conjoined twins; there's no theoretical distinction; there's no morality nor responsibility that can universally be applied to modern forms of journalism in this context because it is merely a technological extension of earlier storytelling. If we are ever to agree that codes of conduct (individual and/or collectively based) are essential for objective accounts to attain truth in journalism then surely we must firstly set out clearly what is so distinctive about journalism in relation to how it mediates news distinct from ordinary storytelling. Journalism, then, was and is a distinct and different way for telling a story from ordinary folktales. But more importantly, journalism as a practice, assumed a higher moral ground, pertaining to be more reliable, truthful and trustworthy by using objective means for accounting events. All this, of course, is highly contentious considering the manner in which the press can mislead on important debates of the day, but that for the moment is not the point; the point is that journalism became a high priest for distributing information.

As noted above, the first reference to the fourth estate was made during the eighteenth century by the English philosopher Edmund Burke and later documented by the nineteenth-century writer Thomas Carlyle in his works *The French Revolution* in 1857[3] and then again in *On Heroes, Hero-worship & the*

---

3   See Part VI, Section V of Carlyle's book *The French Revolution.*

Heroic in History published in 1894. In the former there was reference to 'A Fourth Estate, of Able Editors (Carlyle, Part VI, Section V, *The French Revolution*), but the discussion was extended in the latter:

> Or turning now to the Government of men. Witenagemote, old Parliament, was a great thing. The affairs of the nation were there deliberated and decided; what we were to *do* as a nation. But does not, though the name Parliament subsists, the parliamentary debate go on now, everywhere and at all times, in a far more comprehensive way, *out* of Parliament altogether? Burke said there were Three Estates in Parliament; but, in the Reporters' Gallery yonder, there sat a *Fourth Estate* more important far than they all. It is not a figure of speech, or a witty saying; it is a literal fact, – very momentous to us in these times. Literature is our Parliament too. Printing, which comes necessarily out of Writing, I say often, is equivalent to Democracy: invent Writing; Democracy is inevitable. Writing brings Printing; brings universal everyday extempore Printing, as we see at present. Whoever can speak, speaking now to the whole nation, becomes a power, a branch of government, with inalienable weight in law-making, in all acts of authority. It matters not what rank he has, what revenues or garnitures. The requisite thing is, that he have a tongue which others will listen to; this and nothing more is requisite. The nation is governed by all that has tongue in the nation: Democracy is virtually *there*. Add only, that whatsoever power exists will have itself, by and by, organized; working secretly under bandages, obscurations, obstructions, it will never rest till it get to work free, unencumbered, visible to all. Democracy virtually extant will insist on becoming palpably extant. (Carlyle, 1841, 'The Hero as Man of Letters. Johnson, Rousseau, Burns', Lecture V)

For Carlyle, there is a clear distinction between men of letters (essayists who wrote on literature) and the journalists in terms of the object of enquiry, the latter conditioned primarily by reporting on government business. Journalists, however, also wrote on literature during the nineteenth century and therefore were akin to men of letters, but this also is a distinct subject matter. What is important for our purposes is Carlyle's belief that the formation of the fourth estate is chiefly responsible for extending what limited democracy there was in the lines: 'The nation is governed by all that has tongue in the nation: Democracy is virtually *there*'; and: 'Democracy virtually extant will insist on becoming palpably extant.' Carlyle was in essence writing on the necessity for a free press to exist in order to ward off what Mill would later refer to as despotism, and although in relation to the fourth estate Conboy (2004, p. 108) has claimed that 'it lacked clear substance', Carlyle at least laid the foundations on its purpose in society. The question to be asked in this context in relation to a discourse on media ethics could be as follows: is the fourth estate's purpose closely aligned with Carlyle's founding thoughts and does it benefit society and extend democracy in contemporary times?

Carlyle couldn't be described as a liberal in total spirit, but there's no doubt that a *spirit of liberalism* with respect to the press–government relationship was a part of Carlyle's view of the fourth estate. We can also see that within Carlyle's approach is the spirit of civil society and the public space where the press are able to bring forth matters of government hitherto unknown to the public, necessary for the formation of public opinion and free discourse. Within civil society, the public space is, theoretically speaking, a space where rational ideas are circulated, accessed and discussed as public communication. The *idea* of the fourth estate in this context is that it is activated from within civil society with relative autonomy from the state enabling it to contribute to the public space as it sits in contradistinction to government power. This notion of the fourth estate was and continues to be radical and subversive in the sense that it confronts power and thus creates its objectives from a different rationale, creating a new rationality in the process that challenges authority. It's argued that one such objective is to create the basis for public discussion or public opinion and it could be further argued that this theory of the fourth estate is a means to achieve what Kant (1991) called 'publicity'. The idea then is that the fourth estate, armed to the teeth with a new confronting rationality, distributes information into the public domain enabling and empowering the public to produce new forms of critical thought not imposed by the state or any imposing authority such as the Church for example.

The importance of such a space is that it creates publicity, which in turn encourages public participation in the communications process to progressively more citizens, whilst defining the limits of legitimate state interference. Habermas (1989) used the principle of publicity and formulated a view that it was *the* basis for the political and ideological ethic that underscored and shaped the actual structure of the public realm. Perceived as such, the principle of publicity is a heuristic device in which to measure the legitimacy of communication regulation and thus the definitions of civil society. Under strict liberal interpretations, civil society permits the fourth estate to erect the building blocks of public opinion.

Habermas also argued that Kant's philosophy with specific reference to publicity provided the clearest image of how a public sphere could be seen to operate. Habermas focused on Kant's work concerning enlightenment arguing that 'publicity' was a bridge between the political and the moral. The provision of such a space either as Habermas's public sphere or Kant's publicity requires rules of engagement not that dissimilar from Rorty's theory. For Kant the public would need to acquire skills of reasoning; what Rorty (1998) later called 'competences'. That aside, the gist of this argument is that we can see that irrespective of abilities to comprehend information the press can be perceived as providing some of the raw material on which we base knowledge. Here is what Kant says on enlightenment: '*Enlightenment is man's emergence from his self-incurred immaturity*'. Immaturity is the inability to use one's understanding without the guidance of another (from Reiss 1970, p. 9). Essentially, one is required to think independently, but this requires the building blocks of knowledge plus access, which can be subsumed under the liberal notion of free speech and freedom of the press when the notion of the fourth estate was becoming established; this is how Kant's theory of publicity can be applied.

John Stuart Mill would later use the idea of publicity as a means to effective voting and of being in the public interest, a principle that would later be used in relation to the fourth estate. Amongst other concerns the notion that a public interest principle could be applied in relation to the fourth estate rested upon the further notion that within the fourth estate a series of ethical responsibilities should be upheld in order to satisfy and fulfil public interest demands. Edgar's work (2000) 'The "fourth estate" and moral responsibilities', although not directly speaking in terms of a public interest, is nevertheless based in that spirit, for Edgar outlines some of the key ethical principles that underpin the liberal theory of the press.

As noted earlier in Chapter 1, Hunt's (1998) book title begins *The Fourth Estate* ... and it opens in the first chapter with a significant question: 'What is the Fourth Estate?', stating further: 'that newspapers have grown upon us until they have become a positive necessity of civilized existence – a portion, indeed, of modern civilization' (Hunt 1998, p. 1). Accordingly, newspapers are necessary because they, and journalists, serve a specific purpose in *civilized society*, as Hunt would have it, which serves as the basis of journalistic practice. In fact, it's entirely reasonable to deduce from Hunt's claims that without newspapers and journalists, there would be no modern civilization; for Hunt, both are interrelated with other important parts in society, and each part serves a specific function: 'the newspaper is a daily and sleepless watchman that reports to you every danger which menaces the institutions of your country, and its interests at home and abroad' (ibid., p .7). The idea that the fourth estate is a 'watchman' to protect us from wrongdoing is one embedded in popular consciousness and indeed is central to the liberal theory of the press. However, the purpose of journalism according to Hunt is deeply conformist and conservative; protection means to conserve existing values, established norms and established traditions, including relations of power not only 'at home' but equally 'abroad'. Hunt was writing during what Hobsbawm called *The Age of Capital* (1849–75), which preceded *The Age of Empire* (1875–1914). Britain's interests abroad preceded these dates, but the idea that newspapers enthusiastically support and comply in maintaining class division at home and colonial ambition abroad is to throw journalism to the whims of governmental interpretations of a national interest; not that dissimilar from the way in which Rome dictated the news of the day, also detailed in Chapter 1 of this book. Hunt continues in a likeminded vein: the newspaper 'conduces to the maintenance of order, and prevents the stern necessity for revolution' (ibid., pp. 7–8). Hunt's view of the fourth estate was clearly functionalist, a view that has been held by many within the broad field of mass communications. McQuail (1993, p. 237), commenting on the functionalist as opposed to 'critical theories of mass communication', primarily 'attributes to the mass media the "function" (or hidden purpose) of securing the continuity of a given social order, maintaining control, establishing a broad consensus of values, integrating activities, anchoring individuals and groups in society'.

Whilst this may be true in established liberal democracies, the role of an emerging fourth estate in societies lacking overall democratic structures will be significantly different and thus the liberal theory of the press can have *radical leanings*. This is detailed by Lawson (2002) in *Building the Fourth Estate* in Mexico, where the themes of the text have a familiar ring to them. For instance, the fourth estate has an important role for creating public opinion, particularly in emerging democracies. Lawson argues that an independent press can aggressively promote a democratic transition and political liberalization, which is a direct reflection of the thoughts of Thomas Carlyle, some 161 years earlier.

In relation to the US, Mott (1962, pp. 31–38) details how the trial of Peter Zenger in 1735 paved the way for the freedom of the press when his lawyer Andrew Hamilton produced a stout and convincing defence of the right of Zenger to publicly challenge authority: 'This was an historic moment … in the long struggle for the freedom of the press' (ibid., p. 36) and 'upon the development of the concept of liberty in general' (ibid., p. 38). The early liberal notion of the fourth estate is partly based on the ideal to challenge the power and authority of the establishment, but assumes that challenge stems from the periphery of power and not within. However important the Zenger trial was for establishing press freedom in the US, the process of the development of the fourth estate had, according to Emery (1972, p. 32), begun much earlier in 1704 with the publication of the *Boston News-Letter*, which 'was like the biblical mustard seed. From it stemmed the mighty American Fourth Estate … .'

Equally, Rutland (1973, p. 24) states that the '*Courant* and other obstreperous newspapers signalled the rise of a new kind of journalism in America that would not truckle for long to officialdom' referring to it as 'a defiant breed of newspaper' (ibid.). Although it is true in any country that establishing a press has had its problems, perhaps in many respects establishing it wasn't as traumatic or difficult as maintaining an essence or integrity that is befitting of its original position. Much later in Rutland's book the exasperation at the failure of the US media to maintain a critical edge is summed up with reference to the American broadcaster Ed Murrow, who argued that journalists seek out 'controversial' issues: 'Murrow lashed out at the newsmen attitude that "… we must at all costs shield the sensitive citizens from anything that is unpleasant"' (ibid., p. 371). Murrow held an orthodox liberal view of the fourth estate whose primary function in a democratic system was one based on holding established power to account and certainly upholding freedom of speech with responsibilities that would reform rather than subvert society.

In general terms, even though the economic and political circumstances differ greatly today from the mid to late nineteenth century, the *spirit of liberalism* can be effectively invoked even if it is to simply justify *what is*, which in real terms contrasts greatly with *what was*. Nowhere is this *spirit* more realized and effective than within the historical liberal notion of free speech.[4] Put simply, the fourth estate is seen to guarantee free speech built on the foundations of individuality; the latter is justified in economic terms (individual ownership over state control) and then filters down to journalists who, although they may work within certain

---

4   The term 'freedom of expression' is also used, but is a broader concept than 'free speech'. The former normally includes the latter.

confines, nevertheless can express their individual creativity in the act of news production, even though the reality may be at odds with this view. The fourth estate, therefore, according to the liberal theory of the press, becomes the social space that guarantees a vibrant public sphere within the productive confines of civil society. This current discussion isn't about whether free speech should exist absolutely in any ethical sense; rather, it is simply an expression of liberal wishes and desires that is seen to guarantee democracy.

Haworth (1998, p. 174) reminds us that Mill and later Rawls regard free speech as a 'basic liberty', in other words, free speech is both fundamental and absolute to the functioning of a liberal-democratic system, and because it is seen as a basic liberty it must be protected. The reason for protecting free speech is mainly because it is a means or a vehicle towards attaining the truth, which is afforded great value in liberalism; this is the fundamental reason for the existence of the fourth estate, to pursue the truth in a politicized environment that more often than not breeds corruption, lowers standards and ferments bad practice. There is accordingly a moral purity afforded to the fourth estate as a harbinger of truth in the face of adversity and what at times appears to be proclivity to immorality. Ironically, today, rather than the fourth estate being the seat of critique, it has now had the tables turned on it and has become the object of inquiry and critique espoused by the academic discipline *media criticism*; something indeed has been lost in (liberal) translation! I've always found it interesting and contradictory that liberalism espouses representative government only then to recognize à la Machiavelli that it is essentially flawed, and that the fourth estate acts as a guarantor to both expose wrongdoing and pursue the truth. So what happens to the liberal theory of press when the 'guarantor' also becomes a perpetrator of falsehoods; becomes conformist with government policy and is the source of wrongdoing? Who then do we rely upon?

According to liberalism, the press has an ability to freely articulate language and content (within legal confines) not only because the fourth estate is conditioned by autonomy from the state (relative or otherwise), but perhaps more importantly because of the centrality of free speech to notions of democracy. In Haworth's book titled *Free Speech* (1998), the author explores the importance of the aforementioned concept in relation to the extensive work of John Rawls and asks: 'So, why should Rawls think that freedom of speech can be so easily and straightforwardly grouped together with "political liberty (the right to vote and to be eligible for public office?"' (ibid., p. 177). For Rawls the answer lay with the 'principle of (equal) participation' (ibid.), for all are freedoms of equal status *vis-à-vis* political citizenship.

Free speech and individualism underpins the liberal theory of the press and, more importantly, the function of the fourth estate, and in this context the fourth estate's role in society, at least at this theoretical level, is moral in context. However, the *idea* of the fourth estate is deeply ideological, mainly because liberalism is economically and politically tied in with capital and the free market.

Thus values and beliefs transcend morality within a framework dictated by the pursuit of profit.

Within the economic and political capitalist framework, the press are allowed certain degrees of autonomy to operate and this is its 'watchdog' role, there to ensure that political wrongdoing is revealed and kept in check. Thus the *idea* of the fourth estate is extremely influential for its influence over the development of journalism and has greater impact in Western systems with liberal-social democracies; we can witness its impact in the formation of new press systems in the former Stalinist societies since their collapse in 1989. Equally, the *idea* of the fourth estate can also be perceived as a metaphor for a press independent of state control and power within liberalism. In this sense also the *idea* of the fourth estate is an ideological construct; a mirror within mirrors! Further to this, Conboy (2004, p. 109) states:

> The claim to constitute a Fourth Estate was … an important contribution to the discursive formation of journalism. Despite the fact that it lacked clear substance, it contributed to the establishment of journalism as a mainstream economic and political force … .

Carey's idea of what constitutes good reportage is for some writers the essence of what constitutes the *idea* of the fourth estate. In other words, the ideal is based on individual autonomy to document events without external restriction and with all its glorious peculiarities and perspectives: *vive la difference!* As previously noted, the purpose of reportage is to bring a reality to the public by efficient use of language that captures a moment in history. More importantly for Carey, the style must be so individualized that it avoids a 'daily slide into sameness' (Carey 1987, p. xxxii). Quite clearly this is a celebration of diverse and distinct voices on which plurality of interests are built. The emphasis appears to be placed on rights and free speech and to be heard, accepted or even dismissed. This further emphasizes the toleration of diverse ideas and quite possibly competing claims about society, which is seen as a major element of democracy because it avoids consensus. But for Carey, reportage has a distinct 'social value' in that it 'supplies modern man with a constant and reassuring sense of events going on beyond his immediate horizon' creating 'reality greater than himself' (ibid., p. xxxv), all of which isn't entirely unreasonable if it were not for the fact that Carey neglects to discuss the important issue of power. I am not talking about the power of journalism, not yet at least, but rather the purpose of journalism *vis-à-vis* the power of the state-politic. The main concern of Carey is rather the power of language to convey the reality of events to an audience. In this context what then is the idea of the fourth estate that journalists apparently inhabit? Why is it important that the fourth estate is, in theory at least, seen to be independent from power? Following on from the second question, what exactly is the relationship between the fourth estate and state-political power? In sum, what is the fourth estate meant to be doing? Some feel that the fourth estate has now reneged on its main social responsibilities, articulated in: 'The Fourth Estate is Fatally Wounded and Dying a Slow Death':

> The Fourth Estate was suppose to keep all the enemies of freedom exposed. It was supposed to alert us all to really bad government. Now it's like a dirty rag on the kitchen sink. It's smells and only good for pushing dirt around the surface of our lives. I have read several articles about how the circulations are dropping at alarming rates. 8 per cent in some cities. There are all kinds of reasons they are giving but none are saying how they have lost the confidence of the American people. (Gary2idaho 2007)

Shultz (1999) in *Reviving the Fourth Estate* in Australia details the decline of press responsibilities and the need or indeed urgency for this to be addressed if the integrity of the fourth estate is to remain intact. Shultz's focus on ethical issues is familiar terrain, emphasizing the increase in commercialization, on the one hand, and the need to respond to the challenges that commercialization brings with an increasing emphasis on ethical responsibilities, on the other. The basis of any such possibilities to attain a new moral obligation is firmly rooted in political independence, which in theory should ensure journalistic autonomy. If anything, Shultz's work only confirms the paradox that haunts liberalism as a political and philosophical framework that governs the fourth estate, namely the natural tension between the ideals of the press and the increasing concentration of ownership; a point also made by Belsey (1998).

Hadland (2005) in *Changing the Fourth Estate* in South Africa explores similar issues to Shultz concerning the relevance of the press and its role within a liberal framework for attaining a democratic informational sphere. The collection of essays in Hadland's book is a journalists' guide to good practice with strong ethical overtones. One essay that demonstrates the very best of 'popular journalism' is written by Peta Thornycroft, foreign correspondent for UK newspaper *The Daily Telegraph*, detailing the financial difficulties of ordinary people. Here too we can see the ethical relationship between journalism and responsibilities. In a similar spirit, Jan Schaffer, Executive Director of the Pew Center for Civic Journalism wrote:

> The news media can treat democracy as a spectator sport – or as a participatory exercise. How journalists frame their stories, who they include in their stories, and whether they provide entry points for participation usually determine the difference. Democracy begins to feel like a spectator sport when the news media focus on elected officials or elites engaged in some high-level exercise or in some sort of civic 'freak' show and ordinary citizens can't figure out what their stake is. It becomes participatory, when the media position citizens as more than a piece of colourful furniture in a story, but as people with a role to play. (Schaffer 2008)

The works of Shultz, Hadland and the comments of the Pew Centre are attempts to address the comments of the blogger above. In other words, the answer lies within a discourse on media ethics, emphasizing the relationship and indeed commitment to journalistic social responsibilities and society. How convinced the blogger is by this is another matter but what they collectively have in common is an agreement that something is indeed rotten in journalism today; it's only the solutions that may differ.

The discussion on liberalism in relation to individualism, free speech and the fourth estate is important for this discussion on ethics because to a large extent many writers within the field of media ethics argue that the liberal view of the press has failed. Indeed, the reason for media ethics existing is exactly that; in other words it seeks to remedy this failure in a variety of ways. However, the notion that the press and therefore journalism should confront power for the benefit of society still holds and in this context, despite neo-liberal economic structures, the *spirit of liberalism* continues to reach *residually into the present*; but is it any more than an *idea*?

Chapter 4
Media Ethics and Society: Journalism and Responsibilities

Media Ethics and *Enlightenment Journalism*

There are many dimensions to the debate on media ethics but some of the important ones with respect to this current discussion concern an approach to the meaning and purpose of both news and journalism discussed earlier in Chapters 1 and 2, particularly in relation to mainstream press and media organizations. The approaches can vary but they nevertheless assert or even reassert discussions on the production of news, and what function and purpose journalism *should* have in society. Whatever the differences of opinions within the broad scope of media ethics, all engage with liberalism, the *idea* of the fourth estate, and therefore the meaning of news and journalism and their relationship with democracy and society. Some, like John Merrill, reassert the individualism central to liberal philosophy and others, such as those belonging to the US-based Public Journalism movement, argue that it is liberalism with its emphasis on individualism that is essentially the root of the problem in contemporary journalism.

It's in this context that the liberal view serves as a basis for the emergence of public journalism, which has been the most vigorous group of writers within the field of media ethics. Amongst many other issues, one reason for the emergence of public journalism is a critique of liberalism and the types of individualism that have influenced the meaning and purpose of news and journalism, and it is in this context that public journalism has offered an alternative journalistic model free from the ideals of the fourth estate with its emphasis on individual liberty. This is quite evidently audacious, for it attempts not only to critique the contemporary monopolized condition of the media and journalism, but perhaps more importantly to undermine the philosophical and theoretical basis of the historical notion of the fourth estate by making an appeal not to the individual but rather to the community and its place within wider society. Above all else, it is an attempt to redress not only the contradictions, but also the failures of the fourth estate that operate within broadly defined liberal structures.

This approach to redress practice can also be seen in the emergence more recently of the 'media literacy' programme within the EU and is highly significant within this current debate. Briefly, 'media literacy' is a media policy that equally sets out to confront liberalism's influence over the meaning and purpose of news and journalism, albeit in a novel and different way from public journalism. It also confirms the many contradictions within liberal theory that permit media owners such as Rupert Murdoch and Silvio Berlusconi to amass control of the media landscape, which is largely perceived as having negative effects within a European context – or should that be European society? After all, the EU promotes 'European Citizenship' in context of culture (differences or otherwise), identity and shared values that occupy communities within broader societal levels. Whatever the differences of emphasis between public journalism and the EU towards how journalism should operate within society, they nevertheless share common ground on the issue concerning the value of information for society and thus the EU's media policy is de facto also an alternative model of how information that is primarily beneficial to society can effectively be mediated to broaden not lessen the scope of democracy. Both viewpoints relate strongly to Thomas Carlyle's comments on the fourth estate in *On Heroes, Hero-worship & the Heroic in History* (1894) concerning the role of the press and democratic expansion.

In general terms, the debate on media ethics in relation to the press, elements of broadcast media (news and advertising) and society is one based on function and purpose. At its most basic, it is argued that above all else the function of the press and broadcast news media is to maintain democracy, not erode it. How it achieves this status is a part of a more complex debate concerning the relationship between journalism, ethics and society. Once again, in general terms, the philosophies that underpin academic concerns over practice, however different, are in essence debates on public policy, unofficial or otherwise, towards a view of society.[1] Once again, despite philosophical differences over achieving objectives, there is by and large agreement that something is rotten or at least not quite right about current forms of practice under mostly monopoly conditions. Therefore, the broad discussion on media ethics, despite the various positions, is to correct current practice and therefore to bring tangible benefits to the public based on higher journalistic standards and a higher quality of performance, and once either of these are lowered, as they apparently are, then benefits no longer flow from the site of production to the level of consumption. Rutland (1973, p. 390) in the very last paragraph on the very last page of his book sums up this concern with maintaining this important balance between two points of contact:

> Before the purveying of information becomes a lost art, the newsmongers must accept the fact that the real test of professionalism is not whether one can protect sources or hang out a shingle but how well one performs a task that is vital to society.

Both public journalism and the EU have different and opposing views on how the media *ought* to operate in society, and both therefore have respective views on

---

1 The use of the word 'society' is purposely put forward here as opposed to the use of 'community', which is more often used in reference to communitarianism and liberalism to emphasize the broader aspects of the debate on the objectives of a discourse on media ethics.

the meaning of society. I would argue that this latter view is more based on Max Weber's (1949) notion of an 'ideal-type' or a model built on value-judgements. It is this normative context that informs us much of the way in which academics in media ethics view the relationship between journalism and society or rather how it *ought* to be. This context is one built on constant struggle – it is, to use an old phrase from British Cultural Studies – a site where a 'battle of ideas' of how it should be exists. This normative context contains the social function of journalism and what journalism is expected to be doing in order to bring benefits to society. Here, then function and purpose co-exist in a teleological end game – benefits are, after all, a part of the grand design, and journalism is seen as an essential element for society to achieve this status. As we shall see later, both the debate in the US on public journalism and in the EU on the role of journalism are essentially teleological equations made for the benefit of humankind. But they also serve as a form of mystification, as they mask the real relations of society.

A brief summary thus far: in Chapter 1 I provided an assessment of news and the importance of newspapers for the development of journalism. Then, in Chapter 2 the discussion proceeded with an assessment of the meaning of journalism before discussing the liberal theory of the press in Chapter 3. Liberalism and the ideological notion of the fourth estate have had a profound impact on the meaning of journalism *vis-à-vis* its relationship to society and development. This chapter now begins to expand on the previous three and introduces a new element to the discussion, namely normative theory, particularly in relation to the academic discipline media ethics. This chapter is not simply interested in what constitutes news, but rather what constitutes 'good' news and thus begins to introduce judgements on how news can be socially useful. The next logical step is then to expand on the *meaning of journalism* by introducing philosophical debates concerning responsibilities of journalists, and this comes into direct conflict with the liberal theory of the press because, as we shall see, liberalism defends the rights of an individual journalist to act and behave according to their self-determined moral conscience, whereas much of the debate within media ethics prescribes external resolutions and attempts to impose them onto the individual; a code of practice is one good example of this.

The critique of liberalism is equally an attempt to reformulate the ideological perspective of the fourth estate, particularly in relation to what the press *should* be doing in order to bring substantive change and substantial benefits to society. In sum, much of what is discussed within media ethics is a debate on the *function* of the press and how best it can achieve this. At the heart of this is a debate on democracy, even though it is either understated (public journalism) or aligned closely with free market principles (EU) and visions of society. Even though media ethics is concerned with the lowering of standards and the negative role and influence an unfettered commercial market has on the press, it is, nevertheless, a discipline driven by the belief, ideal perhaps, that the press can act for the good of society. It therefore holds to a vision of *enlightenment journalism* and is thus prescriptive because change for the good can only come about by accepting morally defined judgements.

Many of the discussions that occur within media ethics reflect concerns over standards of journalism and quality of performance in relation to the value of news in society. Interestingly, an essential part of these discussions are concerns not only over production, but also consumption, but rarely do discussions on media ethics traverse into the area known within cultural studies as 'media effects'. It is interesting because within media ethics there is an assumption that news has negative effects on the 'good' of society; for why else be concerned if the opposite were true? The lack of empirical data to substantiate claims made about effects is, in my view, a major flaw in moral judgements made against the negation of responsibilities, and there is certainly room for ethnographic research to assess how news is received *vis-à-vis* ethical concerns. The lack of empirical data doesn't, however, influence our ability to make moral judgements on production, but this invariably only makes sense in relation to consumption; that is the nature of journalism to mediate from one point to another. As we shall see later in this chapter, both public journalism and the EU's key debates on how the press/media should function are discourses based on bringing benefits to society and are indicative, as well as providing evidence, of the assumption that the press/media impact upon the development of society.

There is perhaps one other important issue emanating from discussions within public journalism and the EU that should also be considered at this juncture and that is the assumption that presently the press (and media in general) operate separately, away from society rather than a part of society. This view is made more obvious and is explicit in public journalism with emphasis on *communitarianism*, whilst I would argue that it is less obvious but nevertheless implicit within the EU's media policy initiative 'media literacy'. Whatever the differences in emphasis, both positions create media policies on the basis of a press/media–society dichotomy. Public journalism explicitly calls for a return of the media away from an unnatural external logic towards the community that is inherent in society. The EU's emphasis on citizens rescuing information by having democratic access to new technology is equally an admission that media monopolies exist within a separated external logic determined by commercial imperatives.

Interestingly Allan (2004, p. 3) has critiqued the media–society dichotomy as unhelpful for our comprehension of the relationship between processes of journalism and public understanding, using the term 'news culture', which 'resists the analytical separation of the "cultural" from the "economic" and the "political" prefigured by the media-society dichotomy'. Although it's not referred to, it seems to me that this model of approach or method is one that Leon Trotsky once referred to as dialectics, read in Hegel and Marx, but used as a method by Trotsky, which runs the risk of negating an observation of institutions that have externalized 'immanent logics'. Although Allan is not specifically referring to either of the two viewpoints above, the emphasis on the analytical doesn't take into consideration the emphasis on normative precepts so evident in public journalism's and the EU's perspectives; thus the moral imperatives produce an interesting perspective on the media–society relationship. The sum total of this argument is that a system of mediation, which is at least perceived as separate, fails to bring substantive benefits to society; thus the recommendations by public journalism and the EU are prescriptions to remedy this division, and both share a conviction of strengthening citizenship through new media policy directives.

I would argue that despite the unification of systems operating within society, the press/media nevertheless have developed and operate within what Simmel called an 'immanent developmental logic'.[2] I have previously argued that this 'forms a separation between media forms and society and constitutes a contradiction, and therefore becomes a crisis which can be measured dialectically' (Berry 2000, p. 31). Bourdieu (1992) used a similar term, 'immanent law of the structure' (ibid., p. 42), which 'internalises' logic 'in the form of *habitus*' (ibid.). Therefore, 'The autonomy of the media (perceived as having its own logic) – in Simmel's language would constitute a "hostile autonomy" as opposed to unity and harmony – is however a part of a contradictory unity'(ibid., p. 45). I would argue, therefore, that the moral and ethical concerns are consequences of the immanent developmental logic that is empirically, theory applied in practice and a reaction to a hostile autonomy by academics that perceive press/media institutions as operating largely separate ethical systems from society; thus the desire to intervene and correct by using normative theory as a guide to good practice that would bring benefits to society.

Media ethics as an academic discipline within universities is historically speaking relatively new. However, the types of news production that academics are concerned with span further back than this development. In Bleyer's impressive work titled *Main Currents in the History of American Journalism*, the author reminds us just this:

> A brief survey of current criticism of English newspapers in the seventeenth and eighteenth centuries shows that such faults as inaccuracy, 'faking', colouring of news, triviality, venality, and inconsistency between editorial professions and advertising policies are not of modern origin but are as old as journalism itself. (Bleyer 1927, p. 42)

Equally, concerns (ethical or otherwise) and criticism of news production also pre-date media ethics and are as old as news production that appeared on paper in a more or less regular form from the early 1600s. Ben Jonson's satirical play *The Staple of News*, first performed in 1625, was partly based on a scathing attack of news production and served more as criticism than ethical inquiry requiring a resolution on moral grounds. In the prologue to Act III, Scene I under 'To the Readers' Johnson makes a clear distinction between the news of 'any reasonable mans' and 'News made like the *Times* news, (a weekly cheat to draw money)'. Following on with 'publish'd Pamphlets of news, set out every Saturday, but made

---

2   See 'The Culture of Crisis' in Frisby and Featherstone, *Simmel on Culture* (1998), pp. 90–101.

all at home, and no Syallable of truth in them', continuing that 'there cannot be any greater Disease in Nature' (Jonson 1631). Much of Jonson's concerns were echoed much later by the Austrian satirist Karl Kraus and both perhaps leant more towards criticism than ethics with the latter expressing moral resolution of practice. In other words, unlike media ethics, Jonson and Kraus believed that journalistic practice was a lost cause if one was seeking objective truth.

In the early period of the twentieth century in the US, similar concerns emerged over the manner in which the press both gathered and disseminated news and a corresponding concern over ethics emerged much earlier and more thoroughly in the US as Keeler et al., (2002, p. 49) explain:

> Amid this general debate, concerns about ethical abuses and solutions formally became part of the journalist's world through development of professional codes. Movement toward formal journalism ethics began as early as the 1860s when the *Philadelphia Public Ledger* introduced '24 Rules', stressing accuracy and fairness during the Civil War. The word 'ethics' first appeared in an 1889 essay on press criticism by W.S. Lilly titled 'The Ethics of Journalism'.

In 1922 the American Society of Newspaper Editors was formed and as Bleyer (1927, p. 428) states: 'One of the most important steps taken at the first meeting was the appointment of a committee to draw up a code of ethics, and, accordingly, at the second meeting, in 1923, seven "Canons of Journalism" were adopted by the Society.' Amongst other matters, some of the chief concerns that were raised and debated at this second meeting were 'the responsibility of the newspaper ... truthfulness, accuracy, impartiality, fair play and decency'. Bleyer goes on to state that 'Since 1910 various attempts have been made to *improve* the profession of journalism' (ibid.; my italics) and this attempt at *improvement* continues to this day, not only in the US, but also elsewhere.

Under the sub-heading: 'The Rise of Social Responsibility' Keeler et al., (2002) explain how important the Hutchins Commission was in the late 1940s for affecting a public debate on responsible journalism with the publication of its report titled 'A Free and Responsible Press' in 1947. As Mott (1962, p. 797) states, the report set preliminary standards and 'restated the principles of press freedom, with a sound insistence on the corollary of press responsibility'. Ethical instruction within universities also started much earlier in the US: 'In 1908 the first school of journalism was established at the University of Missouri' although there had been earlier attempts at providing specific 'academic instruction in journalism' in the 'thirty-five years following the Civil War' (Bleyer 1927, p. 427). Equally: 'The Columbia University School of Journalism was established in 1912 with $2 million from Joseph Pulitzer, who insisted that ethics should be at the center of all instruction' (Mott 1962, p. 49). According to Rutland (1973, p. 387) the concern with ethics and standards can be found in the writings of Henry David Thoreau (1817–62) stating:

Thoreau's observations still made sense 130 years later. Thus one challenge to the mass media is to revise its priorities, giving a lower one to the means of gathering or transmitting news, and assigning the highest to improvement of the quality of information it delivers each day. More attention should be paid to the content and less to the package. By pandering to the lowest levels of the American's taste since 1833 the mass media have surely helped citizens lose their identity and intensified 'their moral isolation from each other, from reality and from themselves', as Ernst van den Haag has noted.

The priorities noted by Rutland, centre on social responsibilities in journalistic practice. Responsibilities work on many levels but my only concern here is to evaluate ethical journalistic responsibilities concerning the maintenance and expansion of democracy as outlined originally by Carlyle. For John Pilger, responsibilities are deeply rooted within investigative journalism that confronts rather than consorts with power, and this is the foundation of ethical journalism. With reference to Primo Levi, Pilger (1998, p. 544) states:

> Journalists ought not to stand outside the closed doors of the powerful waiting to be lied to. They are not functionaries, and they should not be charlatans ... . They ought to be sceptical about the assumed and the acceptable, *especially* the legitimate and the respectable ... . Their job is not to stand idly by, but to speak for 'the true witness, those in possession of the terrible truth ...'.

Quite often responsibility is conflated with duty but in fact they differ substantially in theoretical composition, in particular in their meaning and in their application. The one is voluntary, the other a demand. The one is built out of the subjective–objective relationship between individuality and structure where the individual is freely permitted the final decision, the other an exogenous virtue in which the individual submits. The one is intrinsically linked to the utilitarian principle concerning the moral consideration of consequence of both speech and action, the other is based on Kant's categorical imperative overriding free will. In essence, developing an awareness of responsibility rests on a self-decision-making process; it is the formation of *habitus* and the reordering of biographical narratives in relation to the outside world – it alerts individuals that they are not isolated islands, but rather are a part of a community of speakers in which actions or words may affect others. Ultimately, one can ignore whether one has a responsibility, whereas a duty confirms its authority; consider the following quote by Giddens (1994, p. 21):

> As compared to duty ... responsibility implies the spelling of reason, not blind allegiance. It runs counter to fanaticism, but it has its own compelling power, for commitments freely undertaken often have greater binding force than those which are simply traditionally given.

So accomplished is ethics in journalism that there is today an academic discipline referred to as media ethics, which has its roots historically in the US. As Keeler et al., (2002, p. 51) state, the publication of the Hutchins Commission Report 'led to the publication of several books and monographs related to the report that were read and studied by many hundreds of students enrolled in journalism schools'.[3] Equally, Evensen (2002, p. 258) explains this early interest:

> When journalists gathered at Philadelphia's press club on the first day of the centennial year [1900], they celebrated journalism's contribution 'to the grandest century in the history of men' [referring to the nineteenth century]. The nation's newspapers could claim credit for raising the intelligence and sense of justice of the average American. This, the press saw, as fundamental to 'the onward sweep of progress'.

It was assumed that progress rested on responsible journalism to convey truth and enlightenment. However, the development of a media ethics discipline is proof of this failure. In comparison to the US, media ethics, as an academic discipline, has barely registered in Europe, with few books being published in the UK. However, there are concerns over standards of performance that in the UK at least have been detailed in various Royal Commissions on the press, and there is a very important debate within the EU on the function of the media in general, which I will later contrast with the very rigorous debate that has taken place in the US.

Whatever the differences in scope and output between countries, the focus of media ethics is predominantly if not entirely on production, although the inference from this is equally a concern with consumption. However, as mentioned earlier, media ethics doesn't concern itself with 'audience research' or detailed ethnographic studies, which is peculiar considering its concern with effects on society. A few British-based writers have loosely referred to media effects in the context of ethics, but unfortunately they lack academic rigour and intellectual precision concerning consumption. For instance, Chapter 1 of Brian McNair's (2003) book *News and Journalism in the UK* titled 'Why Journalism Matters' is an assessment of the importance of journalism in society. Under the sub-heading 'Journalism's Social Role', McNair says journalism is 'arguably one of the key social and cultural forces in our society' (McNair 2003, p. 21), indicating the influence that journalism has on the social construction of meaning. However, much of what is discussed is highly suspect, particularly the material concerning effects with little empirical data to substantiate many of claims forwarded by the thinkers referred to by McNair.

---

3   The Hutchins Commission was established in 1944 under the title of the 'Commission on the Freedom of the Press'. In 1947, the Hutchins Commission published *A Free and Responsible Press* which as Keeler et al. (2002, p. 51) state: 'provided a framework for discussing media ethics during the next several decades'.

Equally, Chapter 1 of Karen Sanders's book *Ethics and Journalism* titled 'Ethics and Journalism' has a sub-section identical to McNair's title chapter, which is also titled 'Why Journalism Matters'. Somewhat surprisingly considering the sub-title, it only consists of just over two paragraphs.[4] Sanders begins: 'There is a view that journalism matters very little' and ends with an emphatic two-worded claim that 'Journalism matters' despite acknowledging beforehand that 'It is notoriously hard to *prove* media effects' (Sanders 2005, pp. 8–9). This overall weakness is universally applicable to media ethics as an academic discipline, but despite this, issues such as the primacy of truth and objectivity in practice are detailed as vital for society to function properly. I don't want to expand on this point, but simply to indicate that it is an assumption of writers rather than proven fact that the public share their concerns. Perhaps detailed audience research would provide an understanding of public needs – after all, as we shall see, many in the field speak in terms of achieving the 'common good', which in most cases is paternalistic and without the involvement of those for whom the 'good' is to be held in 'common'.

What we know is that media ethics as an academic discipline is primarily concerned with the conduct of practitioners or what Jempson (2000) calls 'bad' journalism. Media ethics is based on normative theory and is grounded in moral philosophy (Kieran 1998), which is principally concerned, amongst other things, with social and self-responsibilities, duties, rights, consequences, truth, trust, objectivity-subjectivity, public interest, representation and purpose; in sum, it is interested in how news is framed.

As a formal discipline, it belongs to the philosophical branch of applied ethics and, as Belsey (1992, p. xi) states, it is concerned with news practice: 'We are … concerned with the nature and possible resolution of the issues that arise in … practice.' Much of the discussion that follows in this chapter on media ethics relates to the abstract form of responsibilities, although there is the occasional reference to empirical application. The key or indeed controversial issue concerning responsibility is based on *who* performs the act and *how* that act is applied. In other words, is it the individual who is ultimately in control of their actions or can it be ethically justified to have others determine the character of responsible action? The *how* part is solely based on consequences, for what are the consequences of acting responsibly or not? In its empirical form, responsibility will work on many levels; for instance, I believe that I have a duty to act responsibly in public or towards my neighbours in order to achieve a state of well-being. But this performance is one of equals, for I have no more power than others in these instances. In many respects, if the responsibility is reciprocated towards myself then it is one of mutual respect. To behave in a thuggish or anti-social manner is not one based on differences of power between ordinary people (state power or abuse of power being different), but is rather based on equal status. Why some need to behave anti-socially is another matter.

---

4   It's worth stating that Sanders's treatment on 'objectivity' (p. 42) is equally meagre, barely spanning one page.

The issue concerning responsibility changes significantly when there is an unequal distribution of power in society, and it is at this level that journalism and responsibility operates because of the power to persuade and influence society. Stanley Baldwin's statement regarding 'power without responsibility'[5] was aimed at the abuse or misuse of power and privilege of press owners and whilst I am interested in that issue here, I am, however, more interested in the issue of responsibility and the individual journalist within the context of other power structures.

Before we proceed further it may be helpful to look at the dictionary meaning of responsibility in its abstract form, 'the state or position of being responsible', while responsible is defined as 'having control or authority ... being accountable for one's actions or decisions ... able to take decisions without supervision; accountable for one's own actions'. There is also the duty of an individual to act responsibly *vis-à-vis* their 'commanding officer', which is understandable in war, although even officers sometimes make the wrong decision – the Charge of the Six Hundred, or Light Brigade, in the 1854 Crimean War is a case in point – but is debatable between a journalist and their boss. This latter point rests on many issues to be decided upon, such as the function of journalism, the purpose of information and the role that journalism plays in a democratic system; would for example the public interest outweigh commercial imperatives or ideological interests of owners and, if so, how best to proceed? What has been demonstrated thus far is that responsibilities are seen to be the product of an individual and not of outside forces such as the state, and more benignly perhaps codes of ethics, which attempt to offer guidance on how to behave responsibly.

A discourse on ethical behaviour in the media straddles these two divergent points between, on the one hand, the individual having absolute control over actions and responsibility and, on the other, whether it can be ethically justified for a code to be able to persuade an individual to act morally. A discourse on ethics in relation to media activity is a debate on how the individual *ought* to act based on a privileged position in society; the dispute doesn't concern the viability of abstract notions, but rather *who* can apply them. As we shall see, the empirical application of responsibilities becomes extremely complicated by the very way in which journalism works: owner (commercial interests) – journalist (mediation) – public (recipients). It's the latter point that really muddies the commercial-capitalist waters, because whether owners or journalists like it or not, the community exists and its members have certain interests that information is required to fulfil, and this negates a lot of the so-called *rights* owners or an individual journalist may have, not legal rights, but moral rights.

---

5 Stanley Baldwin was leader of the Tories and three times British Prime Minister, 1923–24, 1924–29 and 193537. The quote in full is 'Power without responsibility – the prerogative of the harlot throughout the ages' and was directed at Lord Beaverbrook the owner of the British *Daily Express* newspaper in 1931.

In this context, there is the consideration of privilege, for some thinkers, such as those that constitute public journalism, it translates into a justification for reducing any rights that we assume individuals have in Western systems; as we shall see later, this is because the communities within society and their interests are of prior value to the individual. For supporters of the Liberal Enlightenment school of thought, this constitutes not only unnecessary interference in the rights of the individual, but is equally an immoral invasion of an individual's ability to decide independently from outside forces. In essence, what this highlights is that media ethics as an academic discipline is indeed a broad church in which anything goes. Everything is up for debate, but what is at stake is whether anyone can impose a system of practice upon journalists in the name of responsibility to the principles of a democracy.[6]

The discourse on media ethics is an academic discipline that attempts to resolve some of the contradictions that journalists face in their daily practice and offer resolution or guidance towards behaving ethically in an economic and political climate dominated by commercial interests. As we shall see, there are differences between various thinkers in the field of media ethics on how best to proceed; that is, whether we offer more protection to the individual journalist, whether the individual journalist needs to put duty to the community before self-interest, or even indeed whether journalists shouldn't just be the eyes and ears of the public, the fourth estate model, but should be active in social change. Whatever the difference in emphasis towards conduct, what is held in common in various degrees amongst thinkers in the field is that media ethics is about alerting journalists to the task at hand; it's about 'reawakening', or 'to see'. In essence, media ethics is about *enlightenment journalism*.

Before we proceed, we need briefly to make clear what exactly is being stated here with reference to *enlightenment*. As Kant rightly stated, there is a distinction between the actual empirical Enlightenment of the eighteenth century and *enlightenment* as abstract idea and theory. The Enlightenment was an actual condition and as a movement was as an amalgamation of ideas of the relationship between individual and society. But for Kant, the empirical form was riddled with imperfections, natural or otherwise and the actual Enlightenment in this context was distinct from the abstract notion of *enlightenment* to be achieved as demonstrated by the following quote from Kant: 'are we living in an *enlightened* age today? ... no: but ... we are living in an Age of Enlightenment'.

---

6   As far as liberal thinkers are concerned, the duty to protect individual choices, free from unnecessary constraints, *is* an intrinsic element of democracy, whilst others who hold contrary views will argue that such stress upon individuality is to result in a dereliction of duty to serve the interests of society as *the* fundamental premise on which practice should be organized.

It's the empirical reality of Enlightenment that forms the basis of Merrill's article titled 'Communitarianism's Rhetorical War Against Enlightenment Liberalism' (1997), which is to argue that any critique of the status or value of the individual is not necessarily a critique against *enlightenment* in any abstract form yet to be achieved, but rather opposition to the liberal view of how the individual is morally situated in society. In essence, any critique is one of rationality produced from the actual Enlightenment project; that is, the rational-reasoned justification of the value of individualism. This is an important point, because the rational belief by so-called reasoned beings from the Enlightenment period have become legitimate forms of structure, or accepted as a natural part of the human condition. In essence, the way in which we view individuality is a product not of a natural condition, although we may think it is, but rather it is the product of ideology.

It's in this context that the many diverging debates with media ethics is about the abstract form of *enlightenment* in relation to journalistic practice, and this works on many levels, either on the more day-to-day level of persuading a journalist not to invade a person's privacy on unethical grounds or to be more responsible when writing articles on asylum seekers, taking care not to harm others unnecessarily, or even on the larger issue of responsibility towards the maintenance of democratic principles. Either way, media ethics is about education and guidance to a more enlightened stage of realization and there are benefits to be gained by this, first, by the individual and, second, as a consequence of a journalist's education and realization of their standing in the world, there are benefits to the wider community: society. But what those benefits should be exactly is very much a point of argument within the field.

Media ethics is a response to standards of journalism occurring within a media framework dominated and conditioned by the liberal theory of the media and at the heart of this debate is the issue concerning the role of journalists, *vis-à-vis* society and the responsibilities that they have for both expanding and maintaining democracy. A discourse on media ethics is partly an attempt to alert us to the fact that commercialism, a central generating force of the capitalist system, is chiefly responsible for the slow and steady decline into the moral abyss. But equally, media ethics attempts to come to the rescue by philosophically prescribing solutions to the unethical tasks at hand; similar to a General Practitioner, media ethics theoreticians provide the broad framework of the remedy that one can use to cure the journalistic disease. Journalists are required to become aware of their environment, role and responsibilities in the production of information and, in order for them to *see the light*, they are required to embark on a process of moral reasoning, which would enable an individual to walk from the darkness of banality, delusion and self-interest into a new ethical kingdom. Thus, a discourse on ethics in the media is primarily about *enlightenment*; one would require greater cultural capital in order to dispense the ethical remedy to the practical solution.

In broad terms, media ethics is an academic discipline that evaluates media performance (McQuail 1993) and assesses standards of media practice. In terms of the press, the emphasis is upon self-regulation and maintaining press freedom against unwarranted state interference in the everyday practice of the journalist. In the UK, the issue concerning self-regulation is premised on the privileged position the press has occupied within a liberal system; we know it as the fourth estate and its theoretical position is to keep a check on powerful institutions such as government (Edgar 2000) and big business.

The theory behind the press then is based on the notion that once state legislation is accepted as a legitimate form of control, this is to accept censorship that infringes upon the very freedom that the press relies upon to investigate wrongdoing. Hence the reason why numerous codes of conduct or practice exist; they are there to fill the gap between legislation and unethical conduct. The defence of self-regulation is, however, premised on the theory that the press won't abuse its privileged position of power, so one of the key issues for media ethics is to find a reasoned balance between maintaining self-regulation and self-proclaimed statements on freedom of the press and to discover through logical argument methods that halt unethical forms of journalism. If state legislation and regulation of the press is rejected, the emphasis rests with individual journalists to heed the advice of a code of ethics and/or to become more self-reflective about the consequences of their actions. The question is, of course, what happens when an individual or editor freely chooses to ignore a code and embarks on what may be considered unethical behaviour?

Theoreticians of media ethics tend to stress responsibilities, duties or moral obligations towards news discourse, and this is premised in pure educational terms; turn to *moral reasoning*, it is claimed, and effective responsibilities may ensue. There are, of course, no guarantees that an education in moral reasoning will have any impact at all, but it's widely assumed that the recipient of an education in morality is a reasoned mind, and to act immorally requires moral justification in itself, if you see what I mean. Moral reasoning is essentially a call to *enlightenment*, and this, it seems, brings substantive benefits not only for the journalist, who will invariably become a wiser, knowledgeable and virtuous being, but also, correspondingly, it inevitably has a beneficial impact upon the community and the wider society, because to think ethically is to increase the standards of media performance, which then impacts on the good of society, which roughly translates into becoming *more democratic*. The link between the pursuit of ethics as a path to *enlightenment* for both the individual journalist and the recipient of news is clear. The path to a greater understanding invariably requires discipline and a rigorous selfless understanding of the essential requirements of good practice. As Splichal (1994, p. 77) clearly explains, amongst other things, enlightenment journalism 'stresses the importance of objective information, education, and the development of a critical consciousness and considers journalists a part of "progressive social forces"'. On the one hand, this belief in the path to a more enlightened form of journalism is only possible if the self submits to a greater authority, not the state, but codes of practice, conduct or ethics, that have been drawn up by another authority. The difference, however, is that whilst the former is, and here I shall paraphrase Habermas, an oppressive form of increased bureaucratization implemented by legal means, the latter is purely voluntary. There is an implicit threat held therein

– submit voluntarily, an oxymoron of course, or the state will force one to submit. All this leads to the onus being squarely placed upon the individual journalist's fragile shoulders, and this is where moral reasoning enters the fray.

Burns (2002)[7] is one such writer who clearly rejects any type of state interference, preferring the idea that journalists self-regulate by willingly submitting, a contradiction in itself, to the more ethical-preferable authority of either a code or the moral guidance of the Potter Box Theory (Christians et al. 2001). One could also, I imagine, use Louis Day's (2006) model for moral reasoning called the Situation Analysis Definition, or SAD, as a guide to becoming a better, more ethically inclined journalist. Burns claims that her book *Understanding Journalism* is essentially premised on three simple propositions. The 'central proposition' argues that it is only journalists who are fully aware of a decision-making process that constitutes everyday journalistic activity who can 'negotiate the challenges involved' in the collection and dissemination of news. The 'second proposition' argues that contrary to some students' beliefs that journalists have little power in the decision-making process, Burns argues that in fact journalists *do* actually have the ' power to act responsibly' and that once a student/journalist is aware of this fact it is to realize that they are empowered to take control over actions.

The 'third proposition' is that journalists must accept their responsibility in relation to affecting 'people's lives' (ibid., p. 11). What this form of ethical conduct or good journalistic practice depends upon is 'critical self-reflection'[8] (ibid., p. 12), which is an essential requirement of the decision-making process. The underlying reason behind critical reflection is the principle of the public interest: 'a journalist must be guided by public interest' states Burns (ibid., p. 41). Even though Burns doesn't realize it, or at least it isn't discussed in her work, the public interest principle is given greater weight in ethical decision making and is therefore given priority; in effect, the public interest principle becomes the main principle that underpins responsibility and to all extent and purposes the public interest principle in this context principally overrides the self-responsibility, inadvertently turning it into a *social* responsibility. This highlights a contradiction in Burns's work because critical self-reflection, which is the central tenet of moral conduct, is a voluntary act, and how can this be satisfactorily achieved when one is to be guided by the public interest? Surely, critical self-reflection is governed, as I understand it here, by *existentialist* criteria. Burns has unwittingly turned self-responsibility into a duty and/or moral obligation; one has a duty or moral obligation to perform ethically because the public interest demands so! But what exactly is the public

---

7   Lynette Sheridan Burns is a former Australian journalist of 25 years turned academic, who recognizes the need of ethical training in journalism.

8   Most of the debate concerning 'critical reflection' takes place in Chapter 3, 'Journalism as Decision Making' where it is stated in the conclusion that: 'Critical reflection as a part of journalism should never be confused with the personal navel-gazing [that] … journalists sometimes engage in at the bar … It is an active commitment in journalists to scrutinise their own actions' (Burns 2002, p. 41).

interest? Unfortunately, Burns doesn't explain the meaning in any detail at all; it's simply assumed that it exists and that it is the driving force behind ethical conduct.

Newspaper editors and journalists also refer to the public interest to justify content, particularly if sales are healthy. Writers in the field of media ethics constantly refer to the public interest and politicians claim they are acting in the public interest. The public interest is perceived as an interest that is common to all and is central to the idea of the common good. As we'll see, the notion of public interest is central to public journalism and the EU's differing views on what constitutes the common good. As Frost (2007, p. 253) rightly states, the public interest is 'poorly defined', but nevertheless it is continually invoked. As Mitnick (1980) reminds us, the idea of a public interest has a long history and was initially concerned with regulating what was seen as an unfair economy during the medieval period, to suppress and control the overzealous market in favour of reform for the community. What is more, this benevolence was based on a sense of moral and political obligations in order to produce a modicum of justice. It is obligations that we are partly concerned with here in relation to the duties that the mass media have towards the public interest. There is no doubt that these obligations exist in many legal documents across various countries, but the problem is: (1) defining the public interest; (2) that often other provisions in legal documents gain greater weight against a mostly unspecified and generalized notion of the public interest; and (3) that obligations are often reduced to the field of ethics and that there are no real effective measures to ensure that the obligations are met.

The public interest often translates into a 'common interest' (See McQuail 1993) that also reflects the idea of the 'common good'. In journalism, both truth and objective reporting are often used as justification for invoking the public interest principle. Under the sub-title '"Objectivity" as a professional ideal' Allan (2004, p. 22) states 'that over the course of the 1920s the ideal of "neutral" reporting gradually became synonymous with the invocation of the "public interest" for many news organizations'. The idea that objectivity can bring benefits to society has now shifted more substantially towards academics who now hold to the view that objectivity can act as a remedy for a press that has lost its moral compass and, what is more, objectivity is only ethically and socially useful in that it is in the public interest.

Intrinsically linked to the public interest and responsibility is the principle of the 'public right to know', which has its origins in the liberal idea that information distributed in the public space by individuals unconnected to government is a means in which to keep a check on political life, abuse and wrongdoing. This, in essence, can be traced back to Edmund Burke's observation regarding the fourth estate; the gentlemen of the press were in the gallery of Parliament to satisfy what was being formally established as the 'public right to know', which eventually was subsumed within the idea of a public interest. Writers that defend the public right to know principle often do so as long as the actions of the journalist do not fall outside what is considered to be proper moral behaviour. All in all, this means that the journalist must weigh up the situation and base their decision on firm ethical criteria, but there are no real sanctions that can be imposed if a journalist refuses to abide by a code of conduct that is too weak to be taken seriously in the competitive commercialized world that governs modern journalistic practice.

The notion of the public interest governs Christians et al.'s (2001) work in their demonstration of the value of moral reasoning in relation to the Potter Box and its application to practice, which is necessary they claim for good ethical conduct: 'The Potter Box *forces* us to get the empirical data straight, investigate our values, and articulate an appropriate principle' (ibid., p. 21; my italics). This is a rather audacious claim, because, in reality, rather than the Potter Box 'forcing' people to express their actions appropriately (whatever that is), people can reject guidelines; in other words, there are no guarantees. Under the sub-heading: 'To whom is a moral duty owed?' Christians et al. list so many duties that any student is left with their head spinning; they include: 'duty to ourselves', 'duty to clients', 'duty to our organization or firm' and 'duty to society' (ibid., p. 22).

What is apparent is that the public interest and public right to know principles serve as a basis for the critical self-reflection that Burns spoke of and, in this context, media ethics provides an intellectual space in terms of *enlightenment* and the *benefits* such critical thinking and doing can bring to society, captured by the following:

> Most societies in the world feel strongly about some area of media ethics and ensure appropriate behaviour by legislating in that area. It is perfectly legitimate for societies to reach a consensus about what is acceptable for the media to publish or, more usually, not publish. (Frost 2007, p. 45)

Gordon et al. (1996, p. xi) have claimed: 'Media Ethics is not an oxymoron ... Rather, it is a necessity.' In a similar vein, Smith (1999, p. 7) states: 'To many "ethical journalism" is an oxymoron' and then argues the case that journalists should subscribe to 'ethical demands' (ibid.) because other professions such as lawyers and doctors do. Kieran (1997, p. 1) has also noted the distaste in certain quarters when ethics is spoken in the same terms as media: 'Despite an increasing concern with media ethics there are many who remain sceptical about the very idea.'

This scepticism mostly comes from the world of journalism, where some practitioners believe that ethical journalism is indeed an oxymoron. But there is also scepticism within academic circles, whose critique emanates from the idea that moral philosophers claim to have all the answers to the ethical dilemmas or unethical practice. Joost van Loon (2000, p. 55) has claimed that normative views are 'paternalistic', further stating that 'Such moral philosophy sets itself up as the Law, from which universal rules can be deduced' (ibid.), to which I would add 'imposed' as legitimate values that give the appearance of consensus, where in reality they are the values of an elite. Van Loon denounces the elitist claims of moral philosophers who preside over the meaning of ethics and states:

> In good Kantian fashion, he [Kieran] claims that social consensus about moral issues cannot provide us with a definitive judgement on the rights and wrongs of particular acts, as 'people's preferences and moral judgements can be mistaken …'. In doing this, he places his philosophy on a different, indeed higher, level of knowledge than common sense. (ibid., p. 54)

In a similar vein to Merleau-Ponty, the understanding of consciousness and ethics lay elsewhere and for van Loon the modes of media discourses and the processes of morality therein are mediated via technologies; and, of course, by the good hand of the journalist. Ethics are ultimately disclosed within the dialectical-discursive relationship between 'enframing' and 'revealing' of the message. In sum, reading a text is likened to accepting a gift, and in the act of acceptance the ethical issues are revealed. Or at least that's the theory! There are no guarantees, of course, but unlike moral philosophy, of which van Loon is critical, his ideas are not based on some elitist notion of applying a universal law of ethics and then applying it. The reason that moral philosophy is accused of being elitist according to van Loon, who bases his argument on Lyotard, is because in reality it is an 'expression of a *particular* collective will', or using Vattimo's ideas, is an assertion of a 'particular value' (ibid.), imposed by moral philosophers who believe they know best.

The understanding or, to use a term from Stuart Hall (1993), 'decoding' of the 'encoded' message lies in the ability to interpret data, and interpretation relies upon social activity with others. Interpreting data on the basis of learnt experience from others is to inculcate the ideas from elsewhere; a process of domination and submission itself, an issue that van Loon is out to discredit. Unless we can all somehow recycle information into a meaningful interpretation uniquely, which is a retreat into hyper-subjectivity or cultural relativism, which van Loon is out to avoid, or at least that's my interpretation of his works, then there are always another authority's values slipping through the media net conditioning the very processes on ethics.

In a similar vein to Kieran, Frost (2000, p. 2), under the sub-heading 'Do Journalists Need Professional Morality?', states: 'Being part of society means that we need to adhere to rules that help society work.' Although Frost doesn't directly answer his own question, the inference that journalists *should* be moral beings is evident, but only by reading between the lines. The reason that Frost's views are similar to those of Kieran is apparent by the reference to 'rules', for who ultimately decides what the rules of the game are to be? Who sits in the high moral office offering their virtuous guidance to society, which must then play by *their* rules? Further on, Frost asks: 'What is a good journalist?' and says nothing more than it's a journalist having a 'moral duty' (ibid., p. 61) with their own conscience. However vague this may be, the measure is clear: thinking and applying is to be enlightened. This theme of ethics as a source of enlightenment is carried on by Merrill (1989, p. 172) who has claimed that for a journalist's work to be effective, they must be aware of the responsibilities in the act of mediation: 'I use the term *responsible* in a moral context to mean ethical', claims Merrill, claiming that:

'Responsible journalism is ethical journalism; a responsible reporter is an ethical reporter' (ibid.).

Thinking about morality and performing an action in the context of the journalist–society relationship entails reflections on responsibilities, actions and consequences. In Nozick's *Invariances* (2001), under the sub-heading 'The Genealogy of Ethics', one cannot be coerced to enforce moral objectives; individuals should always act on personal choice that prioritizes self-development. This view, whilst not identical, is reflected in Merrill's notion of *existential journalism*, whilst Eagleton (2003, p. 155) expresses the opposite: 'morality is basically a biological affair ... rooted ultimately in the body'. Because the body is what is common to all humans, morality can be perceived not as purely subjective, closed off in some hopeless relativism, but rather it is universal: 'The material body is what we share most significantly with the whole of the rest of our species, extended in both time and space' (ibid.). Of course, we can freely choose to ignore this shared sense of belonging, but what are the consequences of doing so? What happens if we simply fail to recognize this shared otherness? If morality is born out of the body's existence and therefore has a universality of presence, what happens when we stray from the essential features that are core components of morality? In other words, at what point does recognition of that universality occur or how can it emerge from the depths of immorality? As Eagleton has claimed, to pursue and act upon an ethical life is to excel 'at being human, and nobody can do this in isolation' (ibid., p. 142). Neither can they achieve this if the 'political institutions' (ibid., pp. 142–43) aren't in existence in order for the ethical life to flourish. Taking his lead from Aristotle, Eagleton argues that ethics is intrinsically linked to the social and political spheres. To think morally, detached from those spheres, to believe dogmatically in rules outside of those fields of influence is to reduce morality or at least conflate it with 'moralism', which has more in common with ideology; this perspective towards morality–others–society is critically expressed by Edward Said with regard to media representations of the Palestinians in terms of thinking and acting on social-responsible criteria:

> Never have the media been so influential in determining the course of war as during the Al-Aqsa Intifada, which, as far as the Western media are concerned, has essentially become a battle over images and ideas. (Said 2001)

Said spoke of the 'falsification of history' further claiming that such distortions of truth is what 'Orwell called ... misinformation newspeak or doublethink' (ibid.). The moral responsibility Said spoke of is based purely and simply on fact, context and understanding. The ability of the press to reduce full, disclosed information to a series of sound bites negating relevant issues to a case is at the centre of the debate on media ethics. In February 2008 a similar issue arose when the Archbishop of Canterbury, Dr Rowan Williams gave a lecture on whether parts of Islamic Sharia law would or should be incorporated into English law. Writing in the *Independent* in an article titled 'Williams is snared in a trap of his own making' Paul Vallely (2008) explained what happens when complex issues enter the public domain:

> The error is assuming that the leader of a major church has the same intellectual freedom that he had when he was merely an eminent theologian. The cold fact is that the semiotics are entirely different. An academic may call for a nuanced renegotiation of society's attitudes to the internal laws of religious communities. But when the Archbishop of Canterbury does that the headline follows, as night follows day: 'Sharia law in UK is unavoidable, says Archbishop'. This is not what he was saying, and yet it is. News has little room for the subtleties of academic gavottes around delicate subjects. A canny religious leader – or at any rate his press office – ought to know that.

A letter appeared in the *Independent* (11 February 2008) titled 'A travesty of what the Archbishop said':

> Sir: We never thought we would be moved to write to the press in defence of the Archbishop of Canterbury, or indeed any other religious leader. However we have been dismayed and outraged by the press and radio reaction to his lecture on Thursday. We were there, and when we left the Royal Courts we felt we had heard a cogent, thoughtful argument, eloquently delivered, which is not to say we agreed with the points being made … . The reports we read the following day, and the sensational furore that they created, were a travesty of what we heard for ourselves. If this is an example of a responsible press, then we despair. If newspaper editors had any sense of responsibility, they would print the lecture in full … .

However reasonable or even desirable some of the claims moral philosophy raises and attempts to resolve, there are concerns over its practicality or, to put it another way, how applicable and realistic is a discourse on ethics in relation to the actual working conditions of journalists? Essentially, the problem that ethics is faced with is the harsh realities of the commercial world in which the press operate and that the practice of journalism is confronted or exists between two extreme poles of a dialectical continuum: on the one hand, ethics and on the other, commercial journalism. This represents what Day (2006) has referred to as a 'conflict of interest', a term borrowed from the legal world, but in ethical terms it means that on two sides of an equation each side will have a number of legitimate points that warrants justification for action; the point, ethically speaking, is to resolve the moral dilemma. In this context at least, ethics is there to help to resolve the dilemmas between the moral conscience of the journalist and the practicalities of their working environment. The examples above presented by Said and the letter to the *Independent* demand broad disclosure of the issues that reflect responsibility and truth, which I take it, should outweigh other criteria. The further issue raised by Vallely demonstrates the difficulty of achieving this in the present climate.

Sanders (2005) devotes an entire chapter to 'The good journalist', and states: 'Ethically good journalism begins with competent reporting' (ibid., p. 160). This view of the ethically good is intrinsically linked to the purpose of journalism by posing the question 'What is journalism for?' (ibid.). An essential part of the academic debate concerning media ethics is to view training and education in virtue ethics as a form of *enlightenment* that acts as a conduit or vehicle for attaining journalism's true purpose. The idea of *enlightenment journalism* posits purpose as a teleological aim for the betterment of society and the notion of the 'good' is reflected in virtue. In this vein Sanders argues: 'For journalism to be good, it must have good aims' (ibid., p. 161) and this view is one that promotes social responsibilities over and above self-responsibility if we are to understand the latter as *existential journalism*, but somewhat contradictorily launches into a brief defence of Aquinas's theory on 'conscience'. This misunderstanding of the distinctions between self and social responsibilities unfortunately makes for uncomfortable reading, and therefore the discussion on 'good' is seriously devalued. This confusion exists further on with reference to 'a standard of excellence in journalism' (ibid., p. 169) contrasted with an elaborated discussion on conscience by asking 'What is conscience?' before answering that it is the ability to know right from wrong, which is confusingly placed in context of virtue ethics. In other words, it's not entirely clear that 'good' is a product of self-knowing or externally imposed, thus it isn't clear whether 'good' is a responsibility or duty. Being or becoming a virtuous journalist is perfectly acceptable but on what basis is virtue constructed? In other words, do the values of society or the individual's moral perspective condition virtue and subsequent action? The answer perhaps lies with a commitment by Sanders towards 'universal values' (ibid., p. 165) 'the chief of which is a commitment to truthfulness' (ibid., p. 167).

Frost (2007, p. 11) claims: 'A reasonable definition of a *good* journalist is "someone who gathers, in a morally justifiable way, topical, truthful, factually-based information of interest to the reader or viewer and then publishes it in a timely and accurate manner to a mass audience"'. Once again, there are serious shortfalls in this extremely brief description and there is no philosophical argument and justification on what constitutes a morally justifiable way, and no thorough discussion on what constitutes news that would be of interest to the reader who is but one within a mass audience. How can Frost scientifically measure or know what is of interest? Frost also dedicates an entire chapter to 'The Good Journalist', which is an identical title to that of Sanders. Curiously, Frost begins with asking 'What is a good journalist?' only then to state: 'There is no one answer to this question' (ibid., p. 56), to which I would ask: so what exactly is the point of the question? Moreover, why dedicate an entire chapter to the notion of the 'good journalist' if there appears not to be an exact definition? However, this all seems to contradict Frost's earlier statement above where he claims to have provided a 'reasonable definition', further posing a question: 'Is a good journalist one with high principles or one who brings his employer, within the deadline, stories that will boost circulation? (ibid., p. 12).

The idea of being good or even dutiful is central to most discussions on media ethics, but nowhere, as far as I have read, is there a convincing definition of what 'good' constitutes. Later in this chapter I'll look at the other related notion of the 'common good', which is a central feature of public journalism and the EU's view of information, both of which argue that it is servicing the public in beneficial ways mostly pertaining to a view of democracy, obscurely defined or otherwise. The idea of the 'good journalist' currently expressed by Sanders and Frost can't be directly connected to the idea of the 'common good', with the latter expressing a sense and a view of what constitutes community and society. The emphasis for Sanders and Frost is less community/society and more upon the individual, although it is only fair to state that both include a discussion on readers and viewers, and therefore the idea of the 'good journalist' is positioned *vis-à-vis* the public. To what extent the public interest impinges upon the individual to act properly isn't, however, very convincing. That said, Sanders stresses the conscience of each individual and Frost states with reference to 'characteristics' that 'it is up to each individual journalist to decide which ... are important' (Frost 2007, p. 57); a retreat into *existential journalism*.

Sanders and Frost's emphasis also differs from Kieran's (1998) vision of 'good journalism', which is based on a philosophical structure irrespective of individual fancies. 'Good journalism' accordingly is structured by a non-negotiable commitment to method, principally objectivity and impartiality, which in turn differs significantly from the common good because it principally focuses on production, standards and quality of performance, and says nothing about *uses*, and, as we shall see, the common good is based on a vision of society and a campaigning journalism that helps to bring about that vision, whereas Kieran's view of 'good journalism' is free from additional value-judgement. Whatever the differences, what is being expressed in both Sanders and Frost is that thinking ethically is educative and ethical instruction is a form of enlightened thought, for it seeks to elevate our understanding about the human condition. What Sanders (2005) calls 'Thinking about ethics' seems to be standard fare in most books on media ethics, which detail ethical discourse and values (see Bertrand 2000; Alia 2004; Day 2006; Frost 2007 as some of many examples).

Media ethics isn't governed solely by thinking but also by acting on ethical instruction and by putting theory into practice; this is applied ethics and the application of ethical instruction in practice is media ethics as a means to producing *enlightenment journalism*. This normative notion of *enlightenment journalism* is based on the dialectical interconnectedness of theory and practice. The first stage is ethical instruction for the individual journalist to think self-critically about actions. The second stage, based on the impact on society and overall the theory behind *acting* ethically, is to bring substantial positive benefits to citizens in society; social benefits that include truth and knowledge, which are essential elements of enlightened thinking; knowledge as opposed to opinion in the Platonic sense.

Moreover, other benefits are trust, for this would increase happiness because distrusting, as Bok (1980) has claimed, is a destructive force in society, the implications being that happiness is a consequence of trust: 'When it [trust] is damaged the community as a whole suffers; and when it is destroyed, societies falter and collapse' (Bok 1980, pp. 26–27). This viewpoint on trust may appear melodramatic, but nevertheless it informs us of the importance that Bok and others attribute to trust. Luhmann (1979) also viewed distrust as pernicious and counter-productive to a cohesive and harmonious society. In this context, I have previously argued the following: 'In essence what we have here is a reflection of the Hobbsian insistence that society is held together through trust in powerful institutions and, in contemporary life, trust in the media industry and by definition in media practices' (Berry 2000, p. 30).

Much of this, however, rests upon *enlightened journalism* as a social agent and producer of a wider social enlightenment. Truth and knowledge are important because it has been claimed that readers of the so-called quality press[9] are more enlightened or better educated than those who read tabloids because of the differences in journalism and the product therein. Much of this debate is extremely dubious, but interestingly our very choice of the newspaper we buy is based on trust, so therefore trust is absolutely fundamental to academic thinkers in media ethics and increasing trust is the aim of ethical instruction and *enlightenment journalism*.

Belsey (1998) has discussed the tensions and contradictions between what he refers to as 'industrial journalism', which is another term for commercial journalism and ethics in an article entitled 'Journalism and ethics: Can they co-exist?' Industrial journalism is mainly driven by the financial interests inherent in corporate capitalism with its emphasis on the pursuit of profit; in this context, news becomes a commodity, and using Marx and Adorno as guides, its value is measured more on exchange-value rather than use-value, which would entail some moral consideration. 'Use-value' is particularly apt for media ethics as *enlightenment journalism* because it signifies the social benefits of ethical journalism for society; its 'use-value' in this context is bound up with the value of information and can also be conceptualized in terms of 'uses' and 'gratification' criteria. Belsey simply notifies us of what are termed organizational imperatives governed not only by financial requirements but also by an *ideology of content*, and it's within this broad context that Belsey alerts us to the apparent contradiction between industrial journalism and ethics. Belsey concludes his article by stating:

> But there is, I fear, no resolution of the contradiction, no solution to the paradox of industrial journalism co-existing with ethical journalism ... good intentions are fine, but they can only operate within the existing system ... good intentions are not sufficient, as they need to be matched by corresponding good actions. This is why I put the emphasis on virtue in journalism, as virtue is a disposition to act in ethically correct ways ... . (ibid., p. 13)

---

9 See Schramm in Rutland 1973, for example, detailed in Chapter 2 of this book.

Whether it's virtue in journalism or the critical self-reflection as in Burns (2002), the fact remains that journalists freely choose to ignore and reject moral responsibilities; in other words, we can only hope that journalists will express virtue as a guiding principle. In the absence of self-discovered virtue there are codes of practice and conduct, but like virtue they remain largely voluntary and, even when transgressed, there aren't any effective means of punishment.

The argument concerning ethical journalism more often than not is centred on two possibilities: either a journalist adheres to a code or codes unnecessarily restrict an individual's ability to freely develop a sense of morality, which should be premised on conscience in relation to the external world. John C. Merrill is an advocate of this latter perspective, arguing that journalistic freedom is *the* basis on which news is built. Journalistic freedom equals *existential journalism*; here a personalized system of rights is invoked to protect the individual from oppressive exogenous forces such as codes of ethics. As Merrill (1989, p. 35) claims, 'journalistic freedom *individualises*' the process of newsgathering free from 'direction and interference'. For Merrill, the importance of achieving journalism freedom is based on his notion that press freedom is distinct from the former in that it is formally institutionalized and 'tied in with economic control and power', therefore 'Press freedom is not democratic at all' (ibid.); accordingly, real freedom lies within the individual, who is free from restraint and this is apparent despite the fact that organizational imperatives permeate all practice.

Merrill attempts to resolve this problem by arguing that somewhere in between the two extremes of existentialism and authority lies a 'middle way'; this, Merrill claims, is 'social existentialism'. This appears to be an oxymoron because it implies that the individual must play by rules external to the self. This attempt is unsatisfactory because Merrill had denounced governing bodies and authorities such as codes, press councils and editors, as oppressive even undemocratic features of the capitalist landscape, but replaces one authority by another, namely the collective will of the community. This is a rather big leaf taken out of the works of Jean Paul Sartre, who also attempted and failed to reconcile the differences between the individual and the collective. Sartre, who had Marxist sympathies, was conscious of the fact that the Stalinist dictatorships in the former Soviet Union and the Warsaw Pact, had brutally suppressed individual freedom, but was equally conscious that capitalist societies placed too much emphasis upon the individual and self-interest. The contradiction for Merrill, as it was for Sartre, is that at some point the individual submits to the collective will, because to ignore is to retreat into the hermit world of relativism. Here is a quote that just about illustrates the contradiction in Merrill's thought:

> Existentialism stresses personal freedom, of course, but the middle way emphasizes that this personal freedom is to be used rationally and ethically. In short, the individual must think of society as well as the self … . The existentialist is no island (ibid., p. 132).

But how can one think or more appropriately act on two different positions without sacrificing core principles? Surely, one must eventually submit to the other. Notice also the reference to 'of course', this is the proviso, this signifies that society and the collective will is ultimately superior, for why else say it? Merrill's position is diametrically different from the perspective on how to achieve ethical conduct that is proposed by Claude-Jean Bertrand (2000), who has claimed that there are legitimate social institutions that can justifiably govern and act as a guide to ethical conduct. In this context Bertrand claims that there are 'Media Accountability Systems' (MAS) that can effectively supervise practice: 'Media ethics faces one crucial problem: finding means to enforce its rules that are acceptable, that is to say non-governmental' (ibid., p. 107). For Bertrand, MAS are perfectly acceptable because they are non-governmental bodies, and the MAS Bertrand has in mind are Press Councils, an anathema to Merrill, codes, journalism reviews, consumer groups, letters to editors, and so on.[10] In sum, as long as they emanate from within civil society then MAS are legitimate in forcing individuals to 'behave well' (ibid.).

In 'Codes and Cultures', Dring (2000) raised some important issues on the discussion concerning codes of ethics and rightly claims that there are many obstacles yet to be overcome before any universal system can be accepted. The obstacles to achieving a consensus is based on the varying histories and traditions of different press systems, and in terms of Europe there can only be a European-wide code of ethics if these differences are properly ironed out. For Dring, there is a model in which to base a code of ethics on and that he claims is the Swedish model. Dring claims that in some way it satisfies the US system with its emphasis on freedom of expression, as discussed by Merrill, and, despite the differences, European codes with an emphasis on social responsibilities by claiming that the 'Swedish system ... is characterised by a mixture of libertarian theory embracing issues such as freedom of information, wedded to a strong influence derived from notions of social responsibility'. As Dring states, the Swedish system contains an ombudsman and a deputy-ombudsman who can either assist members of the public with a complaint or refer their case to the Press Council who have the power to fine newspapers according to their readership size. What exactly those responsibilities should be is a matter of debate depending on how one perceives the real purpose of journalism.

In sum, whether or not we agree on leaving the final decision to the individual and live with the consequences or whether a code should be adhered to doesn't really address the key issue of interest here and that is the impact of the legacy of liberalism and commercialization on the practice of journalism and its relationship to democracy. The discussion on ethics is constrained by the commercial imperative that imposes itself upon the individual, and this has led to a degree of hopelessness and frustration in the field concerning possible resolutions. However, frustrations

---

10   See Chapter 6 in Bertrand's (2000) book particularly p. 124 for a complete listing of MAS.

are not always negative because they produce new solutions, and the current condition of commercialized journalism has led some in the field to address the fundamental issues of journalism and responsibilities in relation to democracy, an issue that is discussed next.

Public Journalism

'Few controversies in the twentieth century have generated as much division and animus within American journalism as the arrival in the 1990s of "civic" or "public" journalism' begins *Assessing Public Journalism* edited by Lambeth et al. (1998, p. 1). Whilst public journalism remains relatively unknown outside of the US, the controversy there hasn't extinguished it from the US academic environment as demonstrated by the public journalism network.[11] Many of the issues that have concerned public journalism are equally applicable elsewhere where journalism operates within broad liberal boundaries, so why it hasn't exported elsewhere to any great effect remains a mystery. Nevertheless, in terms of the debate on media ethics there is no more important body of thinkers than that of public journalism and the controversy is partly based on its almost religious zeal towards journalism as an *ethical practice*. In fact, it is referred to as the public journalism 'movement' mainly because of its emphasis on campaigning and because it perceives media ethics as *enlightenment*.

The public journalism network refers to itself as an 'online think-tank' and promotes 'representative journalism', a 'term coined by Leonard Witt'. Representative journalism it is claimed 'aims to build sustainable journalism one small group at a time'. This contemporary viewpoint is based on public journalism's historical support of communitarianism; a philosophy diametrically opposed to liberalism with the latter's emphasis on individualism. The social existentialism proposed by Merrill, which is part of his critique of public journalism, is rejected by the latter; public journalism's emphasis is on the community and small 'Representative Journalism Groups' or 'Representative Journalism Community'. The theory therefore is to impact on society as a whole even if it emphasizes 'decentralization' towards community control. It views journalism's purpose in crusading terms as to bring substantial benefits to small communities but within the larger society, but it differs significantly from liberalism in that it stresses social not self-responsibility. The collective is king, with an equal emphasis on journalist obligations to public life, which led Merrill to argue that public journalism has dictatorial tendencies that seek to annihilate the individual and subsume it into the community whose morality is greater. The emphasis on community and its chief characteristics can be understood in relation to Tönnies's (1957) idea concerning *gemeinschaft*, particularly the issue of responsibility within community and the place of communal relations within society (*gessellschaft*).

---

11   See http://pjnet.org/.

Despite the claims of liberal writers, public journalism writers have argued that rather than journalism broadening out public participation and therefore expanding the horizons of democracy, they claim that the contrary is true, that journalism and the media in general have systematically failed in this project and what's more there is a worrying decline in democracy and a widening of the gap between those who make policy and those who are the recipients of it. The result is an attack on the failing of capitalism and liberalism in producing the economic and political environment that permits divisions in society and a loose manifesto of kinds on *what is to be done*. In essence, it's a call to arms to journalists and citizens to rise up and take full responsibility for their present actions and to rectify this, in other words to adhere to a form of *enlightened journalism*, and this debate centres on what function or role journalism can adopt to best achieve a more democratic system. There is, therefore, a normative perspective involved in this debate because public journalism ascribes a set of fundamental principles to the role of journalism in contemporary life, one of which is the crucial relationship between public participation and media organization. As we'll see in the following section, public participation is a policy central to the EU's view of media, but their emphasis on how to achieve this is radically different (less emphasis on 'community' within society – more emphasis on the larger 'European Society' and new technologies). But whatever the differences in emphasis and how to achieve it, both public journalism and the EU perceive public participation in relation to achieving an expansive view of democracy.

What is central to the public journalism project then is the issue concerning public participation, particularly how journalists can encourage participatory politics, and public journalism writers argue that public participation is essential for a political decision-making process to be truly democratic. Perhaps the best way to demonstrate the concerns of public journalism is to briefly outline some of the thoughts of Robert Putnam, who although not directly connected to public journalism, does however express the issues that lay behind it. Putnam (1995) argues that there has been a substantial decline in public association coupled with mutual distrust between people. Putnam (1996) was concerned with the decline of social and civic engagement in the US and argued that television was mostly responsible for the decline in socialization. For Putnam it is television that is primarily responsible for public disengagement; it is television that has eroded community networks and 'social capital'. Putnam claimed strategies should be developed in order for participants in the community to actively engage with each other to secure shared social interests.

Putnam was stressing a common good criteria and this effectively underpins the ideals of public journalism, which was founded in 1994 by the Ethics and Excellence in Journalism Foundation at Oklahoma City, US. It grew out of a concern with the unethical standard of journalism in the US and one of the central questions it was concerned with was posed by Black (1997, p. v): 'To what extent is the ethical journalist an isolated "individualist", and to what extent is he/she a "communitarian" or a committed member of the wider community?'

Friedland et al. (1994) claim: 'Civic journalism is about making connections between journalists and the communities they cover, and between journalism and citizenship.' This is premised on the 'fundamental responsibility for *strengthening* civic culture'. This they claim is based on their understanding of the role of the press as outlined in the American Constitution with regards to its relationship with sustaining a democratic system. Under the subheading 'Journalists as Citizens', Friedland et al. (1994) argue that improving journalistic standards concerning the coverage of politics is a way of 're-establishing the bonds of trust between journalistic institutions and public life'.

Public journalism is campaigning journalism because it encourages public involvement into the political policy-making process. The theory is that public participation can influence the political agenda. Public journalists are not specifically calling for the overthrow of American capitalism, but rather are attempting to reform it through greater public participation, which produces political accountability. As Friedland et al. (1994) claim, civic journalism is about taking a more proactive role in conditioning and shaping American democracy. It is this interventionist role that has led critics to claim that this campaigning aspect is an abandonment of one of the central tenets of journalistic practice, namely objective reporting. In many ways, public journalism is extremely close if not identical to Martin Bell's theory of the 'Journalism of Attachment' (see discussion on objectivity in Chapter 5), which is a critique of objectivity and a claim supporting passionate and attached forms of journalism to a *just cause*. It is this *just cause* that is the driving force behind public journalism; this cause is based on building a better and more morally aware community in the pursuit of happiness.

There are numerous projects (movements) such as the Civic Journalism Initiative based in Minnesota, whose aim is to 'gather citizens to talk about public policy issues',[12] the Community Journalist Interest Group,[13] the Civic and Citizen Journalist Interest Group,[14] and many more. The Pew Center for Civic Journalism is another project publishing its '10 Tips on Award-Winning Civic Journalism' in its *Civic Catalyst Newsletter* (2001). One of the tips is entitled: 'Listen to people who aren't normally heard' and states: 'It's important to go way out of our comfort zone and our homogenous newsrooms and listen to all voices.' Accordingly, journalists are means through which to communicate the concerns of the community. But there is a problem here, for what if the concerns are the ideas that civic or public journalism detests most of all, that is, absolute individualism and self-interest? On some readings or interpretations of the aims one may be tempted to apply the word radical, for instance Friedland et al. (1994) state under the sub-heading 'The Public Nature of Journalism' that it is about 'reclaiming the system as public property'.

---

12   See http://www.mpr.org .
13   See http://comjig.blogspot.com/.
14   See http://ccjig.blogspot.com/.

At the heart of the project is the public discourse concerning politics and how citizens can both engage and affect political decision making by publicly expressing their opinions. There are two important goals, one of which is explicit and the other not. The first is that it attempts to reorganize the community into a collective whole, more intimate, more cohesive, more understanding; ultimately, the goal is the betterment of society and this is based on the notion of the 'common-good'. The second, less explicit goal relates to the question of power, for how is the common good to be achieved *vis-à-vis* the state?

Campbell (1999) has written a defence of a more heroic form of journalism based on enlightenment at the site of production with the specific, dialectical aim of enlightening at the point of consumption. This is clearly demonstrated by both the sub-heading of Campbell's piece, entitled 'Journalism as Contributing to Understanding' and Campbell's reference to Edward O. Wilson's claim that we are 'Drowning in information, while starving for wisdom'. The focus on enlightening the public is further examined under the subsequent sub-heading, 'Journalism as a Philosophy of Attentiveness', where Campbell states:

> If we cast journalism as a philosophy of attentiveness – a system of thinking about what to pay attention to and how to pay attention – we begin to see its real, enduring value. Our main contribution is not information and understanding but a kind of ordering of topics worthy of contemplation, conversation, and further enquiry. (ibid., p. xx)

Using Ronald A. Heifetz's model of 'effective leadership', Campbell argues that journalists must set out to get the public to pay attention to 'what matters most' (ibid., p. xxi). Of course, all of this depends on achieving consensus within diverse communities, who perhaps have diverse and irreconcilable concerns. Besides, who actually decides the ordering of topics? In sum, isn't Campbell simply replacing one model of hierarchy for another? What happens if only a small number of the community are willing to air their concerns and will this minority dominate the proceedings of what constitutes a worthy news item?

The emphasis on journalism as an enlightening force for society is based on a positive view towards consumption and thinking. For the public journalism movement much of this would depend on the value of information in the first instance, and this is not simply based on truth and objectivity but relevant, meaningful information that any given community can relate to in their everyday lives, and the idea that the public would be responsive in any participatory role is a positive moment in the development of democracy.

The EU's View of Media: Public Participation and the Cohesive Society

Whereas public journalism emphasizes community, the EU perspective emphasizes society with bureaucrats and academics mostly determining both media policy and the public interest in relation to the common good. It's no accident that the EU mostly refers to the word society rather than community in many of its key documents on media policy. Society in this context captures the breadth of geographical scope plus political, economic and cultural objectives on a grand scale. Society here is no longer referred to in terms of a nation state either, but rather is pan-nationalistic – hence the idea of a 'European Society'. On the EU's website[15] titled 'European Information Society: Thematic Portal' there's a link to 'Culture and Society', the former not entirely replacing the use of community but rather taking precedent. The Commission of the European Communities (1993) claimed that 'European culture is marked by its diversity. But underlying this variety is a common European identity' and 'Culture is at the very heart of the European project' (Morley and Robins 1995, p. 76). The European Research Council states:

> European integration and European cooperation is already very high on the political agenda in most European countries. No matter what we think and feel about the EU, the European question is already deeply imbedded in our public life, in our media culture and in our everyday life.[16]

Terms such as 'cultural convergence' are used in tandem with 'United in Diversity' (*In Varietate Concordia*) and the means to achieve this state of being is aided by information technologies and industries, which are elevated as one of the most important cultural industries within Europe. The Audio-Visual Space is there to improve relations and understanding amongst Europeans. Politeia (Holland) is the self-proclaimed 'Network for Citizenship and Democracy' actively promoting information networks; information is the key to unlocking understanding and the idea of society. This builds on the Treaty of the European Union (1992)(Maastricht) Article 2, which states: 'This treaty marks a new stage in the process of creating an even closer union among the peoples of Europe.'

What we may call the European media landscape is built upon the premise that media technologies are currently transforming the public space in Europe. The importance of how technologies can help democratize Europe through public participation was outlined by The European Council of Ministers, who had requested a report on the information society in December 1993. The result was the 'Bangemann Report' (1994), which made a number of recommendations, one of which was the 'Complete transformation of the social and economic structure of public space in the EU'. Influenced by the Delors White Paper (Commission for the European Communities 1993) this was a vision of public policy and media law concerning the information sector of which the liberal conception of public access

---

15 See http://ec.europa.eu/information_society/.
16 European Research Council (2001). Also printed in *Nordicom Review* 22(1), (http://www.nordicom.gu.se).

to a variety of media was central. Essentially, it argued that competition was good for society because it produces more choice.

The new vision to emerge would be a 'European Information Space' and it would form a 'new industrial revolution ... based on information, itself the expression of human knowledge ... and ensure the cohesion of the new society'.[17] The Commission of the European Communities policy is to link information and a European public space with the public interest. The ultimate aim of this new *informational space* is human emancipation and cultural enlightenment. It's envisaged that a European public space is necessary for democracy to exist because it is anti-state. It argues, rather dubiously in my opinion, that a public space in democracies is somehow dependent on equality in terms of access to the *means of communication*.

The main criticism of this perspective is that it's not based on public participation, but rather it depends on private interests of individuals that own the media, who do not have a moral duty to the public in the first instance, but must primarily satisfy shareholders' financial interests. The problem lies with the liberal system in that it awards *proprietary rights* to individuals who can compete for an audience share. Some theorists may argue that the individual ownership of the press and media could be offset by the existence of Public Service Broadcasting (PSB), but even here there are problems because according to legal precedents in Europe, PSB is seen as undemocratic because it is anti-competition.

This is clearly defined in the 1957 Treaty of Rome, whose objective was to develop 'competition rules' in nation states that eventually transferred into placing non-commercial PSB forms of communication on a de facto illegal footing. Accordingly, providing special status to non-commercial systems is undemocratic because rights of this kind only seek to reinforce monopoly over commercial economic rights. Such non-commercial rights were and continue to be seen as economic restrictions over 'free competition', thus further restricting freedom of consumer choice over products. Accordingly, commercial rights translate into the public good and therefore the PSB model, because of its apparent monopolistic nature, is seen as harmful according to the legal reasoning of EU liberalism. The European Commission's objectives have been to ensure the free flow of ideas by emphasizing competitive values rather than public-service values for communications development. The importance of this is that it invalidates the regulatory authority of the state. The EU continues to recognize economic rights of ownership and competition rights embedded in the Treaty of Rome, which is responsible for creating a largely undemocratic environment allowing for media monopoly and media concentration to develop. This the EU has claimed is no longer acceptable, but what exactly is the EU's answer to media concentration? More regulation? Consider the following quote from the Information Society and Media Commissioner, Viviane Reding:

---

17   From Chapter 1, 'The Information Society – new ways of living and working together' (Bangemann Report 1994).

In a digital era, media literacy is crucial for achieving full active citizenship ... . The ability to read and write – or traditional literacy – is no longer efficient in this day and age. People need a greater awareness of how to express themselves effectively, and how to interpret what others are saying, especially on blogs, via search engines or in advertising. Everyone (old and young) needs to get to grips with the new digital world in which we live. For this continuous *information* and *education* is more important than *regulation* (my emphasis).[18]

The EU's media policy isn't simply based on *empowering the individual*, but is also a perspective on what constitutes news. We have seen how public journalism in the US also has attempted to reinterpret the social meaning of news, and here too the EU is attempting to redefine both what news is and its purpose in society. There is no doubt that the 'media literacy' policy within the framework of public participation is akin to the notion of 'citizen journalist'. However, unlike public journalism, the emphasis is not on community journalism and localized newspapers, but rather it's on the internet. Once the means of expression are in place, that is, a computer, then citizens not only engage with others and critique mainstream views on news production, they can also contribute to the construction of news. Ironically, according to this view, the net takes us right back to the beginning of history where news was a product of social interaction and not of a journalist! This has implications on the meaning and purpose of journalism when we consider the atomization of news production, and it equally has implications on newsgathering, training, method, objectivity and truth once we open up the production of news to the world.

Even though the EU doesn't specifically refer to media ethics, there is no doubt that its 'mission' is driven and as campaigning, as public journalism and its emphasis upon itself to provide a wider framework for participation and democracy is deeply normative in relation to the value of information. The major difference between the EU and public journalism, however, is the philosophy that guides media policy; this is our return to liberalism, which in this context 'strives to articulate a political system that will serve to defend individual freedom' (Edgar 2000, p. 74).

In the EU today there is a bureaucratic officer responsible for widening public participation called 'Information Society and Media Commissioner':

The media are changing, and so is citizens' use of such media. New information and communication technologies make it much easier for anybody to retrieve and disseminate information, communicate, publish or even broadcast. The ability of people to critically analyse what they find in the media and to make

---

18 Ibid.

more informed choices – called 'media literacy' – therefore becomes even more essential for active citizenship and democracy.[19]

'Media literacy' is driven by the *ethical concerns* mainly over the vast concentration of ownership under neo-liberal conditions, power, content and the social influence that media conglomerates have in the 'European Society'. 'Media literacy' is also based on the recognition and a reaction to the paradox, or even contradiction at the heart of liberal philosophy *vis-à-vis* capitalist development. For example, the EU acknowledges the propensity of capitalism to develop exponentially into monopoly structures, thus negating the very soul of liberalism; namely individualism. 'Media literacy' is therefore a *means* to retrieve and perhaps return to the central doctrinal practices of liberal theory by empowering the individual via new technology. The internet therefore represents a democratic moment for the EU in the continued and ever-changing historical development of liberalism; hence the *spirit of liberalism and residual meaning in the present* is approximated to new social conditions in contemporary times. The EU acknowledges that the original spirit or idea of liberalism has been lost in the context of the mainstream media, and the ethical concerns revolve around the notion of 'content' and 'regulation', and the ethical certainly takes precedent over the political and economic. The emphasis on ethics over 'content' and regulation of content dominates discussions because of the acceptance, reluctant or otherwise, over the rights of individuals within liberal theory. These rights include *economic rights* of ownership and these are forcefully expressed in EU documents dating back to the Treaty of Rome in 1957. The EU, however, appears to make no distinction between 'media literacy' and 'media education', using the terms interchangeably under 'What is Media Literacy?'

> Media literacy may be defined as the ability to access, analyse and evaluate the power of images, sounds and messages which we are now being confronted with on a daily basis and are an important part of our contemporary culture, as well as to communicate competently in media available on a personal basis ... Media education is part of the basic entitlement of every citizen ... . (European Commission n.d.)

This view differs from Media Awareness Network (2008), who clearly make distinctions between 'media literacy' and 'media education'. Under an identical heading 'What is Media Literacy?' they outline the differences stressing that 'critical thinking' is key to 'media literacy', whilst 'Media education encourages a probing approach to the world of media' followed by: 'Media literacy is the expected

---

19   Taken from Europa 2007. 'Media literacy: Do people really understand how to make the most of blogs, search engines or interactive TV', at: http://www.europa.eu, accessed January 2008.

outcome from work in either media education or media study.' Confusingly, it is stated elsewhere that: 'Critical thinking is a process not an outcome' (ibid.).

Whatever the subtle or otherwise differences, the emphasis on 'the ability to sift through and analyse the messages that inform, entertain and sell to us every day', which is indicative of media literacy and critical thinking reflects Hall's (1993) work concerning the decoding/encoding model or what is referred to as 'Reception Theory'. I don't wish to elaborate further other than Hall's view was to argue that each individual had the ability to critically engage with powerful media messages, rather than absorb uncritically, and what's more each engagement would proceed to each subjective position, making each reading different according to each circumstance.

Reception, understanding, rationalizing and thinking are important attributes for the EU's view of media literacy, but the key difference is to link public participation and the intercultural exchange between citizens of Europe; in other words, it stresses a public interest perspective in normative terms. Equally, the EU's vision of community and society is driven by a moral responsibility to provide or at least make the public aware of sources of information other than the mainstream media on which they are reluctant to place regulatory restrictions. This sense of moral responsibility or even obligation is actually conveyed as a 'media literacy movement' (Silverblatt 2001, p. 8) and the emphasis is on 'awareness' (ibid., p. 3), and under the sub-heading 'Purpose of Media Literacy' Potter (2005, p. 25) succinctly states: 'The purpose of media literacy is to empower individuals to control media programming'; control being used in terms of critical thinking.

The Common Good and Democracy

The political issues and ethical values that underpin both the EU's and public journalism's theories towards media is largely based on the idea of the 'common good' and its relationship and influence in expanding democracy. Both espouse the shared commonality of the collective community with common aspirations, but both have a very different view of what the common good is according to their different standpoints and interpretation of this philosophical ideal. The EU's perspective towards the common good is based on the multiple identities concerning national cultures; both internal identities within sovereign states and boundaries and 'externally deduced identities' in relation to *others* exogenous to internal structures. However, whilst recognizing substantial and substantive cultural differences within Europe, the EU has claimed that Europe is also built on shared histories and traditions common to all European nations. A substantive element of the recent European political project is liberalism, which has existed in one form or another and to varying degrees and time according to which country one chooses to focus on. The forces of liberalism are seen to have conquered the fascist regimes of Italy and Germany in the Second World War, and then continued victorious to topple the fascist regimes in both Portugal and Spain in the 1970s. Equally, the forces of liberalism were seen to have smashed the Stalinist regimes that culminated in the 1989 revolutions, which led the American political scientist, Francis Fukuyama to claim that the defeat of Stalinism and the victory of the *idea* of liberalism represented the 'End of History':

> Of the different types of regimes that have emerged in the course of human history ... the only form of government that has survived intact to the end of the twentieth century has been liberal democracy. What is emerging victorious ... is not so much liberal practice, as the liberal *idea*. (Fukuyama 1992)

The end of history means that there will be no alternative forms of political-human development other than what we currently have, although Fukuyama did claim that it is possible to improve upon the pretty wretched condition that most people find themselves to be in. So, for the EU, the common good embraces the political objectives of the liberal ideal and the dual form of identity is summed up in its slogan 'United in Diversity', which recognizes difference, but at the same dialectical moment quite clearly states that there exists an objective common to Europeans and that can be achieved via both the audio-visual landscape and the press, if not so much in content but in forms of ownership. Moreover, the common-good principle underpins the EU's view of expansive media usage by European citizens and subsequently their public participation within liberal democracy; in this context, it is premised on bringing substantial benefits and rewards to the public. The common good is, in this context at least, premised on preserving individualism as a human right and as an ethic of democracy.

Public journalism's emphasis is very different where the starting point is an intellectual critique of liberalism for elevating the individual over the community needs within wider society. For Christians (1999, p. 67) liberalism has failed the public because of its preference to prioritize individualism over shared communal requirements and has produced an account of the theory that lay behind public journalism: 'The future of public journalism depends on the notion of the common good' arguing that the common good is based on the shared interests and concerns of all citizens 'rather than that of factions or special interests' (ibid., p. 68). According to Christians, the common good is based on a 'normative principle' and one that is defined in terms of collective rather than individual interests: 'The individualism of liberal democracy has left the common good in tatters' (ibid.).

Carey (1999, p. 63) states that public journalism 'emphasises local democracy ... and citizenship' in a world dominated by large state and corporate structures, but as Glasser (1999) has noted, public journalism has failed to provide a clear definition over the meaning of democracy and how the press can actually help to achieve it. Under the sub-heading 'Journalism's Role in Democracy' Merritt (1998, p. 4), one of the key architects of public journalism, states: 'Begin with the proposition that *public life* – the way in which *our democracy* is expressed and experienced – is not going well' (my italics). But what exactly constitutes public life? And what does Merritt actually mean by 'our' democracy? Indeed, what does Merritt mean by democracy? In fact, the word democracy doesn't feature at all in the index of Merritt's book. On the other hand, in the index it states: 'Public life, defined'. However, the terms are vaguely referred to such as: 'Public life "going well" means that democracy succeeds', and then states: 'If people are not engaged, democracy fails' (ibid., p. 142).

Public journalism's theory of the common good is premised on communitarian principles and, taking a lead from Sandel's work concerning communitarian criticism of liberal philosophy and its emphasis on individualism, public journalism strove to offer a radical alternative not only to the practice of journalism, but equally proposing a variant social system consistently at odds with liberal theory. Freeden (1998, p. 248) reminds us of the following:

> The initial so-called communitarian critique of philosophical liberalism was offered by Sandel, who pointed out the individualistic biases in Rawl's original position – the position in which only the thin theory of the good holds. Specifically, Rawl's theory is individualistic, argues Sandel, because its subjects are beyond the reach of experience and have a static existence independently of the values to which they subscribe. Conversely, common purposes and ends can inspire self-understanding, describe an individual in terms of others, and define a community as constituting a subject. For Rawls, Sandel maintains, a sense of community is only an attribute and not a constituent of society.

Freeden argues, however, that this view of a distinct philosophy from liberalism is to all extent and purposes a false logic: 'it is a fact that communitarianism has been accommodated within liberalism' … and 'To assert, therefore that communitarianism is opposed to liberalism is true only if we take some instances of either term to represent their entire semantic field' (ibid.). The common good is in reality open to interpretation and can serve the purposes of liberal philosophy with an emphasis on individuality or communitarian philosophy with its prior emphasis on a collective community and is, as such, not an entirely convincing or useful concept to construct a theory of the media in relation to ethics and democracy.

Despite these criticisms, the debate in the US concerning public journalism has served as a positive reminder of the concentration of power and ownership of the press. It has equally alerted us to the fact that market-driven journalism is premised on the commercial imperative rather than a solid ethical foundation. Public journalism is mainly a critical response to the liberal theory of the press, which argues that the individual journalist is nothing more than a servant to the good of society, or perhaps to put it another way, the journalist is there merely to satisfy a public interest not self-interest. But whilst we may be able to criticize public journalism for its simplicity, naivety, inability to persuasively construct a convincing theory of democracy and a woolly version of the common good, we can equally accuse the EU for failing to address media monopoly and concentration of media ownership; failure to address commercial journalistic practices; failure to fully address and in fact ignore and by definition support an unregulated media market. Lastly, we can accuse the EU of failure for providing what amounts to a thoroughly unconvincing 'media literacy' policy that is designed to bring democracy to Europe via alternative new media networks.

Chapter 5
Truth and Objectivity

'Truth' has never been harder to define because information comes to us quickly from all over the globe, overwhelming our ability to sort out 'the truth'. (Burns 2002, p. 23)

Truth in Journalism

In light of the discussion thus far, the concerns within media ethics relate to news, its meaning and purpose in society, and this also concerns the meaning and purpose of journalism, particularly its role and effectiveness in society and its capability for aiding and even helping to create democracy. Media ethics therefore is partly a debate over normative perspectives towards applied ethics and journalistic practice. In this context, media ethics is concerned with the function of journalism and the purpose of news. With respect to what defines journalism it's clear that method is integral to newsgathering practices and production; however, there are, as we'll see in this chapter, different perspectives on how to achieve this. The most popularly discussed method and perhaps the most controversial is objectivity, and there are just as many detractors as there are supporters of objective reporting. Objective reporting is a desirable ethical value and seen as a *means* for achieving truth. The discussion on objectivity and truth profoundly impact upon both the meaning and purpose of journalism and news. Moreover, they impact upon the validity of news and journalism, for it's reasonable to argue that if objectivity isn't applied at the newsgathering process then how can an event be justified as news once we assume that news differs from both gossip and opinion? Truth is also perceived as a desirable ethical value and is seen as an end-goal developed by methodological rigour, for once subjective opinion fuses with facts then truth has become infected – unless we hold to the view that humans produce truth rather than truth existing externally to us.

These are some of the issues raised within media ethics and there are equally attempts to resolve what are complex philosophical issues pertaining to both truth and objectivity. Media ethics is an academic discipline and it's no surprise that many practitioners perceive many of the debates that occur within media ethics as no more than ideals, bearing no relation to the empirical reality of day-to-day journalistic practice. One prominent critic of the debate concerning ethics in relation to journalism that continues to pervade throughout large parts of the industry is the former assistant editor of the *Observer*, David Randall (1996)[1] who had claimed that the objectives and resolutions of ethical debates are unrealistic in the real world of practice: 'There is no more nonsense written and spoken about ethics than any other issue in journalism' (from Dring 2000, p. 311) further claiming that ethics are 'an irrelevant exhortation to standards of behaviour which are doomed to be unmet ... there is not much point to them' (ibid., p. 312). I doubt that Randall is claiming that ethics is a waste of time *per se* but rather that ethics in journalism is, which begs the question: what is so special about journalism that ethics becomes invalid? Arguing that ethics cannot be applied to practice would send shock waves through the philosophical traditions dating back to Plato with his discussion on the validity of morality in the *Republic*. Randall appears to be unaware of the branches of moral philosophy that exist which have varying meanings for practice including meta-ethics, normative ethics and applied ethics.

Borrowing a term from C.P. Snow, what Randall's viewpoint actually reflects are the 'Two Cultures' concerning ethical debates in journalism, and these differences over the applicability and practicality are mostly between academics and practitioners. However, it's important to bear in mind that not all practitioners are sceptical about ethics and some have even crossed the divide embracing academia with all its contradictions *vis-à-vis* journalistic education and research. The tensions that exist between ethics and industrial journalism have been addressed by the philosopher Andrew Belsey (1998), who argued that ultimately only the virtuous journalist will reasonably negotiate the demands of commercial journalism; something that Randall would reject no doubt.

Unfortunately for Randall, his argument contains a substantial contradiction because he states that: 'Every story should be an honest search for the truth' (Dring 2000, p. 313) leaving himself wide open to criticism because inadvertently he has transgressed into the world of moral philosophy. This invariably leads to an immediate intellectual inquiry on my part in relation to the issues Randall has now raised. For instance, what is honesty and truth, that's assuming truth exists, other than a deeply, intellectualized discourse in philosophy? If truth exists, how can we achieve it; by objective means? If so, what exactly is objectivity? Are we inherently immoral or even amoral so much so that truth can only be replaced by mere opinion? The questions are endless, but what this argument highlights is that we can't escape discussing moral philosophy in relation to journalistic conduct, however much people like Randall and others would like to do so. What we can't escape is an engagement with truth, which is fundametal to practice and the manner in which people engage with news that reflects perceptions of journalism. For instance in a blog titled 'The Fourth Estate and The Future of Truth' (Gronbach 2007) the following reads:

---

1 I have stressed that Randall was critical of the 'debate on ethics' and not dismissive of ethics per se because he does argue in this book that journalists can negotiate their way through the moral maze of journalism.

I was watching the six o clock news last night surfing with my remote control between CBS, ABC and NBC. The news is important to me because after all it is *The Fourth Estate*. The name was coined long ago in England signifying that the press was an important fourth part of government representing the people. The press keeps government honest. It is one more element in our wonderful system of checks and balances here in the United States. So off I go in search of the news. Sometimes you can catch a story on one network while the others are airing commercials, but not always. It seems that the networks have an agreement to air their commercial spots at exactly the same time. It forces people like me to watch commercials, which is really my part of the deal. The networks provide us with valuable information and entertainment in exchange for our attention to their commercial messages. It is the system and it has worked for generations, until now.

In amongst the commercials the writer reminds us there are 'sound bites' of news that are 'shallow' and 'brief' and in a similar vein to the blog detailed in Chapter 3 titled 'The Fourth Estate is fatally wounded and dying a slow death!', the author continues 'it's the end of *The Fourth Estate* as we know it. So I ask you, who will keep government honest?' (Gary2idaho 2007).

Gordon et al. (1996) once claimed that truth is the first principle of journalism; in his wisdom Hiriam Johnson also stated that 'truth is the first casualty in war' (Knightley 2002) to which I would add 'truth is a casualty in most areas of journalism'. Under the chapter heading 'The Value of Truth' Haworth (1998, p. 83) says in relation to Mill's vision of a liberal condition: 'In this chapter I ask what justification there can be for placing such a high valuation on truth.' I would like to broaden out this point by asking: 'On what justification and moral grounds can the fourth estate, as a product of liberalism attain the truth?' The two points here are not mutually exclusive, for if truth can be striven for, the fourth estate has traditionally been perceived, in theory at least, as one means amongst others for achieving truth. Most certainly, if not entirely realistic and convincing, truth seeking is a central feature in discussions on media ethics. The notion that truth exists as a universally applied principle is based on objectivist notions that truth exists beyond subjective and/or cultural boundaries. Haworth is right to remind us that elevating truth as a valued principle is subject to relativist rejection using 'value relativism' and 'epistemic relativism' to press his point home. The former is identical to 'cultural relativism' and therefore value is susceptible to cultural conditions that vary from place to place. With regards to the latter, Haworth states: 'in its moderate form epistemic relativism threatens the classic defence with its implication that there is no single destination – "the truth" – to which the road of logical reason leads' (ibid., pp. 113–114).

According to pragmatism or postmodernism advocated by Rorty, there is no truth in the single or absolute sense. In *Objectivity, Relativism and Truth* (1991) and later in *Truth and Progress* (1998) Rorty claims that truth can be established but not in relation or correspondence to a reality, but rather by inter-subjective agreement between speakers who have entered into public discussion. Grenz (1995, p. 8) explains clearly that postmodernism:

> affirms that whatever we accept as truth and even the way we envision truth are dependent on the community in which we participate … . There is no absolute truth: rather truth is relative to the community in which we participate.

Transfer this to the press and we suddenly understand why media critics focus on power, ideology and influence (or effects) because statements are privileged at this productive level and inter-subjective agreement (or shall we call this 'public opinion'?) can at times be constructed on information mediated from media outlets and is reason enough to reject Rorty's naïve claims considering the lies and deceptive practices many media institutions utilize.

That said, Rorty awards free speech great value in the traditional liberal sense discussed previously in Chapter 3. What Rorty (1998) refers as the 'free discussion' of the members of any given community is in essence both a product and an intrinsic part of free speech. As Rorty has maintained, the outcomes of any discussion are always uncertain, but it would be unwise to ignore the fact that some voices dominate proceedings or at least set the agenda for discussion. Here is what Rorty (1998, p. 51) says:

> 'Free discussion' here does not mean 'free from ideology', but simply the sort which goes on when the press, the judiciary, the elections and the universities are free, social mobility is frequent and rapid, literacy is universal, higher education is common, and peace and wealth have made possible the leisure necessary to listen to lots of different people and think about what they say.

There is room here to launch a critique, particularly if we consider the possibility that some people may have limited sources of information on which to make judgements from which free discussion may flow. For instance, someone who religiously watches Fox News, perceiving it as an authoritative and trustworthy source of news may have a skewed, distorted, stereotypical and limited view of the world. For example, according to World Public Opinion (2003):

> A new study based on a series of seven US polls conducted from January through September of this year [2003] reveals that before and after the Iraq war, a majority of Americans have had significant misperceptions and these are highly related to support for the war in Iraq.

Rorty would perhaps argue that this is immaterial because, as a member of society, any individual can contribute in free discussion to help create reality, despite the fact that defining truth boundaries is based on competences or what Bourdieu and Passeron (1973) refers as 'cultural capital' on which domination in terms of contribution rests. However, the concerns of many within media ethics is to create the correct conditions on which judgement is based and this would be primarily based on factual accounts of news universally accessed and more often than not realized through objective reports; something that Rorty would emphatically reject considering his objections to objective truth. Pragmatists argue that this is clear evidence of the impossibility of truth in any coherent and universally agreed sense. According to Rorty: 'All there is to talk about are the procedures we use to bring about agreement among inquirers', and in a critique of this view Michael Albert says: 'Yet there is virtually nothing in *Truth and Progress* about such procedures. Having rejected correspondence, should we mesmerize, manipulate, lie, fabricate, bias by partial reporting, coerce, or submit to the authority of the Pope?'

As Albert says, 'bias by partial reporting' (ibid.) would entail not being faithful to the truth and thus deviating from matters directly relating or corresponding to reality, which is constituted of facts. Reality can be natural occurrences, human made or a combination of the two. An interesting question to ponder upon is this: what exactly is the role that journalists play in the production of what I term a 'truthful framework'? For instance, should journalists simply reflect and present the truth or do they actively engage in the production of truth? What I equally term 'Reflective Truth' is essentially premised on the mediation of factual occurrences that correspond to reality and can only be achieved by objective analysis. This corresponds to objectivist claims that truth is independent of subjects and available for collation. The second proposition is what I term 'Interpretative Truth' whereby subjective modes of interpretation impose upon reality constructing a new reality. Whatever the substantive differences in procedures and outcomes, both seek to construct a 'truthful framework' based on being *in reality* and *of reality* and both ultimately rely upon modes of consumption whereby truth is filtered through various dispersed social contexts. There is another viewpoint to consider, which was advocated by Hunter S. Thompson, that subjects are the source not the donkey that merely and benignly transports truth. It's fair to state that most ethical discussions defend 'Reflective Truth' based on the notion of social responsibility that effectively overrides self-interest. Accordingly, the journalist is perceived as being in the service of society, a servant and loyal documenter of a reality detached from the self.

Establishing truth occasionally entails degrees and variations of representation that form the essence of mediation through language or visual imagery. Representation can be false, true, seriously impaired, constructed by accident or even incompetence. A representation that is true adheres to the *correspondence theory* of truth; one that is faithful to objective conditions and that is verifiable by investigative inquiry. False representations of truth can be the product of value-judgements, opinion, stereotypes that distort information deliberately or otherwise. They can be the result of deliberate bias that seeks to set an ideological public agenda and to manipulate public opinion. They can also be the result of ignorance and ineffectual approaches to newsgathering.

In this context, the process of representation produces specific forms of social engineering, a term normally associated with authoritarian systems, but here it exists within the social democratic empirical form. Essentially, representation manufactures and imposes distinct ways of *seeing the world* and is a part of a process in which cultural meanings occur. Representation is a social process and a fundamental feature of news production and is a way of reaching out to an audience with distinct characteristics.

Representation is in fact passed as reality and perhaps the Factist Perspective is useful for a critical approach to news discourse. As Alasuutari (1995, p. 47) points out, the Factist Perspective 'makes a clear-cut division between the world or reality "out there", on the one hand, and the claims made about it, on the other'. According to Chambers (1994, p. 22), representation 'stands in for something else' and according to Theobald (2000, p. 14), with reference to Karl Kraus, it replaces 'the pure water of information with the seductive perfume of the cliché'. The result can be distorted information of the original unadulterated form. The relationship between truth and representation is important because, as Walter Benjamin argued, 'The newspaper is an instrument of power ... not only with regard to what it represents but regards to *how* it expresses it' (Benjamin quoted and translated in Theobald 2000, p. 12).

According to Davis and Raynor (2000, p. 90), representations are 'often based upon selective and dramatic cores of information' and in this context framing news is not only ideologically loaded, but also intrinsically limited because it excludes other information pertinent to events. Representations always attempt to connect with the targeted audience, what can be described as a *discursive bond*. The authors go on to state that a news item 'is based upon similarities between the *habitus*[2] of the journalist and that of the audience' (ibid., p. 96), and therefore journalists/editors always have their audience in mind when constructing a news item that invariably impacts on method and truth. This, however, doesn't detract from nor deter a discourse in media ethics because resolving unethical practice is the aim of intellectual engagement.

The *Dictionary of Philosophy* (1979, p. 305) describes representation as the following: '[Representation] ... refers to the theories of perception wherein the mind is believed not to have direct acquaintance with its objects, but to apprehend them through the medium of ideas that are supposed to represent those objects.' Representation is a form of 'agency', to 'cause' or to 'represent', as in news agency or newspaper. More importantly, there are two uses of representation that are suitable for our understanding of how news discourse is produced, for representation is both to 'describe' and 'act for'. In its denotative (signifier-literal) state, it means to 'stand-in' for something it seeks to represent, to make representation and not necessarily on a group's behalf (consent), but also by taking liberties with the description that the representative invokes. Acting for or on behalf of the community is a taken-for-granted assumption and procedure of

---

2 Bourdieu (1977) in the *Outline of a Theory of Practice* developed the concept of *habitus*, which was an attempt to understand how ideology conditioned the subject and how that very same ideology corresponded to and conditioned objective structures.

the press. In its connotative state, representation is to infer or 'suggest meaning' (Berger 2000, p. 40).

More specifically, the term 'internal representation' is 'a presentation to the mind in the form of an idea or image' (Thinkmap® 1998–2000). This is important to understand on many levels. Internal representations are manifestations of understanding that journalists have and use in their daily activity. Representations become internalized based on an individual's relationship with many influencing factors; the news organization's perception of community or society is but one. There are two useful ways to explain this dialectical process between self and world. We could use Bourdieu's (1977) theory of *habitus*, which is the 'holding frame' for understanding, recycling and the formation of thought; representation is held here. Alternatively, we could use Giddens (1979) theory of 'structuration', which is the ongoing construction of identity managed through the subject-object relationship.

Despite the fact that representation at many levels impacts on performance, Rutland (1973, p. 390) has argued that there are certain 'tasks' that the news media must 'perform' that are 'vital to society'. This view is based on the perception that the function of news is one primarily based on enlightenment, as the following suggests:

> By telling the American citizenry the whole truth, the newsmongers of the future can vindicate professionalism. To tell the truth is still the highest calling in politics, in medicine, in law, and above all, in journalism. (ibid.)

The main reason given for the desirability of objective accounts of news is based on the idea that truth is the ultimate aim of journalism. Knowlton (1997, p. 10) has claimed that regardless of whether one is driven by religious belief, we all live in a society that requires solid functioning and one important element that enables society to function properly is to tell the truth, for truth 'allows society to function', stating further that 'the journalist's primary obligation is to tell the truth' (ibid., p. 14); this, Knowlton claims, is based on both political and moral considerations. It's a political obligation because truth is seen as fundamental for the proper functioning of a democratic system. Some writers such as Allan (2004, p. 191) have questioned whether journalists should pursue the truth in the first instance:

> How does 'truth' relate to 'fact'? Do journalists … have a fundamental obligation to determining 'the truth' of any given situation? … would it be advantageous for journalists to dispense with the notion of truth altogether in favour of concentrating strictly on matters of fact?

But what happens if two accounts of an event are untruthful, non-factual and fictitious accounts? It would be factual to faithfully report the lies without interpretation, intervention of the journalist or omission of any points in the accounts, but we are no closer to establishing the facts let alone the truth. All we have is lies! Of course, the lies are a part of the objective account, that is, they tell us something about the case and perhaps, objectively, the journalist should attempt to understand why people lie about an event. What are their motives for doing so? This can be understood on further enquiry without damaging the road to truth via objective means. The question we must pose is what happens if journalists abandon the idea that truth cannot be attained? What then would be the point of journalism as a social activity? Would it be the case that journalism, in reality, could only achieve part truths and not the whole truth? Surely, 'facts' are the building blocks on which truth faithfully rests? These are fundamental questions regarding the role or function of journalism within a democratic society and attaining the truth is to minimize its entertaining value and maximize its epistemological status. Constructivist theory holds that all truth is socially constructed and isn't external to human mental and physical activity. The realities that are constructed exist as modes of production; the issue for ethics is how constructed reality is gathered and then mediated and not that truth is a chimera.

Objectivity in Journalism

In 1690, when Benjamin Harris published his one and only copy of *Publick Occurences, Both Forreign and Domestick* in Boston, US he was following in the footsteps of Thucydides in attempting to establish a number of principles for journalistic practice namely objectivity, truth and public interest. The debate over whether Thucydides was practicing an early form of journalism is bound to continue, but Harris was one of the first to at least speak of, albeit ephemerally, the need to develop a method that would be fit for purpose in journalistic practice in relation to a form that we recognize as central to journalism, that is, a newspaper. Williams (2002, p. 3) explains thus:

> In his first (and, as it turned out, his last) edition of *Publick Occurences*, editor Harris offered a prospectus that sketched out the purposes and policies of his newspaper. He focused on the need for a 'Faithful Relation' of events.

Williams explains how Harris sought to publish 'credible reports' and how Harris dismissed 'rumourmongers' (ibid.) and 'falsehoods' (ibid., p. 3) that were common practice amongst the British colonies in the US at that time. The title of Williams's paper is 'The Purpose of Journalism' and she uses the insights of Harris as an early example for establishing the essential purpose for journalism and that subsequently 'the American press would strive to do as Benjamin Harris had done' (ibid., p. 4). In other words, the US press would show *reality* in its full glory: 'It could present truth as it was' (ibid.) based on Harris's belief in 'accurate reporting' (objectivity). Finally the author states that 'The press had a purpose of publishing the truth' (ibid.). I believe that the emphasis and wording is mistaken here and that it should read the press had a *responsibility* to publish the truth, thus emphasizing the *purpose* of truth not journalism; thus truth becomes teleological and journalism is the means to reach that end.

However, Williams rightly argues that truth is an extremely complex idea and there were hitherto limitations placed on establishing truth because of selectivity of content, and for Williams, a breakthrough came with the establishment of the 'penny press' in the US in 1833: 'This new press movement would help answer the question "what is truth?" by insisting that the truth was even in dirt and squalor ignorance, not just in lofty party ideals' (ibid., p. 6). And although Harris had only been able to make a brief but nevertheless honourable gesture towards accuracy it was, according to Williams, the penny press that established objectivity more convincingly: 'An interesting outgrowth of the penny press' self-image was the idea that objectivity was part of truth' (ibid., p. 7). The press in the US had previously been dominated by party politics and advocacy journalism, and the notion of objectivity in relation to the penny press was primarily based on independence. But in what way is an independent press more able to speak the truth than politically motivated advocacy journalism? Being independent may be helpful, but is in itself no guarantee for establishing the truth. I can be as independent as I like but tell you sweet lies all day long if I so choose.

In relation to a discussion on investigative journalism, Aucoin (2002, p. 215) claimed that the reporter on the Watergate scandal, Bob Woodward, 'brought cold objectivity to the team' seen to be an essential element of investigation practices. When Thucydides compiled his work on *The Peloponnesian War* (reprinted 1978), he was establishing a principle that Woodward some two and a half thousand years later was emulating on how to accumulate information that reflected the truth of events. The principle of objectivity was and continues to be simultaneously a method on how to approach accounts in which truth can be verified and established. Perhaps one reason that Thucydides hasn't been associated with the practice of newsgathering that later in history became known as journalism is due to the oft-laughable notion that journalism, (newsgathering by another name), in reality, is bereft of objective accounts, and therefore held in a most contemptuous view. So even though there are problems with the account of *The Peloponnesian War*, it's widely believed that the *spirit* of a scientific approach was imbued within it and that *spirit* was an attempt at historical analysis not journalism. It's fair to say that the much-vaunted discipline of history is also prone to collapse into subjective interpretations of past events; thus, sociologists claim that only sociology with its rigid, cold and detached methodological approaches to subject matter can achieve, if not entirely perfectly, an objective account. Whether or not any of these disciplines are more or less objective isn't the point but rather what they share in common, like science, is a belief that objectivity through methodological rigour is ethically desirable.

Scientists constantly complain that journalism is unable to competently mediate the complexities surrounding scientific issues, and there appears to be something ironic about the relationship between science, with its emphasis on method and rigour, and journalism. Scientists may well claim that the core facts become somewhat lost in translation when they are framed as news. Althusser once alerted us to the fact that scientists suffer from ideological impregnation that influences 'scientific-objective' approaches to subject matter. At one extreme, Mengele used science for overt political reasons; at the other seemingly benign but no less extreme, ideology goes unnoticed guiding our every move. Method is believed to relive all known ideological symptoms, not fusing with identity but temporarily eradicating it, if we so freely choose, and if Schopenhauer and hordes of other philosophers from Plato onwards are correct then our free-will if we really desire to 'will it' can surely overcome *prejudice* and *value-judgement*; can't it? The value underpinning objectivity is firmly based on the value of truth discussed earlier; truth is both prior and a consequence of objectivity, or so it is argued. It is prior because it is the justification and reason for objectivity and objectivity then becomes the means on which truth rests; the rest is up to the individual!

The notion that objective journalism is a means and therefore a method to attain truth reflects Mill's rationalism and his separation of method and truth. Accordingly, a truth can be established if it corresponds to a fact and remains in the final analysis unchallenged and accepted as definitive; truth is then established on proven empirical data and not vulnerable to Rorty's claims that counter-positions and counter-arguments can consistently undermine a truth claim. For Rorty, objectivity is not simply undesirable but unachievable. Under the heading 'Solidarity or Objectivity', Rorty (1991) argues that objectivity be reduced to 'solidarity' amongst community members; in other words, it's replaced with inter-subjective beliefs that somehow form the basis of achieving consensus or a reality amongst members that *for them* corresponds to the truth. In this environ, 'preference' commands centre stage and it's 'preference' that constructs social behaviour. For Rorty, 'preference' negates human nature; human beings are what they are because they so freely choose but within confines of established rules and conventions.

In *Contingency, Irony and Solidarity* Rorty (1989) argues that sentences form the world and that sentences are created by human language, which is the product of actual human activity, but importantly Rorty doesn't dismiss that 'The world is out there' (ibid., p. 5), it's just that 'descriptions of the world are not' (ibid.). Describing the world of reality is therefore an end result of sentence production, preference, argumentation and interpretation; in other words, it's human made. Rorty further argues: 'Only descriptions of the world can be true or false.' In the meantime: 'The world on its own – unaided by the describing activities of a human being – cannot' (ibid.). Truth is a product of language and social engagement not *beyond* us, but from *within* ourselves, therefore the negation of objectivity is complete. Rorty may want to consider that despite the claims of the US and UK governments Weapons of Mass Destruction (WMDs) didn't exist in Iraq; false claims on which war was based. The truth has been told and factual-empirical data sustains that; it's not prone to dispute.

As far as McNair (2003, p. 33) is concerned, 'the concept of objectivity has become the key professional ethic, the standard to which all journalists *should* aspire' (my emphasis). If objectivity is a fundamental principle of journalism then it is so despite the political, economic and ideological framework that practice exists within; in other words, it is non-negotiable and transcendent. This also presumes that societal influences that structure our subjective horizons within distinct cultural and political settings are unimportant because objectivity as method is perceived as a universal principle that can be acquired through teaching and understanding, then applied through practice. The universalizing of objectivity over cultural relativism is but one part of the contention over its use and application, for is it possible to negate distinct cultural identities in the formation of language and narrative that eventually formulate a news frame?

The value of objectivity is constructed on the idea that it objectifies subjective analysis and therefore is a method for discovering truth or at the very least is more truthful than subjective accounts because subjectivity is related to opinion. This last point, however, is highly contentious, not least because more truthful is hardly satisfactory, but also because subjectivists argue that truth is unobtainable without the truthful intervention of self into narrative. In other words, self cannot be detached from context. Subjectivists stress the *what ought to be* aspect in relation to social phenomena and are therefore immersed in making moral judgements on events and claim there is no ultimate truth, but rather only moral judgements. In this context, moral attitudes merely reflect personal tastes and having a moral opinion is based on preference. However, moral reasoning is the basis on which statements are made, validated by firm evidence.

Conversely, objectivists maintain that truth exists despite the inconvenience of opinion and therefore truth exists independently of perception. It is in this context that objectivity is seen as a method that attempts to reveal the truth and objectivists stress the *what is* element of social phenomena and therefore desist from making moral judgements because, in sum, objectivists claim that we merely observe and then transmit findings based on scientific application that objectivity allows. It is, however, important to note that decisions made in the first instance on whether objectivity should be a norm are based on moral judgements.

The added complexity of objectivity is that it signifies both a 'state of being' and a 'state of achievement'. A 'state of being' reflects the word objective as an adjective and in this context being objective represents a methodological approach towards the gathering of information concerning a news story. This manifests itself in an approach to accessing news sources that balance accounts of news. This approach negates assumptions that are held prior to investigation and in essence holds that journalists, like scientists, should be value free. There is an argument that this 'state of being' is unattainable because our subjective drives, or our character dominates our identity to such a degree that being objective is a chimera; drives such as moral beliefs, political views and ideological positions are often cited, but all this is an argument against persuasion, reason, training and education. Obtaining objectivity is the 'state of achievement', something to strive towards and represented as a noun. Curiously, to attain objectivity one must be objective and, combined in this way, objectivity is both *means* (method) and *end* within a united structure.

For Niblock, objectivity serves as a key training standard for would-be-journalists: 'News journalists are required to endeavour to report objectively, which means they must not express an opinion or any bias in favour of any of the conflicting sides of a story' (Niblock 1996, p. 15); thus its value is achieved or so Niblock would have us believe. Stephens (2007, p. 253) states:

> Objectivity is a term journalists began using in the 20th century to express their commitment not only to impartiality but to reflecting the world as it is, without bias or distortion of any sort. European journalists have been slower to raise the banner of objectivity, but in the United States this commitment is central to the modern reporter's self-image.

For Stephens, the philosophically oriented debates on objectivity are unrealistic in journalism referring to 'The impossibility of journalistic objectivity' (Stephens 2007, p. 256). Rather, Stephens claims that journalists have 'settled upon a working definition of objectivity' and it 'is this "objectivity for realists" that guides the behaviour of practitioners of the journalistic method' (ibid.). There are, however, two problems with Stephens's analysis; the first, which I am less interested in, but is nevertheless important for wider issues, is that Stephens generalizes without providing empirical evidence and rather produces vacuous statements referring to 'these reporters' (ibid.). The second, which is far more important for the purposes of this book, is that Stephens fails to produce a detailed account of objectivity for realists other than it helps journalists 'reach the end of their stories each day without the feeling of having sinned' (ibid.), once again complete with a generalization.

The US publisher Morton McMichael once claimed that 'Fact finding was the principal purpose of the press' (from Evensen 2002, p. 258) and is an emphatic statement supporting the principle of objective reporting for true replication of reality, which is the 'aim and end of true journalism'. Accordingly, objectivity and truth are interlinked: objectivity the means to achieving truth. McMichael's claim, I would argue, is missing the point, however, of a purpose beyond fact finding. Gordon et al.'s (1996) approach is more realistic, for the principle must first be established and then applied practically, for there is a purpose beyond both objectivity and truth, which is to bring benefits to society. Nevertheless, the point expressed by McMichael is that the press are not merely organs for our entertainment; they should serve the essential democratic needs of society.

Under the sub-heading 'The Penny Press and the Rise of Objectivity', Evensen (2002, p. 261) notes how, in the US, the *Sun* in the 1830s believed that it could present 'an impartial history' of the day's events and that objectivity had been fully incorporated into the journalistic vernacular in the early period of the twentieth century. The emphasis on objectivity in the US at least was not about setting a universal standard for journalists, but rather, as Evensen states with reference to Casper Yoss, 'the founding father of the American Society of Newspaper editors' (ibid., p. 263) that objectivity was a method of newsgathering 'that would separate serious-minded journalists from the tabloid press' (ibid.). This relative rather than universal approach has interesting implications in terms of what exactly constitutes news, for it assumes that non-objective 'tabloid' accounts are of no, or at least have little, social value. This would also have implications not only for production, but also for consumption, for it assumes that readers of 'objective-serious' press are better informed than those who consume tabloids, and here we begin to enter the complex debate concerning *false consciousness*. Evensen claims that by the mid-twentieth century, 'objectivity was beginning to get a bad name, and by millennium end it was no longer fashionable to emphasize fairness, balance, and impartiality as consensus values that shaped journalism', giving way to 'interpretation' that would make 'the day's events more meaningful' (ibid., p. 264). Mott (1962, p. 835) also details this division between interpretation and objective accounts stating that:

> Debate on the question of 'interpretative' or 'objective' reporting was common among newspapermen throughout the 1950's ... . The consensus of thoughtful journalists was that the modern scene required much more from the reporter than bald facts.

Another term used during this period was 'Reporting in depth' – 'digging behind and under the mere news of events' (ibid.) or what is currently referred to as 'investigative journalism', which according to the veteran British journalist John Pilger is the bedrock of all true journalism. Digging beyond the veneer or spin of political events entails journalists in thinking and becoming critical in their analysis, what Mott (1962, p. 836) referred to as 'intelligent initiative'; the question, however, is how is this to be achieved?

The main argument by thinkers and journalists who support the necessity for objectivity in journalism is ultimately based on the idea that news must serve a certain, specific function, which, it is claimed, can provide the public with uncontaminated information on which informed judgements about events can be made. This argument is sometimes placed within a particular context, that is, that objective news is in the public interest, and it is assumed that news concerning politics, education, health and national security are examples of news items that serve the public interest principle because ultimately the public are affected by such news.

Hausman (1990) and Clayton (1992) have claimed that objectivity is both attainable and a desirable outcome for good journalism. The play on truth, balance and fairness, weighing up the propositions through the installation of proper ethical training, can result in objective reporting regardless of any bias an individual or organization may have. According to Westerståhl (1983), whatever the issues, problems and criticisms concerning objectivity, it is nevertheless a model that may provide guidance for journalists to adopt a neutral position. Objectivity is more than an ideal because, as Windschuttle (1998, p. 6) has claimed, journalism has an empirical methodology and has a realist view of the world. According to this perspective, objectivity is seen as a scientific method for gathering news, and one that guarantees truth in the process of mediation. Underwood (1993) has claimed that objective reporting breeds *integrity* towards the truth and Burns (2002, p. 23) states that: 'Integrity is defined as adherence to the social obligations attached to a privileged position', which is based on journalism's ability to influence the social and cultural environment and accordingly 'the power of the media to disseminate information must be balanced with social obligations to truth and justice' (ibid.). Objective reporting is thought to be a full account of an event written in a dispassionate and detached manner so as to avoid subjectivity or the over-use of one's own value-judgements. But being dispassionate or disinterested isn't to lie back idly, but rather it is the result of a committed and determined individual and is itself, ironically, born out of the *passion* for attaining the truth! Ultimately, to be objective is to be aware of one's approach to any given subject matter.

Fishman (1980), at the beginning of his book *Manufacturing the News*, has claimed that journalists share something in common with sociologists and that is the pursuit of facts. To a very large extent, this pursuit is based on discipline and method, which is good, sound practice that finally and hopefully produces truth via objective means. In a defence of objectivity, Dennis (in Dennis and Merrill 1991, p. 115) has asked 'is it possible within the context of human frailty to try to be disinterested, not meaning *uninterested* or *indifferent*, but impartial?' Dennis answers with a 'resounding yes' (ibid.). But this is to miss the point somewhat or, to put it another way, to conflate objectivity with impartiality. Golding and Elliot (1979) have argued objectivity is a much, misunderstood concept and is often confused with impartiality. An objective news account is one that is inclusive of all the facts pertinent to the case at hand. In reality, impartiality is an essential element of objective analysis; if you like, it is one element of the means to achieving objectivity, but it's not to be confused with objectivity, which I'm afraid Dennis does. One can be impartial or indifferent to any given situation such as the brutal murder of one person or another, but still fail to achieve an objective account or a full, unadulterated picture of the scene; that's not to argue, however, that objectivity doesn't exist, is unattainable or can't be striven for.

Schlesinger (1978) has claimed that far from impartiality being value free, in fact it represents the highest form of ideology, often reflecting a news organizations world-view. As Kieran (1998, p. 34) asserts: 'Good journalism aims at discovering and promoting the audience's understanding of an event via truth-promoting methods.' Striving to accumulate the total amount of facts pertinent to an issue and including them accordingly is a crucial part of good practice, because the consequence of not doing so restricts public understanding of important issues. Both the Press Complaints Commission's (PCC) Code of Practice[3] and the

---

3   See http://www.pcc.org.uk/.

National Union of Journalists (NUJ)[4] Code of Conduct purport to the necessity of objective reporting, although the term isn't used. According to the PCC's Code, under 'Accuracy' the following points apply:

- Newspapers and periodicals must take care not to publish inaccurate, misleading or distorted information including pictures.
- Whenever it is recognised that a significant inaccuracy, misleading statement or distorted report has been published, it must be corrected promptly and with due prominence.
- Newspapers, whilst free to be partisan, must distinguish clearly between comment, conjecture and fact.
- A newspaper article must report fairly and accurately … .

The NUJ's Code of Conduct states that: 'A journalist shall strive to ensure that the information that he/she disseminates is fair and accurate.' The belief in objectivity is not only crucial for all news workers, but equally, it is important to the way audiences both perceive and respond to the press. Bogart (1989) has argued that objective reporting is also valued by the audience and, although this does seem difficult to evaluate, it may, nevertheless, be of interest to research the reasons why people purchase certain types of newspapers.[5] In this context, there is a degree of public trust in news practice pertinent to a particular paper if its news is deemed to be based on objective accounts. However, trust in news is equally based on the way in which a person can relate to news accounts in an overt and biased manner; this is particularly the case in the UK.

That said, objectivity is an ideal or value that is seen to be essential for an ethical approach to news; to be objective is to attain good ethical standards, the basis of where journalists' social responsibilities lie. However, in a critique of objectivity similar to Randall's criticism discussed earlier, Burns (2002, p. 62) has equally claimed that it is nothing but an ideal and is unrealistic in the real world of journalism: 'The trouble is objectivity is a value-free concept, whereas journalists' decisions are always a prioritizing of values.' In *Media Debates: Issues in Mass Communication*, Dennis and Merrill debate the merits and viability of objectivity for the practice of journalism with Merrill arguing against and Dennis for. As Merrill (in Dennis and Merrill 1991, p. 107) states:

> Let us consider 'objective reporting': It would be reporting that is detached, unprejudiced, un-opinionated, uninvolved, unbiased, omniscient and infallible … . It would tell the truth, the whole truth, and nothing but the truth. Where do we find this kind of reporting?

---

4   See http://www.nuj.org.uk/.

5   Further to this, Rubin (1978) in a study of American television argued that there are large areas of social life that are ignored because of the perception of the audience by the television programmers, which is equally applicable to the newspaper readership.

Merrill's main point is that journalists, like all of us, are imbued with value-judgements prior to an event: 'Reporters ... do not come to their stories as blank slates on which the realities of events is to be written' (ibid.) and it is this position that disables a journalist from achieving objectivity. Gans (1979), van Dijk (1988) and McQuail (1993) have argued that ideology and subjective positions (value-judgements) come to the fore when journalists encounter an event and that it colours their perception of it, thus making a mockery of objective reporting.

Objectivity has come under some intense scrutiny within studies of the press because it assumes a neutral positioning of the subject responsible for the written text. Two concepts that have been used to undermine objectivity are Weber's (1948) theory of 'value-judgement' and Gadamar's (1979) theory concerning 'prejudice'. Each is based on the idea that individuals cannot escape the true realities of their own subjective and moral personality that ultimately affect the way in which we view matters that ultimately distort the final presentation of a text. According to Golding and Elliot (1979), subjectivity will ultimately bias our accounts. In this context, events become susceptible to processes of interpretation through representation, rather than exact photocopies of reality. Equally, it has been argued that subjectivity coordinates and organizes our cultural horizons (Schutz 1964; Berger and Luckman 1967) prior to our intervention into an event; too powerful to detach from.[6]

Both Rosten (1937) and White (1950) have argued that the selection of news itself entails a degree of subjective judgement. Roshco (1975) has claimed that objectivity is a framework where a selection of items is seen to be of value to the news worker. Others have argued journalistic autonomy is negligible because of external and internal constraints (ideology and organizational directives) either set by advertisers and investors, or from the news organization itself (Tunstall 1971; Schlesinger 1978; Tuchman 1978; Gans 1979). In this context, objectivity may be a 'strategic ritual' (Tuchman 1978, p. 164) that legitimizes selectivity of events as newsworthy according to the values of a newspaper.

Historically, objectivity was a novel way of reaching new and wider audiences, thus potentially increasing newspaper circulation (Schudson 1978); the emphasis was on fact rather than opinion. In this way, a new professional framework was signified by the neutral positioning of the reporter; it was a new method to collate information (Tuchman 1978). Thus, today, the very notion of the production of facts by objective means and criteria is the hallmark for the defence of the claim by owners of the press to be free. This type of methodology, it is claimed, is untainted by ideological intentions of either the owners or the *habitus* of the news workers and editors; they merely report the facts as they are visually

---

6   Andrew Edgar (1992, pp. 112–129) in reference to Paul Ricoeur states that citizens have certain types of beliefs according to the culture they inhabit and that: 'Such beliefs "bias" ... interpretation ...'. This, Edgar claims, ultimately negates objectivity because journalists are shaped by a cultural framework that define their understanding of an event and making sense of it is dictated by 'cultural horizons'.

observed, uncontaminated by exogenous forces. Capturing the whole world in a news item based on restricted time and space may be difficult, but that doesn't necessarily negate objectivity, it just means that more time and space may be required, plus effort and good intentions, of course. Objectivity requires balance in news reporting that is synonymous with fairness. Achieving balance is not only moral in terms of the personal approach by a journalist, it is equally perceived as a means for attaining the truth. The importance of balancing a news text cannot be underestimated; that is not to say that all practitioners agree with the weight or value given to balance.

Perhaps the most detailed account on this subject is in Stephen Ward's *The Invention of Journalism Ethics: The Path to Objectivity and Beyond*, where the author meticulously details the central arguments pertaining to objectivity. It's a fine scholarly work that demands serious attention and reaches out to practitioners, so it's not confined to airy academic debate but it is a demanding work. Ward more or less begins his study by rightly alerting us to the fact that the meaning of objectivity has changed consistently since its beginnings, stating, first, that: 'in the medieval era, objectivity and subjectivity meant the opposite' of what they mean today, and, second, that: 'The English noun "objectivity" goes back to the classical Latin verb "obicere" – "to oppose" or "to place a hindrance before".' By medieval times, the Latin noun "objectum" referred to a visible object placed before someone' (Ward 2004, p. 15). The point of all this is that Ward seeks to offer his own contribution to the meaning of objectivity in relation to journalistic practice. Before I discuss Ward's theory on objectivity, the author explains that there are 'three senses of objectivity' (ibid., p. 16) that help us understand this complex concept. First, there's 'epistemic objectivity', which is normative serving as 'method of inquiry'. Second is 'ontological objectivity', which explains 'the subjective–objective distinction', and, third, there is 'procedural objectivity', which is based on 'fair and reasonable decisions' (ibid., p. 17) in the empirical world. I'm not convinced between the distinctions of epistemic and procedural because the latter incorporates normative perspectives and is certainly based on a method of approach.

Nevertheless, Ward does concede that all three 'are closely related' (ibid., p. 18) and then argues that 'The doctrine of journalism objectivity, with its stress on facts, procedures, and impartiality, is a hybrid of the three senses of objectivity' (ibid., p. 19). Ward explains that journalism has adhered to 'traditional objectivity' developed in the US and central to this model is the notion that journalists report 'unbiased information' (ibid.). Ward details six key features to traditional objectivity, one of which is 'non-interpretation' or expressing 'opinion' (ibid.). Ward finally states that 'Journalists borrowed the term (objectivity) from science to distinguish news from commentary' (ibid., p. 22).

In Europe, objectivity barely registers on the journalistic Richter scale with various codes of practice and conduct simply paying lip service to it, and even then the academic-intellectual debate concerning objectivity is nowhere near as intense or thorough as in the North American context. Objectivity in theory and practice is only traditional in particular cultural contexts and hardly universal as a consequence; the debate on whether it should be a universal principle is another matter that ironically depends on relative application in various empirical conditions. Ward obviously believes it to be crucial to all journalistic practice irrespective of cultural context claiming it to be 'vital ... for responsible journalism' and 'scientific inquiry' (ibid., p. 5).

Despite these flaws Ward argues that the US-based idea of traditional objectivity is unworkable for three reasons: first, because it wasn't precisely defined (ibid., p. 22); second, because it negates interpretation; and, third, because it advances 'neutrality and detachment' (ibid., p. 19) in all cases as set standards for practice. The resolution to these apparent flaws is to propose an alternative, workable model called 'pragmatic objectivity'. Pragmatic objectivity stresses not only the importance of facts and fair application in reporting, but also interpretation, which, according to Ward, can effectively be tested for any truth claims, in my view highly dubious and contradictory considering it is left to the individual to investigate the validity of their own self-inspired interpretation. It's worth recalling that Mott (1962) (see Chapter 1) had rejected interpretation, preferring detached objectivity, which was the only guarantee for producing news. That said, Emery (1972, p. iii) had earlier forwarded a view similar to Ward:

> Journalism history is the story of man's long struggle to communicate freely with his fellow men – to dig out and interpret news, and to offer intelligent opinion in the market place of ideas.

Emphasis on 'interpret' and 'opinion': no mention and indeed no index reference to objectivity in Emery's book and it's not clear that this absence is a latent critique of objectivity. There's nothing latent about former BBC journalist Martin Bell, who conducted a very public attack against objective reporting. Bell claimed that during his training at the BBC to be objective was 'necessary' and was born out of the BBC's 'tradition of distance and detachment', and as a consequence refers to objective reporting as 'bystanders journalism'. Bell also said that 'I am no longer sure what "objective" means' (Bell 1998, p. 18), claiming that objectivity was 'an illusion and a shibboleth' (ibid., p. 16), and Bell proposes an alternative to objective reporting:

> In place of the dispassionate practices of the past I now believe in what I call the *journalism of attachment*. By this, I mean a journalism that cares as well as knows; that is aware of its responsibilities; that will not stand neutrally between good and evil, right and wrong, the victim and the oppressor. That is not to back one side or faction or people against another. It is to make the point that we in the press, and especially in television, which is its most powerful division, do not stand apart from the world. We are a part of it. We exercise a certain influence, and we have to know that. The influence may be for better or for worse, and we have to know that too. (ibid.)

The statement, however, appears to be both obscure and contradictory. For how is it possible to 'not stand neutrally' whilst at the same time not 'back one side ... against another', nor 'stand apart from the world'? Whereas Emery ignores objectivity, and Bell offers a gentlemanly critique, the American Hunter S. Thompson was more forthright and perhaps even more honest in his denouncement of objective reporting. Thompson believed that objective accounts were not only insincere, but also lacked courage to confront what he perceived as morally wrong. For instance, Thompson argued that American politics was generally corrupt and not to say so, as in objective-balanced accounts, was not only dishonest, but the reason for corrupt politicians to survive. Thompson believed in taking sides and 'telling it like it is'!

In a similar fashion to Bell, Knowlton (1997, p. 16) has argued that one should care for the subject but also, confusingly I may add, states in the same breath that he opposes 'advocacy journalism', preferring to strive for that 'elusive impartiality', to which I add if impartiality is so elusive why try to discover something that is beyond our apparent grasp? The contradictions continue, where Knowlton states that being impartial 'doesn't mean you don't care; if you deeply care about an issue, it will show in your effort, and if you attempt to be impartial, it will be a better report' (ibid.). But how can one be impartial, which means indifference to the subject, and care for that very same subject at the same time? Notice also the use of *attempt*, for you are either impartial or not (partial).

Lloyd (2004, p. 18) launched a scathing attack upon Bell's idea concerning the journalism of attachment by claiming that the principles that underpin objective reporting are 'casualties' in the newsgathering process. Lloyd also claimed that 'celebrity journalists' such as Bell have promoted their own 'causes', which take precedence over the principles involved in news production. Lloyd doesn't dismiss the journalism of attachment outright and argues that television programmes can benefit from such forms of journalism. It's not entirely clear what programmes Lloyd has in mind, but it does exclude news programmes, which must be based on an objective form of journalism, a journalism revealing the truth in a cold detached and dispassionate manner. But once again, assuming that we are primarily warm and humane beings, with exceptions of course, becoming cold is to understand the rigours of objectivity; it doesn't mean one doesn't care.

Besides, why should it be so difficult to be a part of the world, to acknowledge that relationship and attain objectivity? And why can't we be *passionate* about the rigours of objectivity and all it may reveal in the process of mediation? Lloyd's view is typical of what objectivity isn't and this misconception is also highlighted by Alia (2004, p. 30): 'Journalists are taught to remain "objective", distant and dispassionate – removed from their subjects' is the claim, and judging by Alia's glowing references to Oriana Fallaci, one can only suspect that objectivity is something to avoid. In fact, Alia, with reference to objectivity, poses the following question: 'Is this not a form of journalistic deception?' (ibid., p. 116), which is based on the following statement 'no one is free of values or opinions' (ibid.) so the upshot of this is why pretend? But neither are we trapped by values and opinions, and to argue that both are obstacles to education and achievement is disingenuous. In a more positive tone, Eagleton (2003, p. 132) states to be objective is to be confronted with one of life's more difficult challenges:

> Trying to be objective is an arduous, fatiguing business, which in the end only the virtuous can attain. Only those with the patience, honesty, courage and persistence can delve through the layers of self-deception, which prevent us from seeing the situation as it is.

Virtue is something that Alia doesn't actually consider as a value that can become the means to objectivity other than superficially stating that 'Virtue and responsibility ethics' was 'founded by Aristotle' (Alia 2004, p. 16). Sanders (2005), however, devotes an entire chapter to this important value titled 'Virtue ethics' (ibid., pp. 27–39), stating clearly and unequivocally with reference to virtue ethics that it is both 'helpful and right' (ibid., p. 27) for practice, although it's not clear whether being virtuous as Eagleton argues is the basis for objective action. Eagleton also enthusiastically argues that the 'universal body' is the basis of morality and it is not subjective because it is something we all share, an undisputable commonality. However, Eagleton goes onto to state that there is something that interrupts the universal and that is culture, 'it is culture that is our primary source of division' (2003, p. 158). One key principle central to the discussion on media ethics is objectivity, a universal principle that in many ways attempts to bridge the gap between morality and culture, because to be objective is to recognize the 'other' and acknowledge their thoughts in the process of mediation. One is not necessarily obliged to do so, for only the virtuous can attain objectivity, argues Eagleton. Belsey (1998) also places emphasis on virtue in journalism, arguing that there is no effective way of compelling an individual to be virtuous and therefore virtue can't be guaranteed and is contingent upon conscience.

Perspectivism

Frost (2007, p. 71) argues that objectivity is a value 'desired by consumers and journalists' and then claims that objectivity is problematically linked to the 'concept of truth' (ibid., p. 75) where in reality 'I can only help present *a perspective*' (ibid., p. 74; my italics). Frost's view is uncannily similar to Ward's theory of 'pragmatic objectivity', if not as thoroughly discussed. Whereas Frost only fleetingly refers to 'perspective', Ward on the other hand spends an entire book on his theory. Whereas Frost uses the word 'perspective', Ward uses 'interpretation'; in sum, they are identical in their empirical application. Even though Ward had claimed that his theory contains many of the principles detailed in traditional objectivity, such as the pursuit of fact by fair means, it is only when we delve deeper into his work that in reality they count for nothing and are in effect completely negated as the swirling winds of self-interpretation begin to assert themselves over reality via self-perception, which is effectively limited and contained within a pseudo-subjective framework:

> Inquiry interprets events with the assistance of conceptual schemes. The inquirer can reform and improve his or her schemes of understanding but can never completely transcend them. (Ward 2004, p. 264)

It's pseudo-subjective because self-interpretation is conditioned by conceptual schemes that I would imagine are externally imposed to make sure the individual doesn't stress or stretch their sense of individuality so far as to distort a reality. But how can interpretation proceed when it is governed or restricted by rules? And who exactly decides what the rules are? If I am to interpret, I shall do so according to my own rules and own sense of interpretation, thank you very much, and without the audacious and pertinent intervention of an outsider, which is the stuff of self-preservation and libertarian notions of the self. In sum, Ward's protection of some of the principles of what he refers to as traditional objectivity collapses into a subjective morass and is no more than paying lip service expressed also in many of the European codes of conduct or practice.

The key word in the quote above is 'transcend', and although Ward doesn't reference either Nietzsche or Ortega y Gasset in relation to *transcendence*, or in this context the inability to achieve *transcendence*, I would suggest that is exactly where we can locate his beliefs specifically in relation to Nietzsche's writings on interpretation and Ortega y Gasset's writings on what he called 'circumstance', to be discussed shortly, and also this, I would argue, is implicit in Frost's reference to perspective. What has been expressed in both cases is a retreat into relativism, which is extremely problematic in my view and reflects the existentialism conveyed by the US thinker John Merrill, although neither references either the concept or the writer. By referencing perspective, Frost is in sum proposing an alternative view on how truth can be attained, although it's not entirely clear what role opinion has in the greater scheme of things. As opposed to the objectivist belief that truth is independent of the knower and absolute in universal terms, what we are now philosophically confronted with here is a myriad of perspectives as opposed to absolute truth. How is it then possible to understand the empirical world in objective terms when there are splits and divisions over perspective and interpretation?

Nietzsche (2003) is the chief architect of the philosophical notion of *perspectivism*, arguing that individuals merely assert their self-perspective through an ongoing process of interpretation and self-evaluation. The notion that there is no universal truth existing outside of any given personalized perspective or account has other discursive problems in the context of Frost's comments when it is stated that any proposed perspective ultimately rests upon others to interpret (accept, reject, indifferent) that perspective from their own personalized perspective, and what we end up with is a further Nietzschean myriad series of interpretations that form a maze of disjunctive and disputed understandings. Objectivists meanwhile would happily say 'carry on' with your erstwhile process of continual and endless interpretation for, in reality, the truth is out there and universal.

In Nietzschean philosophy the pursuit of truth is contained and limited within perspective, thus making *transcendence* to universal truth claims impossible. In many ways there is the ghost of Wittgenstein lurking here: 'the limits of my language means the limits of my world' (1963, Tractus, 5.6), and whilst not specifically referencing journalism as an object of enquiry, this statement nevertheless reflects the limits of journalistic activity, particularly if they are governed by perspective.

In *Beyond Good and Evil* (2003) Nietzsche famously disputes the universal truth claims made by many philosophers and argues that in reality the claims are driven by 'prejudice'. A similar notion of 'prejudice' arrives later in the work of Max Weber as 'value-judgement', in Hans Georg Gadamar also as 'prejudice' governed mostly by moral values and cultural placement and the influences therein, although in Nietzsche's use 'prejudice' seems to be psychological. Indeed Solomon (1996) makes a convincing case, arguing that in the first instance Nietzsche can be seen as a psychologist rather than a philosopher. This would also substantiate the criticisms levelled against Nietzsche that a philosopher he was not because there wasn't a coherent body of thought expressed.

That aside, one of the intriguing arguments made with regards to Nietzschean psychology is his emphasis upon the unconscious (Olson 2001) in *Beyond Good and Evil*. Olson argues that Nietzsche merely sought to make us aware of prejudices by challenging convention. This was also the point of Nietzsche's approach to 'genealogy' (Berry 2006), particularly the approach to history where he argued that systems of thought were governed by particular structures and practices resulting in *a* history rather than *the* history; in this way, Nietzsche was a radical because he sought to think outside of convention and attempted to create another rationality.

So, you may ask, what is the point of all this in the context of journalism? Ironically, perhaps, those that subscribe to and make a case for objective accounts do so on a similar basis to Nietzsche, that is, by ridding oneself of all prejudice; the very same prejudice Nietzsche despised, the difference being, however, that Nietzsche declared only perspective and interpretation can realistically make some ground on truth claims; the awareness therefore is an awareness of the unconscious drives that govern prejudice and not training one to be objective, which for Nietzsche was a fallacy. It's worth recalling that Ward's perspective differs by arguing that both objectivity and interpretation can be united to form a method in news practice called 'pragmatic objectivity', stating: 'Objectivity is not the absence of interpretation. It is the *testing* of interpretations by the best available methods and restraining standards' (Ward 2004, p. 22).

Ultimately, Nietzsche's arguments rest on the 'will' to know what is true, a similar position to Schopenhauer's 'will to life', the former expressed in *The Will To Power*, which in essence is personalized judgement, but one not hopelessly detached as in subjectivism. Indeed *perspectivism* is not to be entirely confused with *subjectivism*, which is a form of relativism because unlike forms of *subjectivism* the philosophical concept of *perspectivism* does not reject the idea of truth as a product of collective experience.

Another important writer relating to *perspectivism* is the Spaniard Jose Ortega y Gasset, who sadly is a much-neglected writer and whose great body of works is yet to be translated into English. However, in the translated *Meditations on Quixote* Ortega y Gasset (2000) sets out his views pertaining to *perspectivist* philosophy, although the author refers to the word 'circumstance' to make his point. Ortega y Gasset espoused the philosophy of phenomenology, arguing against speculation, claiming that matters of truth can only be legitimately accounted for with the production of concrete evidence, which explains his support of *perspectivism*. In the *Meditations* Ortega y Gasset analyses Cervantes's invention Don Quixote to understand the truth or reality of Spain and argues that Quixote's travels reveal universal meanings on humanity and Spanish interventions. This, then, for Ortega y Gasset is the reason that 'circumstance' is so important, for it is the real material world of our experience that is the launch-pad for understanding of other realities beyond ourselves.

Perspectivism is critically contrasted and opposed to objectivism and subjectivism because the former acknowledges a cultural context that conditions our beliefs, but perhaps more importantly, unlike subjectivism, it does not dismiss truth beyond the individual. Objectivism for Ortega y Gasset is far too dogmatic in that it insists on reality or truth to be discovered outside of or greater than 'circumstance'. Subjectivism, a form of relativism, was far too restrictive, denying a collective *truth of experience* and containing the boundaries of discovery only within the knower. Subjectivists either claim that personal experiences so distort reality that there can therefore be no truth or, like the journalist Hunter S. Thompson, argue that only the individual can provide truth and it is limited to self-experience. Either way, for Ortega y Gasset this is to be rejected, but unlike objectivists, the author claims that an individual's contribution is vital and that their immediate environment, their 'circumstance', enables and empowers them to create truth in relation to the empirical world. Reality, then, is neither invented nor is it beyond the *real* empirical experience of the knower.

To what extent Frost was using the word 'perspective' is only known to him, for he does not philosophically elaborate on this important subject. Does he use perspective according to the principles of both Nietzsche and Ortega y Gasset? Or does he mean subjectivism and deny truth? It's difficult to comment further, but it may not have escaped anyone's attention that *perspectivism* and 'circumstance' is the language of existentialism, and it will be recalled from Chapter 4 that the US thinker John Merrill in his many criticisms of public journalism advocated the notion of *existential journalism* known as 'social existentialism'.

Some existentialists believe that 'circumstance' is inauthentic and that individuals are capable of transcending the 'circumstance' of where they belong and this is expressed in Krieglstein's (n.d.) theory of *Transcendental Perspectivism*, whilst others believe that transcending 'circumstance' isn't possible, and this is expressed in both Nietzsche's and Ortega y Gasset's respective philosophies.

A student of Adorno, Krieglstein's theory is a clear rejection of the limitations that 'circumstance' places upon the self and, to use a turn of phrase, *to will the self into cultural submission. Transcendental Perspectivism* is curiously linked to Eagleton's view concerning the value and social need of objectivity, although it rejects truth as objective and universal. Krieglstein argued that transcendence beyond self-experience is vital for our understanding of the other or, in other words, it was to understand better the limitations of the value-judgements that govern our lives in order to understand better the empirical world. Eagleton also argued that the true expression of morality is to understand the other and only the virtuous can attain this.

For journalists, this would require discipline and a rigorous application towards newsgathering practices: in other words, method. To use a Weberian analogy, the integrity of applying method is necessary for attempting to understand the relationship between the journalist's values and the subsequent interpretation and comprehension of cultural representation and meaning in a social context. It was Max Weber (1949) who claimed that research enquiry is primarily driven by a deep sense of morality and that objective accounts of phenomena contain subjective elements. To a certain degree they interfere with objective analysis and Ricouer (1981) has argued that when we enter into an investigation we not only take moral baggage with us, perhaps the 'circumstance' that Ortega y Gasset spoke of, but more importantly that cultural baggage influences our sense of interpretation, which Nietzsche spoke of, and ultimately this is conditioned by the immediate environment we inhabit. Aware of such baggage, Weber claimed that method was a means to objectify subjective, moral-oriented value-judgement. Applying method doesn't necessarily negate value-judgements; they simply make us aware and alert us to their presence. As Weber maintained, our very choice of subject matter under investigation is primarily driven by our sense of morality.

Weber argued there was a paradox at the centre of research that had to be resolved, and influenced by his contemporary Rickert, Weber uses the term 'value-orientation' and further claims that value-orientation is the sphere where subjective motives are to be located, and it thus both limits research enquiry and, paradoxically, is the reason for investigative interest. At its core, the subjective position is non-rational and the application of method is designed to bring about a move towards a rational understanding (resolution). So, in essence, method seeks to separate value from fact. Method is designed to achieve the much-maligned notion of objectivity and, for Weber, resolution proceeds through 'interpretive sociology' (Käsler 1988). Influenced by Weber, Habermas (see Thompson 1981; Thompson and Held 1982; Pusey 1987) also claimed that the subjective–objective relationship shouldn't result in a moral relativism based solely on opinion. Understanding the cause of social action meant going beyond interpretation; therefore, other objective factors must be taken into account if we are to fully comprehend intentions of actions, such as economy, politics, culture and social conditions.

There is perhaps an irony to consider in relation to perspective and interpretation. On one level both Nietzsche's and Ortega y Gasset's use of *perspectivism* can be seen as nothing more than a personal view of the empirical world and without imposing *a* truth governed by 'circumstance' as an absolute-universal truth we may deduce that it is merely one opinion amongst others and openly proclaimed as so. But when we apply *perspectivism* to journalism and mass communication it transmogrifies into something completely different, because now it is transmitted over time and space and, given the fact that newspapers are awarded authenticity, a reliable source of information and considered trustworthy by some then perhaps perspective is inadvertently or falsely turned into universal truth about any given subject. Also, because the press is controlled in large parts by powerful commercially minded individuals that subscribe to the politics of powerful and influential political parties and governing ideologies, it is then for this reason that perspective becomes highly suspect as a form of representation and reason I would argue for objective accounts of news.

If it were made clear in any given news frame that only one perspective was being expressed rather than fact then all well and good. However, we then must ask the following pertinent questions: What purpose journalism? What purpose truth? What purpose or intention perspective? Frost claims that when his perspective on an event is produced it is then ultimately the responsibility of the reader 'to come to a closer understanding of how I view what is happening' (Frost 2007, p. 74), but why do we need to know his thoughts if they tell us nothing of truth? What purpose for society would that fulfil? It is one of the most worrying aspects of *perspectivism* that ultimately we learn nothing objectively beyond the moral and perhaps ideological constraints and values of the self who may in the process be expressing dominant values. Also, does Frost's emphasis on perspective reflect what Kieran (1998, p. 34) calls 'truth-indifferent', which for Kieran represents 'bad journalism' that 'fails to respect truth promoting practices'? I would argue that it does and consequently reflects the cynicism expressed by Richard Rorty.

In the art world, perspective is used in relation to representation and Adorno argued that art is an expression of truth but only because it was the product of a free individual, free from commercial restraint, although that's dubious today, and free from the ideology of external control. But when we apply this art analogy of perspective and representation to journalism where invariably news is a commodity, where exchange value rules use value and where the individual is not free especially from news values then it has to be rejected in this form.

Some Final Thoughts

One leading journalist who has questioned whether truth and objectivity can be attained is one of the BBC's leading correspondents, David Loyn who wrote 'Witnessing the Truth' (2003) where Loyn, echoing a Rortian perspective, states: 'There cannot be a single absolute truth – anyone who has interviewed two observers of the same incident knows that there is no perfect account.' Equally, Loyn argued that 'absolute objectivity is impossible'. No absolute objectivity equals no means to attain absolute truths. The problem here is Loyn's emphasis on no perfect account; what Loyn doesn't realize is that these different accounts of the same event may be opinion or interpretation. They may have nothing to do with truth at all, but there again they may. Perhaps somewhere in between the two points, truth or fragments of truth may be found and surely that is a matter for the journalist to pursue; after all, truth is worth pursuing and one can only pursue truth if it is there to pursue. The trap that Loyn inadvertently had fallen into or if you like the contradiction in his argument is that he states that absolute truth is unattainable, but one must nevertheless relentlessly *pursue* it. Likewise, Loyn states that 'absolute objectivity is impossible', but earlier in his argument states that objectivity is a journalist's 'goal'. How can one pursue the truth if truth doesn't exist and how can one have objectivity as a goal if objectivity doesn't exist? During Ancient times, Thucydides experienced a similar problem when relying on various sources of an identical event: 'Not that even so the truth was easy to discover: different eye-witnesses give different accounts of the same events, speaking out of partiality for one side or the other or else from imperfect memories' (Thucydides 1978, 48, I, 22).

In a reply to Loyn's article, the philosopher Julian Baggini (2003) addresses the contradictions therein and attempts to resolve them, but unfortunately Baggini ends up producing contradictory solutions of his own. For example, Baggini uses Thomas Nagel's book *A View From Nowhere* as a reference point by stating that one must make a distinction between the subjective and the objective, and says: 'The purely subjective is that viewpoint which is entirely determined by the particular perspective of the individual', and then states that by becoming 'less subjective' we then become 'more objective' because we 'expand our frames of reference and thus gain dimensions of understanding that go beyond our own perceptions of the world'. The key words here are 'purely' and 'our own' as if we are innately in possession of ideas prior to speech with others. This phenomenological-oriented perspective is one that argues that we produce 'our own' stream of consciousness and that is why I imagine that it is somehow 'pure', uncontaminated from outside pollutants. On another point, when we become less subjective we expand our repertoire in all its glorious diversity, but whose ideas are we consuming and why should they either be more objective or even more truthful than our own expressions? Finally, and reflecting Nagel's views, Baggini states that 'while it is true there is no pure objectivity' – there's that word 'pure' again, which we'll return to in one moment – 'one can always try to get a more objective viewpoint'. But what does more objective actually mean? To paraphrase Baggini when he criticized Loyn, how can one be 'more objective' if 'pure objectivity' doesn't exist? And what is more, why can subjectivity be 'pure' and not objectivity? In what is now a worn out and predictable statement Baggini goes on to argue that journalists can strive to be objective, even though objectivity doesn't, according to Baggini, exist; purely! Just like Loyn said, contradictorily I may add, you can 'pursue' the truth even though it doesn't exist and like Loyn, Baggini, who accuses Loyn of acting in 'bad faith', does so himself, because you can't strive for something that doesn't exist; purely! Nagel had argued that objectivity isn't total or a complete measure of truth statements but rests upon degrees! What degree of truth based on what degree of objectivity does either Nagel or Baggini have in mind? Perhaps, just perhaps, it's a degree based on *their own pure* subjective accounts of the world around them.

But out of this discussion Baggini raises important issues concerning the retreat from truth and argues that the result is to embark on an 'unhealthy relativism', a point that Loyn himself had made where he stated that one would automatically indulge in a 'moral relativism' if one did not pursue the truth; the truth that is ultimately unattainable! Essentially, Baggini argues that if there is no truth, therefore there can be no knowledge. The epistemological implications are *of course* obvious; we simply inhabit a conscious environment of half-truths based on unsubstantiated opinion.

Considering the points made here on attaining truth and understanding, it's worth pondering for one moment on some of the issues that arose from Plato's work the *Republic* concerning the differences between knowledge and mere opinion. One of the interesting points that Plato raised is the issue of why we either *need* or *desire* the truth, and what's more why we *ought* to pursue it. Even though in his earlier work the *Meno* Plato claimed that knowledge was innate and was the product of an elite, this doesn't detract from his overall thoughts on the distinction between knowledge and opinion. Whilst opinions are important they can only be effectively transformed into statements of truth when they are subjected to the rigours of rational accountability; in some way there is a burden of proof at play here, to move rationally from belief to scientific knowledge. Aristotle in the *Posterior Analytics* took this argument, or if you like the desire to attain truth, a step further. Aristotle argued that there are 'eternal truths' that have stability, unlike opinions, which are inherently unstable until proven otherwise. Truths are immutable and beyond dispute but must be subject to method in order to prove the truthfulness of statements.

The debate in Western philosophy concerning the attainment of knowledge and truth has been dominated by two distinct traditions. On one side of the equation is *empiricism* and on the other side is *rationalism*. Empiricism is the belief that we come to know and understand the world through our own experience of it, whereas rationalists claim that it is *reason* that is inherent within us that allows individuals to acquire knowledge, which is always independent of experience. Kant in the *Critique of Pure Reason* addressed the debate between *empiricists* and *rationalists* concerning how we come to know the world and was critical of both positions. In relation to the former, Kant claimed that although empiricists were correct to argue that we come to know the world mainly by experience, he was critical of Locke's claim that the mind was like an empty room waiting to be occupied by knowledge via our sense perception. Equally, Kant was critical of rationalist claims that knowledge is in a world beyond the empirical. What in fact Kant did was to tread a middle ground and fuse elements of the two theories into a new school of thought concerning knowledge and truth. Kant claimed that there is *pure knowledge*, which he referred to as *a priori*, which is uncontaminated by the real world of objects and, second, there is *empirical knowledge*, which we come to know through experience, which Kant referred to as *a posteriori*. Above all, Kant argued that it is with time and maturity that experience is built 'with long practised attention we have become skilled to do so' (from McNeill and Feldman 1998, p. 9) and this is very close to Hegel's thoughts on the attainment of knowledge. For example, Hegel in *Phenomenology of Spirit* (1979) claimed that there are a number of stages that one must pass through to achieve a higher understanding, which is achieved via a dialectical passage to truth. Hegel called this higher-stage *self-consciousness* and is available to individuals who are conscious of their own being, or to put it another way, aware of their complex environment and able to make sense of it.

Being or having the ability to be aware, which is to be self-conscious, allows one to not simply recognize the symbiotic relationship between mind and object, but more importantly is the *key* to open the door on the world of knowledge. For Kant, the movement from the 'sublime', the obscure or what Kant also referred to as 'reflective judgement' to 'determinate judgement', or that which is unequivocally known is based on this idea of 'transcendental logic'. If one is to attain greater knowledge and understanding, to move towards the truth, one must transcend the restrictive boundaries of the former. 'Reflective judgement' is the *particular*, whilst 'determinate judgement' is the *universal*; the former is incomplete, the latter beyond question. Consider the following extract:

> Our knowledge springs from two fundamental sources of the mind; the first is the capacity of receiving representations (the ability to receive impressions), the second is the power to know an object through these representations (spontaneity in the production of concepts). Through the first, an object is *given* to us; through the second, the object is *thought* in relation to that representation ... . Intuition and concepts constitute, therefore, the elements of all our knowledge ... . (from McNeill and Feldman 1998, p. 16)

But 'reflective judgement' is to a large degree inherently unstable, because it is a space where rules have to be found. There is, therefore, a large degree of risk at this stage of cognitive development, it is as Scott Lash (1999, p. 4) states, a 'space of ambivalence ... where everything is at stake'. But it is also *the* space where opportunity to resolve matters occurs and this is where the pursuit of understanding evolves into resolution as far as the mind can perceive it, for Kant believed that there are things external to the mind that remain unknown. Kant believed that it is only through the categories that humans develop that humans are able to understand the external world, which they also create. As Popper (2002, p. 259) states in relation to Kant 'the world as we know it is our interpretation of the observable facts in the light of theories that we ourselves invent'. For Kant, this is how objectivity works, that is, understanding of objects *only* through the categories we construct. But one of the problems with the Kantian perspective is the uncritical way in which Kant accepts the categories in the first instance. This then is a limited and restrictive view of objectivity because what Kant called the 'thing-in-itself' remains beyond human faculties and comprehension.

It is to both Hegel and Marx that we must look for an answer to Kant's restrictive view of objectivity, and this can be found in the *dialectic*, which presupposes that the categories that humans produce are always being contested, reconstituted and redefined as our understanding of the world evolves. Marx applied this theory in his critique of political economy where Marx employed new categories over and above the ones in existence that Ricardo and Smith had used to define bourgeois economics, whilst in the *Logic*, Hegel questions and expands on prior forms of category. Ultimately, the *dialectic* recognizes the unity of human thought and human practice, a point that Kant failed to postulate; hence the criticism that Kant's theory is what is termed 'subjective idealism', for it is the knowing subject or the ego that provides the essence of knowledge. But what are categories of thought if not taken-for-granted assumptions about the world and what is it that the *assumed* automatically transforms into stereotypes and convention, which are there to be challenged, something that dialectics attempts to achieve in its *revolutionized form*.

What this discussion reveals are the complexities concerning the attainment of knowledge and how we come to know the truth of things. What the David Loyn article raises are important questions concerning the contribution that journalism can or cannot make in the discovery of truth. For our purposes, this debate also raises important issues concerning the role of journalism *vis-à-vis* the audience it serves, for what happens if objectivity is abandoned as a means to the truth?

So why is knowledge and truth so important in journalism? The simple answer to that is based on the *value of information*. The truth is, the relationship between production and consumption is a reciprocal one and the greater the knowledge at the point of production the greater the *value of information* at the point of consumption; as Nestor García Canclini (2001) states, 'consumption is good for thinking' where a new rationality is constructed and where consumption becomes a 'space of interaction' (ibid., p. 38) and this process is highly democratic because it not only entails thinking, but also 'participation' (ibid., p. 159) in thinking processes.

Cultural capital is absolutely central to this discussion and is part of the long tradition of Western philosophical thought on knowledge and truth. The responsibility to truth is solely and absolutely based on the distribution of information in civil society. The pursuit of truth is not about self-gratification but is much more based in the Kantian tradition of 'duty', and what follows is the moral obligation to do so. This is a cultural capital that brings tangible benefits and rewards to the community. Simply put, cultural capital is about the *distribution* of knowledge, which more often than not is unequally so. The unequal distribution of knowledge has partly helped to sustain class differences and helps to form distinctions between peoples. One of course can only lead the horse to water but one can't make it drink it, and this applies to the differences between newspapers or broadcasting channels; choice can be illiterate.

In reference to journalism Sanders (2005, p. 41) states: 'Truth is necessary for the possibility of truthfulness to exist' before proceeding to make a more pertinent point: 'trust in truthful communication is necessary'. Sanders quite rightly alerts us to the importance of public trust as a basis for philosophically defending the value of truth; however, trust is an idea in itself that cannot be legislated; you either trust or don't, which is perhaps reason enough to ensure that objective reporting becomes a duty and not a responsibility.

One of the critical issues confronting the discussion on objectivity is what happens if it is abandoned? As Ward (2004, pp. 13–14) asks: 'If objectivity is bankrupt, what should replace it?', rightly arguing that critics have 'failed miserably in constructing new norms to guide practice' (ibid., p. 13). Do we rely on subjective accounts, leaving it to the audience to 'decode' the 'encoded' message? Pure subjective accounts deny any truth beyond the interpretation of the writer where *perspectivists* argue that truth can be found beyond self-experience, but 'circumstance' conditions this reality and therefore objective-truth is not achievable. In this context, *perspectivists* occupy a middle-ground of rationality between subjectivism and objectivism and therefore truth is always contingent on *being-in-the-world*. Ward rejects subjective journalism and denounces it as irresponsible journalism, as the following quotation on the final page of his book explains:

> Our world needs objective journalists who care about responsible communication. The urgent problem of journalism today is not sterile objectivity but economic and technological forces that encourage subjective and irresponsible journalism, which does nothing to address our global future as a species. (ibid., p. 331)

The word 'our' used twice indicates the 'social' rather than 'self' responsibility of the articulated message; going beyond existential pretensions. Social responsibility accordingly is always to locate the *other* beyond self-experience, which morally speaking, is an honourable goal, but is it achievable? There is another perhaps more serious issue here and that concerns the message implied, namely that journalists are allowed and able to think beyond objective findings. What Ward refers to as 'sterile objectivity' is a non-human method; in other words, it negates feelings, passions, morality, values and beliefs, all of which condition a degree of interpretation, but to what extent does interpretation impinge upon objectivity and truth?

Bibliography

Alasuutari, P. (1995) *Researching Culture: Qualitative Method and Cultural Studies*, London: Sage.

Albert, M. (1998) 'Richard Rorty the Public Philosopher', at: http://www.zmag.org/rortyphil.htm accessed January 2008.

Alia, V. (2004) *Media Ethics and Social Change*, Edinburgh: Edinburgh University Press.

Allan, S. (2004) *News Culture*, 2nd edition, England: Open University Press.

Allan, S. (2006) 'Local news, global politics: Reporting the London bomb attacks', in B. Franklin (ed.) *Local Journalism and Local Media: Making the Local News*, London: Routledge.

Andrews, A. (1998) *The History of British Journalism: From the Foundation of the Newspaper Press in England to the Repeal of the Stamp Act in 1855, with sketches of Press Celebrities*, vol. 1, Routledge/Thoemmes Press: London.

Aucoin, J. (2002) 'Investigative Journalism', in W.D. Sloan and L.M. Parcell (eds) *American Journalism: History, Principles, Practices*, North Carolina: McFarland & Company.

Bangemann Report (1994) 'Bangemann Report, Europe and the Global Information Society', report prepared for the European Council of Ministers.

Baggini, J. (2003) 'The Philosophy of Journalism', openDemocracy, at: http://www.opendemocracy.com, accessed February 2006.

Barker, H. (2000) *Newspapers, Politics and English Society 1695 – 1855*, Harlow: Pearson.

Basner, M. (2000) 'Consuming interests in a culture of secrecy', in D. Berry (ed.) *Ethics and Media Culture: Practices and Representations*, Oxford: Focal Press.

BBC News (2007) 'Murdoch: I decide Sun's politics', 24 November, at: http://www.news.bbc.co.uk, accessed January 2008.

Bell, M. (1998) 'The journalism of attachment', in M. Kieran (ed.) *Media Ethics*, London: Routledge.

Belsey, A. (1992) Preface to *Ethical Issues In Journalism And The Media*, London: Routledge.

Belsey, A. (1998) 'Journalism and ethics: Can they co-exist?', in M. Kieran (ed.) *Media Ethics*, London: Routledge.

Berger, A.A. (2000) *Media Research Techniques*, 2nd edition, London: Sage.

Berger, T.L., and T. Luckmann (1967) *The Social Construction of Reality: A Treatise in the Sociology of Knowledge*, London: Allen Lane.

Berry, D. (2000) 'Trust in media practices: Towards cultural development', in D. Berry (ed.) *Ethics and Media Culture: Practices and Representations*, Oxford: Focal Press.

Berry, D. (2006) 'Popular Culture And Mass Media In Latin America: Some Reflections On The Works Of Jésus Martín Barbero And Nestor García Canclini', in D. Berry and J. Theobald (eds) *Radical Mass Media Criticism: A Cultural Genealogy*, Montreal: Black Rose Books.

Bertrand, C.J. (2000) *Media Ethics & Accountability Systems*, New Brunswick: Transaction Publishers.

Bew, R. (2006) 'The role of the freelancer in local journalism', in B. Franklin (ed.) *Local Journalism and Local Media: Making the Local News*, London: Routledge.

Black, J. (1991) *The English Press In The Eighteenth Century*, Hampshire: Gregg Revivals.

Black, J. (1997) *Mixed News: The Public/Civic/Communitarian Journalism Debate*, Mahwah, NJ: Lawrence Erlbaum Associates.

Black, J. (2001) *The English Press 1621–1861*, Sparkford: Sutton Publishing.

Bleyer, W, G. (1927) *Main Currents in the History of American Journalism*, Boston, MA: Houghton Mifflin.

Bogart, L. (1989) *Press and Public: Who Reads What, When, Where, and Why in American Newspapers*, 2nd edition, Hillsdale, NJ: Lawrence Erlbaum Associates.

Bok, S. (1980) *Lying: Moral Choice in Public and Private Life*, London: Quartet.

Bourdieu, P., and J.C. Passeron (1973) 'Cultural Reproduction and Social Reproduction', in R.K. Brown (ed.) *Knowledge, Education and Cultural Change*, London: Tavistock.

Bourdieu, P. (1977) *Outline of a Theory of Practice*, trans. R. Nice, Cambridge: Cambridge University Press.

Bourdieu, P. (1992) *Language and Symbolic Power*, ed. J.B. Thompson, trans. G. Raymond and M. Adamson, Cambridge: Polity Press.

Bowles, W. (2005) 'Investigating Imperialism: 400 Years of Blogging', at: http://www.williambowles.info/ini/ini-0316.html, accessed May 2006.

Brown, A. (1986) *Modern Political Philosophy: Theories of the Just Society*, London: Penguin.

Burns, L.S. (2002) *Understanding Journalism*, London: Routledge.

Button, J. (1995) *The Radicalism Handbook: A Complete Guide to the Radical Movement in the Twentieth Century*, London: Cassell.

Campbell, C.C. (1999) 'Foreword: Journalism As A Democratic Art', in T. Glasser (ed.) *The Idea of Public Journalism*, New York: Guildford Press.

Carey, J. (1987) (ed.) *The Faber Book of Reportage*, Faber: London.

Carey, J.W. (1999) 'In Defense of Public Journalism', in T. Glasser (ed.) *The Idea of Public Journalism*, New York: Guildford Press.

Carlyle, T. (1857) *The French Revolution*, London: Chapman and Hall.

Carlyle, T. (1894) *On Heroes, Hero-worship & the Heroic in History*, London: Chapman and Hall.

Carter, C., and S. Allan (2000) '"If it bleeds, it leads": Ethical questions about popular journalism', in D. Berry (ed.) *Ethics and Media Culture: Practices and Representations*, Oxford: Focal Press.

Chambers, I. (1994) *Migrancy, Culture, Identity*, London: Routledge.

Christians, C. (1999) 'The Common Good As First Principle', in T. Glasser (ed.) *The Idea of Public Journalism*, New York: Guildford Press.

Christians, C.G., Fackler, M., Rotzoll, K.B., and K.B. McKee (2001) *Media Ethics: Cases and Moral Reasoning*, 6th edition. Longman: New York.

Clayton, J. (1992) *'Journalism For Beginners': How to get into print and get paid for it*, London: Piatkus Publishers.

Cole, P. (1998) 'Instinct, savvy and ratlike cunning: Training local journalists', in B. Franklin and D. Murphy (eds) *Making The Local News: Local Journalism in Context*, London: Routledge.

Cole, P. (2006) 'Education and training local journalists', in B. Franklin (ed.) *Local Journalism and Local Media: Making the local news*, London: Routledge.

Collini, S. (1989) *J.S. Mill: On Liberty and Other Writings*, Cambridge: Cambridge University Press.

Commission for the European Communities (1993) 'Growth, Competitiveness, Employment: The Challenges and the Ways Forward into the 21st Century' (Delors White Paper).

Conboy, M. (2004) *Journalism: A Critical History*, London: Sage.

Davis, C., and N. Raynor (2000) 'Reproducing consciousness: What *is* Indonesia?', in D. Berry (ed.) *Ethics and Media Culture: Practices and Representations*, Oxford: Focal Press.

Day, L. (2006) *Ethics in Media Communications: Cases and Controversies*, 5th edition, Belmont, CA: Wadsworth.

Dennis, E.E., and J.C. Merrill (1991) *Media Debates: Issues in mass communication*, New York: Longman.

A Dictionary of Philosophy (1979) prepared by Laurence Urdang Associates Ltd, ed. J. Speake, Aylesbury.

Dowling, T. (2007) 'I don't think bloggers read', *The Guardian*, 20 July, p. 14.

Dring, P. (2000) 'Codes and Cultures', in D. Berry (ed.) *Ethics and Media Culture: Practices and Representations*, Oxford: Focal Press.

Eagleton, T. (2003) *After Theory*, London: Allen Lane.

Eco, U. (1998) *Faith in Fakes: Travels in Hyperreality*, trans. W. Weaver, London: Vintage.

Edgar, A. (1992) 'Objectivity, bias and truth', in A. Belsey and R. Chadwick (eds) *Ethical Issues in Journalism and the Media*, London: Routledge.

Edgar, A. (2000) 'The "fourth estate" and moral responsibilities', in D. Berry (ed.) *Ethics and Media Culture: Practices and Representations*, Oxford: Focal Press.

Emery, E. (1972) *The Press and America: An Interpretative History of the Mass Media*, 3rd edition, Englewood Cliffs, NJ: Prentice-Hall.

Europa (2007) 'Media literacy: Do people really understand how to make the most of blogs, search engines or interactive TV', Europa – The European Union On-Line, at: http://www.europa.eu, accessed January 2008.

European Commission (n.d.) 'Media Literacy', Audiovisual and Media Policies, at: http://ec.europa.eu/avpolicy/media_literacy/index_en.htm#what, accessed November 2007.

European Research Council (2001) 'European Media, Cultural Integration and Globalisation: Reflections on the ESF-programme Changing Media – Changing Europe', at: http://www.lboro.ac.uk, accessed January 2008.

Evensen, B.J. (2002) 'Objectivity', in W.D. Sloan and L.M. Parcell (eds) *American Journalism: History, Principles, Practices*, North Carolina: McFarland & Company.

Feinberg, J. (1973) *Social Philosophy*, Englewood Cliffs: Prentice-Hall.

Fishman, M. (1980) *Manufacturing the News*, Austin, TX: University of Texas Press.

Fox Bourne, H.R. (1887) *English Newspaper: Chapters in the History of Journalism*, London: Chatto & Windus.

Frank, J. (1961) *The Beginnings of the English Newspaper 1620–1660*, Cambridge, MA: Harvard University Press.

Freeden, M. (1998) *Ideologies and Political Theory: A Conceptual Approach*, Oxford: Clarendon Press.

Friedland, L.A., Rosen, J. and L. Austin (1994) 'Civic Journalism: A New Approach to Citizenship', *Civic Practice Network* (the online journal of the Civic Renewal Movement), at: http://www.cpn.org, accessed February 2008.

Frost, C. (2000) *Media Ethics and Self-Regulation*, London: Pearson Longman.

Frost, C. (2007) *Journalism Ethics and Regulation*, 2nd edition, London: Pearson Longman.

Fukuyama, F. (1992) *The End Of History And The Last Man*, London: Hamish Hamilton.

Gadamar, H.G. (1979) *Truth and Method*, trans. W. Glen-Doepel, London: Sheed and Ward.

Gans, H.J. (1979) *Deciding What's News*, New York: Free Press.

García Canclini, N. (2001) *Consumers and citizens: Globalization and multicultural conflicts*, Minneapolis, MN: University of Minnesota Press.

Gary2idaho (2007) 'The Fourth Estate is fatally wounded and dying a slow death!', View to the Mountains, at: http://gary2idaho.wordpress.com/2007/11/06/the-fourth-estate-is-fatally-wounded-as-his-dying-a-slow-death/, accessed February 2008.

Giddens, A. (1994) *Beyond Left and Right: The Future of Radical Politics*, Cambridge: Polity Press.

Glasser, T.L. (1999) (ed.) *The Idea of Public Journalism*, New York: The Guildford Press.

Golding, P. and, P. Elliot (1979) *Making The News*, Harlow: Longman.

Gordon, A.D., Kitross, J.M., and C. Reuss (1996) *Controversies in Media Ethics*, White Plains, NY: Longman.

Grenz, S.J. (1995) *A Primer on Postmodermism*, Grand Rapids: Cambridge University Press.

Griscom, A. (n.d.) 'Trends of Anarchy and Hierarchy: Comparing the Cultural Repercussions of Print and Digital Media', at: http://www.thecore.nus.edu.sg/cpace/infotech/asg/contents.html, accessed May 2007.

Gronbach, K.W. (2007) 'The Fourth Estate and the Future of Truth', at: http://kgcdirect.squarespace.com/journal/2007/3/20/the-fourth-estate.html, accessed February 2008.

Habermas, J. (1989) *The Structural Transformation of the Public Sphere: An Inquiry into a Category of Bourgeios Society*, Cambridge: Polity.

Hadland, A. (2005) (ed.) *Changing The Fourth Estate: Essays on South African Journalism*, Cape Town: HSRC Press.

Hall, S. (1981) 'The determination of news photographs', in S. Cohen and J. Young (eds) *The Manufacture of News*, London: Constable.

Hall, S. (1993) 'The television discourse – encoding and decoding', in A. Gray and J. McGuigan (eds) *Studying Culture: An introductory reader*, London: Edward Arnold.

Hampton, J. (1997) *Political Philosophy*, Boulder, CO: Westview Press.

Harris, T. (1995) 'Propaganda and Public Opinion in Seventeenth-Century England', in J.D. Popkin (ed.) *Media and Revolution*, Lexington: University Press of Kentucky.

Harrison, D.M. (2006) 'Disruptions in The Fourth Estate', Blogcritics, at: http://blogcritics.org/archives/2006/02/26/125831.php, accessed February 2008.

Hastings, W. (2000) 'The History of Journalism', at: http://www.northern.edu/hastingw/journhist.html, accessed May 2006.

Hatton, J. (1882) *Journalistic London: Being a Series of Sketches of Famous Pens and Papers of the Day*, London: Sampson Low, Marston, Searle and Rivington, Fleet Street.

Hausman, C. (1990) *The Decision Making Process in Journalism*, Chicago: Nelson-Hall.

Haworth, A. (1998) *Free Speech*, London: Routledge.

Hegel, F. (1979) *Phenomenology of Spirit*, trans. A.V. Miller, with analysis of the text and foreword by J.N. Findlay, Oxford: Clarendon.

Herds, H. (1952) *The March of Journalism The Story of the British Press from 1622 to the Present Day*, London: Allen & Unwin.

Herman, E., and N. Chomsky (1988) *Manufacturing Consent: The Political Economy of the Mass Media*, New York: Pantheon Books.

Hetherington, A. (1985) *News, Newspapers and Television*, London: Macmillan.

Heywood, A. (2004) *Political Theory: An Introduction*, Basingstoke: Palgrave Macmillan.

Hinchliffe, P. (2007) 'The Training of Journalists', OhmyNews, at: http://english. ohmynews.com/ArticleView/article_view.asp?menu=&no=381100&rel_ no=1&back_ur=, accessed February 2008.

Hodges, L. W. (1997) 'Ruminations About the Communitarian Debate', in J. Black (ed.) *Mixed News*, Mahwah, N.J: Lawrence Erlbaum Associates.

Hornig-Priest, S. (1996) *Doing Media Research: An Introduction*, London: Sage.

Hunt, F.K. (1998) *The Fourth Estate: Contributions Towards a History of Newspapers, and of the Liberty of the Press*, vol.1, London: Routledge/ Thoemmes Press.

Janaway, C. (2002) *Schopenhauer: A Very Short Introduction*, Oxford: Oxford University Press.

Jempson, M. (2000) 'And the consequence was … Dealing with the human impact of unethical journalism', in D. Berry (ed.) *Ethics and Culture: Practices and Representations*, Oxford: Focal Press.

Jonson, B. (1631) *The Staple of News*, at: http://hollowaypages.com/ jonson1692news.htm, accessed December 2007.

Kant, I. (1998) *Critique of Pure Reason*, ed. P. Guyer and A.W. Wood, Cambridge: Cambridge University Press.

Käsler, D. (1988) *Max Weber: An Introduction to his Work*, trans. P. Hurd, Cambridge: Polity.

Keeble, R. (1995) *The Newspapers Handbook*, London: Routledge.

Keeler, J.D., Brown, W., and D. Tarpley (2002) 'Ethics', in W.D. Sloan and L.M. Parcell (eds) *American Journalism: History, Principles, Practices*, North Carolina: McFarland & Company.

Keen, A. (2007) *Cult of the Amateur: How Today's Internet is Killing our Culture*, New York: Doubleday.

Kieran, M. (1997) *Media Ethics: A Philosophical Approach*, London: Praegor.

Kieran, M. (1998) *Media Ethics*, London: Routledge.

Kierkegaard, S. (1992) *Either/Or: A Fragment of Life*, ed. V. Eremita, trans. with introduction and notes A. Hannay, London: Penguin.

Knightley, P. (2002) *The First Casualty: The War Correspondent as Hero and Myth-maker from the Crimea to Kosovo*, Baltimore, MD: John Hopkins University Press.

Knowlton, S.R. (1997) *Moral Reasoning for Journalists: Cases and Commentary*, Westport, CT: Praegor.

Kriegelstein, W. (n.d.) 'Transcendental Perspectivism: The Third Enlightenment', at: http://www.perspectivism.com/, accessed March 2008.

Lambeth, E.B., Meyer, P.E., and E. Thorson (1998) (eds) *Assessing Public Journalism*, Columbia, MO: University of Missouri Press.

Lash, S. (1999) *Another Modernity A Different Rationality*, Blackwell Publishers: Oxford.

Lawson, C. (2002) *Building The Fourth Estate: Democratization and the Rise of the Free Press in Mexico*, California: University of California Press.

Le Bon, G. (1920) *The Crowd: A Study of the Popular Mind*, Electronic Text Center, University of Virginia Library, at: http://etext.virginia.edu/toc/modeng/public/BonCrow.html, accessed December 2007.

Leigh, D. (2007) 'Are Reporters Doomed', *The Guardian*, 12 November, p. 6.

Locke, J. (1955) *A Letter Concerning Toleration*, with an introduction by P. Romanell, Indianapolis: Bobbs-Merrill.

Locke, J. (1990) *Two Treatises of Government*, London: J.M. Dent & Sons.

Locke, J. (1996) *An Essay Concerning Human Understanding*, ed. with an introduction and notes K.P. Winkler, Indianapolis: Hackett.

Lloyd, J. (2004) 'Martin Bell', *Prospect*, February, pp 18–21.

Loyn, D. (2003) 'Witnessing the Truth', openDemocracy, at: http://www.opendemocracy.com, accessed February 2006.

Luhmann, N. (1979) *Trust and Power*, Chichester: Wiley.

Lumsden, L.J. (2002) 'Press Criticism', in W.D. Sloan and L.M. Parcell (eds) *American Journalism: History, Principles, Practices*, North Carolina: McFarland & Company.

McNair, B. (2003) *News and Journalism in the UK*, 4th edition, London: Routledge.

McNeill, W. and, K.S. Feldman (1998) *Continental Philosophy: An Anthology*, Cambridge, MA: Blackwell.

McQuail, D. (1993) *Media Performance: Mass Communication and the Public Interest*, London: Sage.

Media Awareness Network (2008) 'What is Media Literacy', at: http://www.media-awareness.ca/english/teachers/media_literacy/what_is_media_literacy.cfm, accessed January 2008.

Merrill, J.C. (1997) 'Communitarianism's Rhetorical War Against Enlightenment Liberalism', in *Mixed News: The Public/Civic Communitarian Debate*, ed. J. Black, Mahwah, NJ: Lawrence Erlbaum Associates.

Merrill, J.C. (1989) *The Dialectic in Journalism: Towards a Responsible Use of Press Freedom*, Baton Rouge: Louisiana State University Press.

Merritt, D. (1998) *Public Journalism and Public Life: Why Telling the News Is Not Enough*, Mahwah, NJ: Lawrence Erlbaum Associates.

Mill, J.S. (1989) *On Liberty and Other Writings*, ed. Stefan Collini, Cambridge: Cambridge University Press.

Mirando, J.A. (2002) 'Training and Education of Journalists', in W.D. Sloan and L.M. Parcell (eds) *American Journalism: History, Principles, Practices*, North Carolina: McFarland & Company.

Mitnick, B.M. (1980) *The Political Economy of Regulation: Creating, Designing and Removing Regulatory Forms*, New York: Columbia University Press.

Morley, D., and K. Robins (1995) *Spaces of Identity*, London: Routledge.

Mott, F.L. (1962) *American Journalism*, 3rd edition, New York: The Macmillan Company.

Niblock, S. (1996) *Inside Journalism*, London: Blueprint.

Nietzsche, F. (2003) *Beyond Good and Evil*, trans, R.J. Hollingdale, London: Penguin.

Nozick, R. (1974) *Anarchy, State, Utopia*, Oxford: Basil Blackwell.

Nozick, R. (2001) *Invariances: The Structure of the Objective World*, Cambridge, MA: Harvard University Press.

Ohmy News International (2007) 'Citizen Journalism', at: http://english. ohmynews.com/index.asp, accessed January 2008.

Olson, N. (2001) 'Perspectivism and Truth in Nietzsche's Philosophy: A Critical Look at the Apparent Contradiction', at: http://www.stolaf.edu/depts/ philosophy/reed/2001/perspectivism.html, accessed March 2008.

Ortega y Gasset, J. (2000) *Meditations on Quixote*, introduction and notes J. Marias, trans. E. Rugg and D. Marin, Urbana, Illinois: University of Illinois Press.

Ortega y Gasset, J. (1933) *The Revolt of the Masses* (authorized translation from Spanish), London: Allen & Unwin.

The Oxford English Dictionary (1989) ed. J.A.H. Murray, J.A. Simpson and E.S.C. Weiner, 2nd edition, Oxford: Oxford University Press.

Pew Center for Civic Journalism (2001) '10 Tips on Award-Winning Civic Journalism', *Civic Catalyst Newsletter*, Summer, at: http://www.pewcenter. org/, accessed February 2008.

Pilger, J. (1998) *Hidden Agendas*, London: Vintage

Pilger, J. (2006) 'Journalism as a Weapon of War', at: http://www.johnpilger.com/, accessed June 2007.

Podur, J. (2005) 'Fisk: War is the total failure of the human spirit', 5 December, at: http://www.rabble.ca, accessed January 2008.

Popper, K.R. (2002) *Conjectures and Refutations: The Growth of Scientific Knowledge*, London: Routledge.

Potter, W.J. (2005) *Media Literacy*, 3rd edition, London: Sage.

Pribanic-Smith, E.J. (2002) 'Sensationalism and Tabloidism', in W.D. Sloan and L.M. Parcell (eds) *American Journalism: History, Principles, Practices*, North Carolina: McFarland & Company.

Pritchard, S. (2007) 'The readers' editor on … the new age of journalism', *The Observer*, 27 May.

Pusey, M. (1987) *Jürgen Habermas*, Chichester: Ellis Horwood.

Putnam, R.D. (1995) 'Bowling Alone: America's Declining Social Capital', *Journal of Democracy* 6(1): 65–78.

Putnam, R.D. (1996) 'The Strange Disappearance of Civic America, *The American Prospect* 7(24): 34–48.

Randall, D. (1996) *The Universal Journalist*, London: Pluto.

Reich, W. (1946) *The Mass Psychology of Fascism*, 3rd edition, trans. Theodore P. Wolfe, New York: Orgone Institute Press.

Reiss, H. (1970) *Kant: Political Writings*, trans. H.B. Nesbit, Cambridge: Cambridge University Press.

Ricoeur, P. (1981) *Hermeneutics and the Human Sciences*, trans. J.B. Thompson, Cambridge: Cambridge University Press.

Robertson, J.W. (2006) 'Illuminating or Dimming Down? A Survey of UK Television News Coverage', *Fifth-Estate-Online: International Journal of Radical Media Criticism*, April, at: http://www.fifth-estate-online.co.uk, accessed March 2008.

Rorty, R. (1989) *Contingency, Irony and Solidarity*, Cambridge: Cambridge University Press.

Rorty, R. (1991) *Objectivity, Relativism and Truth*, Cambridge: Cambridge University Press.

Rorty, R. (1998) *Truth and Progress*, Cambridge: Cambridge University Press.

Roscho, B. (1975) *Newsmaking*, Chicago: University of Chicago Press.

Rosten, L.C. (1937) *The Washington Correspondents*, New York: Harcourt Brace.

Rubin, B. (1978) *Questioning Media Ethics*, New York: Praegor.

Rutland, R.A. (1973) *The Newsmongers: Journalism in the Life of the Nation*, New York: The Dial Press.

Said, E. (2001) 'Propaganda and War', at: http://www.mediamonitors.net/edward37.html, accessed August 2008.

Sanders, K. (2005) *Ethics and Journalism*, London: Sage.

Schaffer, J. (2008) 'What role can the media play in strengthening democracy?', e.thePeople, at: http://www.e-thepeople.org/a-national/comment/17037/1/view, accessed February 2008.

Schlesinger, P. (1978) *Putting 'Reality' Together*, London: Methuen.

Schudson, M. (1978) *Discovering The News*, New York: Basic Books.

Schutz, A. (1964) *Collected Papers*, 2 vols, The Hague: Nijhoff.

Shultz, J. (1999) *Reviving The Fourth Estate: Democracy, Accountability and the Media*, Cambridge: Cambridge University Press.

Silverblatt, A. (2001) *Media Literacy: Keys to Interpreting Media Messages*, 2nd edition, Westport, CT: Praeger.

Simmel, G. (1998) 'Crisis in Culture', in D. Frisby and M. Featherstone (eds) *Simmel on Culture: Selected Writings*, London: Sage.

Skapinker, M. (2007) 'Scientists must learn to talk to the media', *Financial Times*, 30 October 30, p. 15.

Skinner, B.F. (1965) *Science and Human Behavior*, New York: Free Press.

Solomon, R.C. (1996) 'Nietzsche ad hominem: Perspectivism, personality, and ressentiment', in *The Cambridge Companion to Nietzsche*, Cambridge: Cambridge University Press.

Smith, R.F. (1999) *Groping for Ethics in Journalism*, Ames, IA: Iowa State University Press.

Spengler, O. (1980) *The Decline of the West*, authorized translation with notes C.F. Atkinson, London: Allen & Unwin.

Stephens, M. (2007) *A History of News*, 3rd edition, New York: Oxford University Press.

Theobald, J. (2000) 'Radical mass media criticism: Elements of a history from Kraus to Bourdieu', in D. Berry (ed.) *Ethics and Media Culture: Practices and Representations*, Oxford: Focal Press.

Theobald, J. (2004) *The Media and the Making of History*, Aldershot: Ashgate.

Thinkmap® (1998–2008), VisualThesaurus®, at: http://www.visualthesaurus.com, accessed July 2008.

Thompson, J.B. (1981) *Critical Hermeneutics: A Study in the Thought of Paul Ricoeur and Jürgen Habermas*, Cambridge: Cambridge University Press.

Thompson, J.B., and D. Held (1982) *Habermas: Critical Debates*, London: Macmillan.

Thucydides (1978) *The Peloponnesian War*, introduction M.I. Finley, trans. R. Warner, Harmondsworth: Penguin Books.

Tomalin, N. (1997) 'Stop the press I want to get on', in M. Bromley and T. O'Malley (eds) *Journalism: A Reader*, London: Routledge.

Tönnies, F. (1957) *Community and Society*, New York: Harper and Row.

Tuchman, G. (1978) *'Making News': A Study in the Construction of Reality*, New York: The Free Press.

Tunstall, J. (1971) *Journalists at Work*, London: Constable.

UK Parliament (2007) 'Communications – Minutes of Evidence', Question number 201–219, 18 July, at: www.parliament.uk, accessed October 2007.

Underwood, D. (1993) *When MBAs Rule the Newsroom: How Markets and Managers are Shaping Today's Media*, New York: Columbia University Press.

Upshaw, J. (2002) 'Characteristics of Journalists', in W.D. Sloan and L.M. Parcell (eds) *American Journalism: History, Principles, Practices*, North Carolina: McFarland & Company.

Vallely, P. (2008) 'Williams is snared in a trap of his own making', *The Independent*, 8 February, Commentary section.

Van Dijk, T. (1988) *News As Discourse*, London: Lawrence Erlbaum Associates.

Van Loon, J. (2000) 'Enframing/revealing: On the question of ethics and difference in technologies of mediation', in D. Berry (ed.) *Ethics and Media Culture: Practices and Representations*, Oxford: Focal Press.

Ward, S. (2004) *The Invention of Journalism Ethics: The Path to Objectivity and Beyond*, Montreal and Kingston: McGill-Queen's University Press.

Watson, J.B. (1924). *Behaviorism*, New York: Norton.

Weber, M. (1948) *From Max Weber: Essays in Sociology*, ed. with an introduction H.H. Gerth and C.W. Mills, London: Routledge and Kegan Paul.

Weber, M. (1949) *The Methodology of the Social Sciences*, trans. E. Shils and A.M. Henderson, Glencoe, Illinois: Free Press.

Westerståhl, J. (1983) 'Objective News Reporting', *Communication Research* 10: 403–424.

White, D.M. (1950) '"The Gatekeeper": A case study in the selection of news', *Journalism Quarterly* 27(4): 383–390.

Williams, J.B. (1907–21), 'The Beginnings of English Journalism: Gainsford and the Corantos', in A.W. Ward and A.R. Waller (eds) *The Cambridge History of English and American Literature: An Encyclopaedia in 18 Volumes*, Volume VII, *Cavalier and Puritan*, at: http://www.bartleby.com/217/1501.html, accessed October 2007.

Williams, J.H. (2002) 'The Purposes of Journalism', in W.D. Sloan and L.M. Parcell (eds) *American Journalism: History, Principles, Practices*, North Carolina: McFarland & Company.

Windschuttle, K. (1998) 'Journalism versus Cultural Studies', *Australian Studies in Journalism* (7): 3–31.

Windschuttle, K. (1999) 'Journalism and the Western Tradition', at: http://www.sydneyline.com/Journalism%20and%20Western%20Tradition.htm, accessed November 2007.

Wittgenstein, L. (1963) *Philosophical Investigations*, Oxford: Blackwell.

World Public Opinion (2003) 'Misperceptions, the Media and the Iraq War', at: http://www.worldpublicopinion.org, accessed February 2008.

Index

For Product Safety Concerns and Information please contact our EU
representative GPSR@taylorandfrancis.com
Taylor & Francis Verlag GmbH, Kaufingerstraße 24, 80331 München, Germany

www.ingramcontent.com/pod-product-compliance
Ingram Content Group UK Ltd.
Pitfield, Milton Keynes, MK11 3LW, UK
UKHW020948180425
457613UK00019B/580